Contemporary Challenges to Conscience

AD FONTES

SCHRIFTEN ZUR PHILOSOPHIE

Herausgegeben von Tadeusz Guz

BAND 14

PETER LANG

Aleksander Stępkowski

Contemporary Challenges to Conscience

Legal and Ethical Frameworks for Professional Conduct

PETER LANG

Bibliografische Information der Deutschen Nationalbibliothek
Die Deutsche Nationalbibliothek verzeichnet diese Publikation in der Deutschen Nationalbibliografie; detaillierte bibliografische Daten sind im Internet über http://dnb.d-nb.de abrufbar.

Scientific reviewer: Prof. dr hab. Piotr Niczyporuk (University of Białystok)

This publication was financially supported by the Ordo Iuris Institute for Legal Culture.

ISSN 1613-947X
ISBN 978-3-631-77555-4 (Print)
E-ISBN 978-3-631-79211-7 (PDF)
E-ISBN 978-3-631-79212-4 (EPUB)
E-ISBN 978-3-631-79213-1 (MOBI)
DOI 10.3726/b15722

Peter Lang – Berlin · Bern · Bruxelles ·
New York · Oxford · Warszawa · Wien

Diese Publikation wurde begutachtet.

www.peterlang.com

Contents

Introduction

Aleksander Stępkowki

Contemporary Challenges to Conscience and Their Specificity

Contemporary medical healthcare system is the place of growing ethical controversies within the society, uncovering conflicting interests and different attitudes to fundamental human values in social life. Moral controversies or moral dilemmas of physicians have always been part of human life. It would, however, be an erroneous reduction if we considered contemporary conflicts around conscientious objection as an aspect of everlasting human moral condition. Today, controversies around the conscience are very much specific.

Strictly understood, conscience refers to specific moral recognition of a particular factual situation. Therefore, conscientious objection should be referred to as an exceptional situation in which a conscientious conflict arises not because of unjust nature of applicable law, but due to extraordinary circumstances giving exceptional effect of an abstract and general statutory rule, which in itself need not to be unjust. However, it is not the case today. When dealing with conscientious objection, contemporary authors refer to regular operation of abstract and general norms rather than extraordinary situations. These are not exceptional, factual circumstances but general rules applied in a regular way, which provoke serious moral conflicts and much of the public debate, far exceeding the academic one. As Jakub Pawlikowski stresses in his contribution, providing the most valuable perspective of a medical doctor, majority of the problems related to conscientious objection in medicine arise from the inappropriate, unnecessary and morally unjustifiable scope of duties imposed on healthcare workers – duties which in some areas are contrary to medicine's internal goals. Therefore, despite the fact that contemporary perspective for conscientious objection is not the most regular way of its understanding in theoretical dimension, in practice it is still the most important and the one that is most discussed. This peculiarity is due to characteristic features of the contemporary culture.

Because of this peculiarity, most of the academic publications concerning conscientious objection within the health care were published within the last decade and refer to medical procedures that became legal during the last three decades of 20th century. Controversies concerning conscientious objection are linked to the statutory regulations waiving protection of human life at early or final stages of its development by means of specific medical interventions, although the very first publications concerned already compulsory vaccinations.[1]

This is, however, not sufficient to explain the phenomenon. As it is again emphasized by Jakub Pawlikowski, when debating conscientious objection, we should first of all analyze the scope, necessity, purposefulness, appropriateness and justifiability of that imposed obligation or duty. The primary questions that need to be asked should relate to the goals of medicine and the principles of medical ethics connected with these goals.

However, conscientious objection would not have become so much of a controversial issue, if the development of public health insurance did not create legal obligation to provide medical services covered with such an insurance. Former Polish Minister of Health, Konstanty Radziwiłł, has pointed out in his short contribution to this volume that coincidence of those two factors (legalization of procedures threatening human life and payment for medical services with public money) has created unprecedented situation, when physicians find themselves under legal duty to take action depriving an innocent human being of life or other actions, of similar ethical quality. Therefore, most frequently, conscientious objection is discussed in the context of abortion, which, in a considerable number of Western countries, has ceased to be considered as a serious crime and has acquired status of a right, frequently attributed with fundamental character. Therefore, the position of the State as a warrant of citizens' effective access to publicly funded services (healthcare service included), places its officials in a position requiring action against those providers, who rise conscientious objection.

However, the freedom of conscience, being a universally recognized principle, provides a solid foundation for conscientious objection. It is not surprising, therefore, that conscientious objection is legally protected in most European countries. The list of statutory regulations adopted in European countries is to be found in a table annexed to this volume. Therefore, its author, Robert Clark, together with Roger Kiska consider "respect to the neighbor's conscience as characteristic for the European culture". They provide also extensive documentation for the consistent protection of the rights of conscience by the international law. It is emphasized that in relation to the freedom of conscience and conscientious objection, there is particularly narrow margin of appreciation, especially in relation to performance of abortion, which doesn't have right status

1 Jakub Pawlikowski, "*Więcej wolności sumienia dla lekarzy – konsekwencje orzeczenia Trybunału Konstytucyjnego w sprawie klauzuli sumienia*," Medycyna Praktyczna, 11/2015, p. 2.

in international law.[2] Therefore, Kiska and Clark are of strong convictions that "any future application to the ECtHR concerning conscientious objection to perform abortion should be looked on favourably". A similar position was taken by Gregor Puppinck and Claire de La Hougue who supplement their account of international law with a very valuable reference to ethical principles confirming physicians' rights of conscience in different countries. On the other hand, Michał Skwarzyński demonstrates how the case law of the European Court of Human Rights concerning freedom of conscience is influencing application of domestic law in Poland.

However, surprisingly, it appears that, the firm affirmation of the conscientious objection in international and national law does not prevent prestigious academic journals from publishing papers denying freedom of conscience in this respect. Recently, C. Munthe and M.E.J. Nielsen have presented conscientious refusal as contradicting fundamental legal ethical requirements and undermining operation of healthcare system.[3]

Those contrasting positions illustrate an intensive contradiction between conflicting approaches towards conscience within the contemporary culture. Freedom of conscience is commonly welcomed and appreciated in areas where it results in the criticism of the established social order and its safeguarding norms. At the same time, freedom of conscience is intensively denied if it is supporting the strongest moral convictions, which ceased to be unambiguously supported with contemporary statutory regulations despite the fact that they are an ethical fundament for social life. This extreme difference of approaches illustrates how big obstacles challenge practical operation of this particular dimension of the freedom of conscience within the contemporary health service.

Intensity of those controversies, involving not only medical professionals but also the state and civil society (including professional organizations) had inspired *Ordo Iuris* Institute for Legal Culture and the Chair for Legal and Political Thought of the Faculty of Law and Administration at the University of Warsaw, to organize an international scientific conference on 5 September 2015. The conference

2 For detailed account see Piero Anders Tozzi, "Sovereignties: Evaluating Claims for 'Right to Abortion' under International Law," in: *Protection of Human Life in its Early Stage*, ed. Aleksander Stępkowski, *Intellectual Foundations and Legal Means* (Peter Lang, 2014), pp. 49–67; Stefano Gennarini, "The Diffusion of Sexual and Reproductive Rights through the UN Human Rights Framework," in: *Protection of Human Life …*, ed. Stępkowski (Peter Lang, 2014), pp. 255–263.

3 See, Christian Munthe, Morten Ebbe Juul Nielsen, "*The Legal Ethical Backbone of Conscientious Refusal*," Cambridge Quarterly of Healthcare Ethics, Vol. 26 (2017), pp. 59–68.

confronted the legal perspective with the experience of physicians, midwives and pharmacists in a wider doctrinal context, as provided by theoretical approaches to social life. Among participants, both medical professionals and lawyers were present. Apart from the synthetic account by the former Polish Minister of Health having been previously for a long time the President of Polish Chief Medical Council, Konstanty Radziwiłł, also the perspective of pharmacists was included with the contribution by Danuta Barańska. However, it seems that, the most significant was participation (though merely as an audience) of constitutional judges. The reason was that an important constitutional verdict concerning conscientious objection was expected in Poland at that time. The judgment was delivered three weeks later, on 7 October 2015 and was very vocal in favor of the right to conscientious objection. Polish Constitutional Tribunal declared that physicians' right to object morally, while performing their professional duties, stems directly from constitutional provisions granting freedom of conscience, regardless of the very fact or extent of its statutory implementation. The reader of this volume has an opportunity to read the argument of the Tribunal, which has been included.

Papers collected in this volume provide extensive insight into the diversity of issues discussed during the conference, including theoretical background for the recognition of conscientious objection as well as international and national legal regulations addressing the issue. In fact, the problem of conscientious objection is only one aspect of a much more general problem, concerning relation between law and morals which I am analyzing in the first chapter.

It seems that contemporary development of the modern state has achieved such a stage of intensity in regulating social life, that it is hardly accepting any limits, including those determined by conscience. In his contribution, David Forte has addressed this political and constitutional dimension of the problem. He asks question about conditions allowing operation of the free conscience in a republican government. The perspective taken by him refers to the US constitutional tradition. One might think that in this context the problem seems to hardly exist, as David Forte identifies the very essence of a republican government in its limiting character. Within this approach, "a true republic, respects religiously based conscience because it represents a different authority from governing power and hence affirms the limited nature of the governing power". This is the basic presumption, which provides also a specific way of understanding popular sovereignty as an intrinsic reason for limitation of the government.

Practical development of Western states legislative activity compels, however, to ask whether this perspective is correct. The legal perspective for the problem of conscientious objection in the United States, as adopted by William Saunders in his contribution to this volume, shows that such an optimistic approach is by no means obvious. Historical development of the modern state as established upon the principle of popular sovereignty provokes substantial doubts in this respect. Alexis de Tocqueville has already pointed out that the state based on the popular sovereignty tends rather to be unlimited, than self-restraint in regulations.[4] This is, however, not surprising. The theoretical concept of popular sovereignty assumes that before the original social contract was established and sovereign power representing people was created, no common normative system was able to provide universal measure of what is good and just discerning it from evil and unjust.[5] This leads to the conclusion, that there are no real alternative rules that could allow social coexistence, apart from the positive law. Therefore, the concept of the natural law being the foundation for the modern political order based on the principle of popular sovereignty was used rather to criticize the old social order (as non-conforming to the natural law) than give a common ethical foundation for social life. In this philosophical perspective, it is reasonably necessary that an individual who is free by nature has to create with others a sovereign which will create for everyone, the only binding common rules.[6] Therefore, it is again worth closer examination, if the "very nature of a republican limited government, ... is grounded in the acknowledgement of the presence of another, higher sovereign, to whom individuals owe their loyalty and into which

---

4 Alexis de Tocqueville, *Democracy in America*, (London: David Campbell Publishers Ltd, 1994), p. 254 ff.

5 Thomas Hobbes, *Leviathan*, ed. Richard Tuck (Cambridge: Cambridge University Press, 1996), p. 90: "*The notions of right and wrong, justice and injustice, have there (in the state of nature – A.S.) no place. Where there is no common power, there is no law; where no law, no injustice*". John Locke, *Two Treatises of Government*, (London 1824) p. 204 § 124: "*The great and chief end, therefore, of men's uniting into commonwealths, and putting themselves under government, is the preservation of their property. To which in the state of nature there are many things wanting. First, There wants an established, settled, known law, received and allowed by common consent to be the standard of right and wrong, and the common measure to decide all controversies between them*".

6 Immanuel Kant, *The Philosophy of Law. An Exposition of the Fundamental Principles of Jurisprudence as the Science of Right*, transl. W. Hastie, (Edinburgh: T&T Clark 1887), p. 164, § 44,: "... the first thing incumbent on men is to accept the principle that it is necessary to leave the state of nature, in which every one follows his own inclinations, and to form a union of all [...]. Men thus enter into a civil union, in which every one has it determined by law, what shall be recognized as his; and this is secured to him by a competent external power distinct from his own individuality. Such is the primary obligation, on the part of all men, to enter into the relations of a civil state of society".

loyalty the government has not a right to intrude". There are lots of declarations supporting this position, however, practical experience shows insurmountable tendency of the popular legislator to produce more and more regulations colonizing all spheres of social life at the sovereign's pleasure. Modern individualistic premises lead to the conclusion that nothing but statutory provisions are allowed to create bounding rules of social conduct. Therefore, declining to follow statutory regulations in the public sphere, because of another concurrent authority, is to be considered as a challenge to the popular sovereign.

It is therefore an open question whether the popular government is to be considered as natural environment supporting conscientious conduct or as its primary threat. David Forte advocating for the earlier position says, "*government should, by symbolic acts, acknowledge its own limited nature*". Indeed, existing statutory provisions authorizing conscientious objection might be considered as supporting this position. In practice, however, those provisions often appear to be narrow and subjected to constantly narrowing construction. Moreover, new statutory provisions emerge, which are contradicting this approach. As William Saunders said in his contribution to this volume, "despite … the existence of constitutional, national, and state laws protecting conscience the actual picture is much darker and more troubling". Therefore, it is really important to take an opportunity to explore broad theoretical dimension of the conscientious objection.

Another important aspect is addressed by David Thunder writing about the so-called "dissenting groups". The problem of conscientious objection appears to be a consequence of enacting laws considered by important part of society as being unjust. One of the often-proposed solutions to the problem is to create a special status for the people sufficiently motivated not to obey laws they consider to be immoral. David Thunder is very skeptical about this solution and he has presented a number of sound reasons for his skepticism.

There is the tendency to consider people morally objecting to follow immoral legal provisions as a specific "dissenters' group". It is closely related to perceiving them as religious groups somehow distinct from the rest of society and therefore "strange" in their moral attitude[7] (if not, in having any moral attitude at all).

---

7 Such a simplicity of approach is spectacularly manifested by Francesca Minerva, *Keeping Hands Clean and Patients Safe: How to Regulate Conscientious Objection of Roman Catholic Doctors*. In: M. Beard, S. Lynch (ed.) Conscience, Leadership and the Problem of 'Dirty Hands' (Research in Ethical Issues in Organizations, Volume 13) Emerald Group Publishing Ltd 2015, pp. 153 – 171.

Indeed, religious inspiration for conscientious objection is by no means rare. At the same time, however, it is a huge simplification of the problem if we reduce objecting conscience to a religious phenomenon. Also non-religious physicians object to the performance of abortion on purely rational grounds recognizing the human status of a child in the prenatal stage of development. Moreover, non-religious motivation is concurrent with the religious one among faith-oriented people. Contribution by Nikolas Nikas and Dorinda Bordley to this volume exemplifies very well purely scientific argument in support of conscientious objection.

Regardless of the complexity of motivation, conscientious objection is widely associated with religion and, therefore, labelled as "freedom of religion and conscience". This approach to conscientious objection has provoked criticism by Jakob Cornides in his contribution to this volume. He has emphasized that the intellectual context set by the contemporary culture makes this approach particularly weak. Cornides raises fundamental doubts whether the freedom of conscience is a proper way of addressing the proliferating problem of "injustice disguised as law" and calls for elaboration of alternative ways in which the problem might be addressed in a rational way.

This "disguised injustice" is always accompanied with some intellectual justifications explaining why it is to be considered morally acceptable what was previously morally condemned. Conscientious objection provokes today, however, not only public discussion among academics or columnists, but also concrete litigation. The volume presents, therefore, apart from the already-mentioned argument of the Polish Constitutional Tribunal,[8] also an intervention by Dorinda Bordley and Nikolas Nikas as delivered to the US Federal Supreme Court in a case concerning conscientious objection of pharmacists. This shows very well the nature of the contemporary controversy around conscience starting with the law waiving protection of vulnerable human beings at early stage of their development and subjecting their existence to interests of more autonomous people. The argument contained in the submission shows also that those supporting today conscientious conduct are by no means operating with vague moralistic persuasion, but with sound arguments based on scientific findings.

This short overview of the volume is already demonstrating that contemporary culture raises serious concerns about our ability to protect freedom

8 For the comment on the judgment See Pawlikowski, "*Więcej wolności…*", pp. 1–7.

of conscience manifesting in conscientious objection. Closer inspection of this problem seems to be of primary importance today. Variety of approaches, including different national and international perspectives, as well as particular experience of different medical professions, makes this volume worth studying.

Part I: General Perspective

Aleksander Stępkowki

Contemporary Conscience-Related Controversies Against Philosophical Background

Abstract: The chapter explains intellectual context underpinning contemporary controversies around conscientious objection. On the one hand, the focus is placed on the status of sovereign power and, on the other hand, the modern shift in understanding conscience. As concerns sovereign power of the state, the chapter describes, how classical liberal philosophers had promoted idea that the sovereign power of the state has no moral constrains. Although, this radical approach was rather disguised than emphasised by the early modern philosophers, careful reading of their writings shows their general unanimity in this respect. Their consistent philosophical constructions explain why, after three centuries of gradual practical implementation of modern social project, contemporary Western societies are ready to accept this controversial approach to sovereign power, even if it is not openly admitted. There is, however, a second reason why conscience, if objecting to certain legislative provisions, is considered as dangerous, anarchical concept threatening social life and public order. Such a depreciation of conscience in Western intellectual culture was possible due to considerable change in its understanding. The chapter presents the way in which conscience ceased to be understood as a faculty of reason and started to be associated with human emotions. Being understood as emotional and not rational motivation, the conscience is not considered as a legitimate reason for objecting to legislative provisions. Those two factors (the modern concept of sovereign power and the modern understanding of conscience) seem to determine contemporary approach to conscientious objection.

Keywords: sovereign power, conscience, practical reason, emotions

1 Introduction

Contemporary controversy about conscientious objection in medical health care is a concrete exemplification of the most fundamental (one might say classical) issue in jurisprudence: interrelation between law and morals. We are discussing problem whether an objective system of positive law should respect personal moral assessment of an action, as required on the ground of a specific statutory provision or other positive legal duty. In practice, it raises a question of general statutory authorisation for objection to perform a specific professional duty, motivated by rational, personal, and moral assessment of a specific situation, that is the *judgement of conscience*. The most confusing aspect of the contemporary controversy is suspiciousness it creates over the very conscience itself. The reasons for such depreciation of conscience in the contemporary debate will be discussed below.

2 Peculiarity of the contemporary challenge

If we are talking about conscience, one important remark is necessary. Conscience expresses itself as reasonable assessment of moral value of a specific, individual action rather than of an abstract and general rule of human conduct. Basically speaking, conscientious objection should rather concern the process of ethical assessment of a particular way of application of general statutory rules and not their content in itself. Conscience should be engaged rather in assessing reasonableness or equity of the process of application of general rules, which, in specific circumstances, might appear to give unjust effects even if the applied statutory provision is not unjust in itself. Necessity for conscientious objection should arise predominantly in a context of specific situations in which, due to extraordinary circumstances, adherence to abstract and general rules might amount to the legal enforcement of a conduct, which a person under the duty may consider intrinsically evil. Aristotle is describing a human virtue allowing to maintain justice in such conflicting situations, with a term *epieikeia*,[1] being traditionally considered as the Greek counterpart for Latin *aequitas*.[2] However, today we experience situations when conscience is objecting already to the very abstract content of the statutory provisions considering them to be true *lex iniusta*. This is the characteristic feature of contemporary Western civilisation inspiring controversies around the conscientious objection. Contemporary law does more and more often contain regulations contradictory to basic moral principles, which for a long time were considered as fundamental for our civilisation.

The Antigona's case comes to mind; however, it differs very much from our contemporary situation. Antigona was objecting to Creon's order affecting only one particular and extraordinary case, having a limited scope of application. Nowadays, we are experiencing regulations affecting millions of human beings.

---

1 Aristotle, *The Nicomachean Ethics*, (Cambridge, MA and London: Harvard University Press and William Heinemann Ltd., 1956), p. 313 ff.

2 See translation by Dionisio Lamino from 1558. *Ethica Nicomachea Donysio Lamino interprete*, V, 14, 1, in: Aristotelis opera. Edidit Academia Regia Borusica. Vol. 3, Berolini 1831, p. 562.

Moreover, these conflicting regulations often inspire subsequent measures aimed at ensuring operations of those first. This is the case of statutory provisions allowing for artificial interruption of pregnancy resulting in depriving of life to a child developing in the prenatal phase of its life. Such a *lex iniusta* requires special protection against information exposing true nature of the procedure known as abortion or IVG in France. Thus, unjust legislation inspires after some time subsequent legislative measures providing for serious restrictions of free speech and other aspects of free communication, as it was the case in February 2017 in France.[3]

Therefore, some more fundamental reflection upon the nature of the state's legislative power is necessary. Is the state arbitrary in its sovereignty, with the exclusive power to define what is good and evil at its pleasure; or is the result of the legislative activity subject to reasonable moral evaluation of a person capable of reasonable moral judgement? The question is a real "hard case" for our contemporary Western civilisation. *Prima facie* we are not willing to accept the totalitarian prerogative of the state to define what is good and evil at its pleasure. However, if we look closer at the contemporary legal culture, real rejection of this standpoint is by no means convincing. Moreover, this unlimited competence of a state was conceptualised long time ago, when intellectual foundations for modern social life were settled in the books. However, it is not clear if we can say it was clearly rejected.

---

3 Loi n° 2017-347 *du 20 mars 2017 relative à l'extension du délit d'entrave à l'interruption volontaire de grossesse,* Journal official de la République française n°0068 du 21 mars 2017, texte no. 2 https://www.legifrance.gouv.fr/eli/loi/2017/3/20/AFSX1632341L/jo/texte (seen on: 03.03.2018). The statutory measure was broadening the scope of application of the article L. 2223-2 in the *Code de la santé publique*, which had introduced in 1993 and subsequently extended in 2004 a tort of obstruction to abortion (*entrave à l'IVG*). The newly introduced provision was intended to ban any information on Inernet, which might prevent a woman from undergoing abortion, including information about human development before delivery. Application of this statutory measure was however restricted by means of interpretation as provided by the Conseill Constitutionalle on 16th March 2017 excluding from the scope of the law information directed to general public and presenting objective information. For the decision of the Conseil Constitutionel see: http://www.conseil-constitutionnel.fr/conseil-constitutionnel/francais/les-decisions/acces-par-date/decisions-depuis-1959/2017/2017-747-dc/communique-de-presse.148789.html (3.03.2018).

3 State's moral sovereignty

Thomas Hobbes was certainly the first, who denied in an explicit way the classical position, that good and evil can be recognised from the very nature. According to Hobbes, notions of good and evil are a product of the man's sensual perception in the pre-social state whereas in the society the only one entity being in the position to determine what is good and evil is the sovereign representing political community.[4] Consequently, the only sensible way of understanding natural law for Hobbes is to equate it with positive law.[5] In such a way, each legislative solution was attributed with the natural law status. This Hobbesian position was commonly found to be repugnant, however, it was in practice strongly influential. Even those who openly condemned Hobbes often were following his line of ethical thinking. John Locke provides the most spectacular example of such a double attitude towards Hobbes' position. It was very well portrayed by Leo Strauss who admitted that Hobbes, being

> *"deservedly punished for his recklessness ... still exercised a very great influence on all subsequent political thought, continental and even English, and especially on Locke – on the judicious Locke, who judiciously refrained as much as he could from mentioning Hobbes's «justly decried name»".*[6]

Therefore, Locke was affirming *prima facie* ability of the human reason to recognise what is intersubjectively good and evil by its very nature through the knowledge of natural law.[7]

---

4 Thomas Hobbes, *Leviathan*, ed. R. Tuck (Cambridge: Cambridge University Press, 1996), p. 39 (chap. VI). "*For these words of good, evil, and contemptible are ever used with relation to the person that useth them: there being nothing simply and absolutely so; nor any common rule of good and evil to be taken from the nature of the objects themselves; but from the person of the man, where there is no Commonwealth; or, in a Commonwealth, from the person that representeth it*".

5 Hobbes, *Leviathan*, p. 185 (Chap. XXVI): "4. ... The law of nature and the civil law contain each other and are of equal extent. For the laws of nature, which consist in equity, justice, gratitude, and other moral virtues on these depending, in the condition of mere nature (as I have said before in the end of the fifteenth Chapter), are not properly laws .... When a Commonwealth is once settled, then are they actually laws, and not before; as being then the commands of the Commonwealth; and therefore also civil laws: for it is the sovereign power that obliges men to obey them".

6 Leo Strauss, Natural Right and History, (Chicago Illinois: Chicago University Press, 1965), p. 166.

7 John Locke, *Two Treatises of Government*, (London 1824) p. 133, § 6.: "every man is following precepts of the same *reason, which is the law of nature teaching anyone (who*

However, having taken this anti-Hobbesian position at the beginning of his Second Treaty of Government, Locke made to it a very important reservation while explaining necessity of leaving the state of nature. Notwithstanding his initial affirmation of the reign of the law of nature in the state of nature, Locke suddenly said, that "The state of nature lacks established, settled, known law, received and accepted by common consent as the standard of right and wrong as the common measure to decide all controversies".[8] Locke is then explaining that the lack of common measure of what is good and evil results from man being biased by self-interest which cause, that the men "aren't apt to accept the law of nature as a law that will bind them if it is applied to their particular cases".[9]

It is even more precisely explained in § 136, where Locke says that natural law "serves not, as it ought, to determine the rights, and fence the properties of those that live under it".[10] As it is impossible to settle the content of the law of nature due to insurmountable power of self-interest over one's ethical perception, legislative power must be accepted as the only one arbiter necessary to reconcile contradicting private moral opinions.[11] Therefore, legislative power appears to have full moral supremacy over the society. As Locke says

> *"this legislative is not only the supreme power of the common-wealth, but sacred and unalterable in the hands where the community have once placed it; ... [A]ll the obedience, which by the most solemn ties any one can be obliged to pay, ultimately terminates in this supreme power, and is directed by those laws which it enacts: nor can any oaths to any foreign power whatsoever, or any domestic subordinate power, discharge any member of the society from his obedience to the legislative".*[12]

This modern concept creates an axiom, that the legislative power "can never be supposed to extend farther, than the common good".[13]

---

takes the trouble to consult it), that because we are all equal and independent, no-one ought to harm anyone else".

8 Locke, *Two Treaties*, p. 204 (§ 124).

9 Locke, *Two Treaties*, p. 204 (§ 124).

10 Locke, *Two Treaties*, p. 211.

11 Locke, *Two Treaties*, p. 211: § 136 "The legislative, or supreme authority, ... is bound to dispense justice, and decide the rights of the subject by promulgated standing laws, and known authorized judges: for the law of nature being unwritten, and so no where to be found but in the minds of men, they who through passion or interest shall miscite, or misapply it, cannot so easily be convinced of their mistake where there is no established judge".

12 Locke, *Two Treaties*, p. 209 (§ 134).

13 Locke, *Two Treaties*, p. 206 (§ 131).

Moreover, this Locke'an approach to legislative power is quite similar to other philosophers like Rousseau and Kant, who have also determined the modern culture with their ideas. They also granted legislature with unlimited power to enact absolutely bounding statutes.[14] It is true, a reservation should be made, that Rousseau and Kant emphasised democratic procedural requirement to such an unchallengeable position of a statutory enactment, namely that all people are involved in law-making process, so that everyone was deciding on everyone else. Regardless of the fact that such a procedural requirement is hardly realistic, this democratic attitude towards legislation still is more and more influencing culture and social consciousness. The standpoint accepting absolute legislative power of the modern state is still more and more persuasive. It is commonly considered to be a much better solution than risking anarchy and war.

Taking into account that Locke's political philosophy is the true foundation of the modern state and social life, contemporary controversies over the conscientious objections are better understood. It seems that we have achieved today such a level of practical implementation of the philosophical concept of the modern state that the absolute moral supremacy of the state has been *de facto* accepted. There is, however, another aspect of this process that is concurrent to the acceptance of absolute state supremacy in moral domain. This parallel process has deprived conscience from its rational character and is directly inspiring contemporary objection to conscientious conduct in medical area.

4 Separating conscience from reason

If we look into classical moral philosophy, that of Plato, Aristotle or Cicero, it is clear that morality is the domain of reason. The reason is considered there as peculiar to human beings constituting their very essence, so Aristotle is saying

14 See also Jean Jacques Rousseau, *Du contract social ou principes du droit politique*, (Lyon, 1792), p. 49 „… le pouvoir souverain, tout absolu, tout sacré, tout inviolable qu'il est, ne passe ni ne peut passer les bornes des convention générales …"; Ibidem, p. 57: „… il ne faut plus demander à qui il appartient de faire des loix… ni si la loi peut être injuste, puisque nul n'est injuste envers lui-même; …"; See also Immanuel Kant, Die Metaphysik der Sitten, ed. J.H. v. Kirchmann, (Leipzig, 1870), p. 62: „§ 9 Das Naturrecht im Zustande einer bürgerlichen Verfassung (d. i. dasjenige, was für die letztere aus Principien a priori abgeleitet werden kann) kann durch die statutarischen Gesetze der letzteren nicht Abbruch leiden"; Ibidem, p. 155: § 48 „der Wille des Gesetzgebers (*legislatoris*) in Ansehung dessen, was das äußere Mein und Dein betrifft, ist untadelig (irreprehensibel)"..

that "… the intellect is the man himself".[15] This reason, in its practical dimension is not only allowing them to discern between good and evil[16] but is also able to direct actions taken by a virtuous man according to judgement of his reason as to what is good.[17] This way of understanding moral knowledge and its relation to human conduct was followed strictly by Cicero, who was insisting that a good man is perfectly able to follow reasonable judgement as to what is good and evil, and respectively, what is just and unjust. In the classical ethics this faculty of reason enabling moral knowledge and practically directing human conduct was called the "law of nature", which is characterised by the Arpinat in the following way:

> *There is a true law, a right reason, conformable to nature, universal, unchangeable, eternal, whose commands urge us to duty, and whose prohibitions restrain us from evil. Whether it enjoins or forbids, the good respect its injunctions, and the wicked treat them with indifference.*[18]

---

15 Et.Nikom IX, VIII, 6; 1168b; Aristotle, *The Nicomachean Ethics*, p. 553.

16 Politics, 1.1253a "…it is the special property of man in distinction from the other animals that he alone has perception of good and bad and right and wrong and the other moral qualities". http://www.perseus.tufts.edu/hopper/text?doc=urn:cts:greekLit:tlg0086.tlg035.perseus-eng1:1.1253a.
Et.Nikom IX, VIII, 6 (1169a): "With the bad man therefore, what he does is not in accord with what he ought to do, but the good man does what he ought, since intelligence always chooses for itself that which is best, and the good man obeys his intelligence". Aristotle, *The Nicomachean Ethics*, p. 553. For on-line version see: http://www.perseus.tufts.edu/hopper/text?doc=urn:cts:greekLit:tlg0086.tlg010.perseus-eng1:1169a

17 Et.Nikom IX, VIII, 6 (1169a): "With the bad man therefore, what he does is not in accord with what he ought to do, but the good man does what he ought, since intelligence always chooses for itself that which is best, and the good man obeys his intelligence". Aristotle, *The Nicomachean Ethics*, p. 553. For on-line version see: http://www.perseus.tufts.edu/hopper/text?doc=urn:cts:greekLit:tlg0086.tlg010.perseus-eng1:1169a

18 Marcus Tullius Cicero. The Political Works Comprising His Treatise on the Republic and His Treatise on the Laws in Two Volumes. Translated by Francis Barham, Esq., Vol. I. The Treatise On The Republic, London: Edmund Spettigue 1841, p. 270, De republica, 3.33: "Est quidem vera lex recta ratio naturae congruens, diffusa in omnes, constans, sempiterna, quae vocet ad officium iubendo, vetando a fraude deterreat; quae tamen neque probos frustra iubet aut vetat nec improbos iubendo aut vetando movet". M. Tullius Cicero. Librorum de Re Publica Sex. C. F. W. Müller. Leipzig. Teubner. 1889, p. 344. For the same Cicero's approach in his other works See: *De legibus* I, 18–19 "… *lex est ratio summa, insita in natura, quae iubet ea quae facienda sunt, prohibetque contraria. Eadem ratio, cum est in hominis mente confirmata et perfecta, lex est. Itaque arbitrantur prudentiam esse legem, cuius ea vis sit, ut recte facere iubeat, vetet delinquere*". http://data.perseus.org/citations/urn:cts:latinLit:phi0474.phi044.perseus-lat1:1.19

This ethical approach became an intellectual standard in Western culture up to early modern times. In the meantime, Aquinas, however, considerably developed it. He acknowledged that the natural law might be understood in certain way as conscience,[19] however, Aquinas wanted to be more accurate and provided some additional distinctions within this approach towards human rational moral faculty. In the second book of his *Scriptum super sententiis Petri Lombardii*,[20] Aquinas emphasises active character of conscience and thus discerning between natural law, *synderesis* (pre-conscience) and the conscience *sensu stricto*. According to Doctor Angelicus, the natural law is therefore to be understood as general moral principles, *synderesis* is to be understood as human faculty to recognise them, whereas the conscience is the imperative force of reason allowing application of general principles to particular case.[21] In this context, the conscience was describing this aspect of the operation of reason, which was directly determining human action.

However, emergence of the modern intellectual culture has brought a radical change in our understanding of reason. Reason, even if still able to discern between good and evil,[22] appeared in practice unable to direct human actions according to that knowledge. It was directly expressed by John Locke, who acknowledged, that, despite rational ability to discern between good and evil, it is not the

---

19 Super Sent., lib. 2 d. 24 q. 2 a. 4 ad 5 „ … conscientia, secundum quod accipitur pro habitu, potest dici lex naturalis, quia ex habitu illo praecipue actus conscientiae elicitur". (See: http://www.corpusthomisticum.org/snp2023.html)

20 For more systematic presentation of Aquinas' account on conscience see M. Mrozek, Tomasz z Akwinu „Komentarz do sentencji Piotra Lombarda", II, D. 24, Q.2, A. 3–4, „Forum Teologiczne" 15 (2014), p. 175–191.

21 Super Sent., lib. 2 d. 24 q. 2 a. 4 co.: „… Et secundum hunc modum patet, qualiter differant synderesis, lex naturalis, et conscientia: quia lex naturalis nominat ipsa universalia principia juris, synderesis vero nominat habitum eorum, seu potentiam cum habitu; conscientia vero nominat applicationem quamdam legis naturalis ad aliquid faciendum per modum conclusionis cujusdam."

22 It is very probable, that by attributing to reason ability of discerning between good and evil, Locke was equating good with pleasure. There are at least two reasons for such a position: 1) in the *Second Treaty* Locke is directly saying (J. Locke, *Two Treaties …*, § 26, p. 145), that "God, who hath given the world to men in common, hath also given them reason to make use of it to the best advantage of life, and convenience"; 2) in the *Essay Concerning Human Understanding*, II, XXI,42 Locke is clearly acknowledging, that "what has an aptness to produce pleasure in us is that we call «good» and what is apt to produce pain in us we call «evil»; for no Rother reason but for its aptness to produce pleasure and pain in us, wherein consists our happiness and misery". John Locke, *An Essay Concerning Human Understanding*, 13 ed. London 1849, p. 163.

reason that truly determines human actions but interests and passions.[23] In this way, moral conduct was separated from reason, as being passive and unable to inspire moral action, and subordinating this to senses and emotions. This radical change of approach was systematically applied by David Hume, who argued:

> *Since morals […] have an influence on the actions and affections, it follows that they cannot be derived from reason; and that because reason alone […] can never have any such influence. Morals excite passions, and produce or prevent actions. Reason of itself is utterly impotent in this particular. The rules of morality, therefore, are not conclusions of our reason.*[24]

This change had immediate consequences for understanding of conscience. Preserving active character of conscience, Hume had to separate it from reason and subordinate to subjective feelings and emotions arguing that

> *Reason is wholly inactive, and can never be the source of so active a principle as conscience, or a sense of morals.*[25]

Hume has made the reason unable to recognise good or evil as he reduced function of reason only to its theoretical dimension focused on discernment between truth and falsehood.

> *Reason is the discovery of truth or falsehood. Truth or falsehood consists in an agreement or disagreement either to the real relations of ideas, or to real existence and matter of fact. Whatever therefore is not susceptible of this agreement or disagreement, is incapable of being true or false, and can never be an object of our reason. […] [A]ctions do not derive their merit from a conformity to reason, nor their blame from a contrariety to it; […] Actions may be laudable or blamable; but they cannot be reasonable or unreasonable […]. Moral distinctions, therefore, are not the offspring of reason.*[26]

It took a long time since Hume's new conceptualisation of the moral issues colonised popular consciousness. This modern conceptualisation of morals, assuming lack of relationship between conscience and reason is growingly influential. It is inspiring contemporary anti-conscience attitude which is particularly vivid in medical healthcare. If the conscience is depicted as subjective, emotional

---

23 Locke, *Two Treaties*, p. 204 (§ 124) "… *though the law of nature be plain and intelligible to all rational creatures; yet men being biased by their interest, as well as ignorant for want of study of it, are not apt to allow of it as a law binding to them in the application of it to their particular cases*".

24 David Hume, *A Treatise of Human Nature in two volumes*, vol.2, (London and New York: Dent and Dutton), p. 167.

25 Hume, *A Treatise*, p. 168.

26 Hume, *A Treatise*, p. 167–168.

motivation of our action, it has a very weak position against statutory law, which is considered to be foundation for social life.

5 Instead of conclusion

The cultural process as outlined above has determined contemporary perception of conscience. Therefore, conscientious objection is often presented today as a challenge of subjective feelings to objective standard allowing social cohabitation. This is, however, not a proper perspective. In fact, situation is quite opposite. Contemporary legislature, supported with the means of social influence, is more and more often challenging most fundamental moral consciousness. In this perspective, conscientious objection is not a means of attacking existing social order, but rather a last-resort defence against the statutory provisions denying fundamental moral principles. Conscience does not provide general capacity to question the law in force on the basis of an individual's personal opinion. It is rather reaffirming existence of an objective moral order and human ability for its rational recognition. If, however, existence of such an original moral framework is practically denied, conscientious conflicts emerge. The question therefore is, why the contemporary state is so zealous in imposing legal obligations which conscience opposes so much?

David F. Forte

Conscience and Republican Government

Abstract: In this chapter, the question is whether an individual can demand an exemption from a law that applies to all. This chapter describes a number of approaches to this problem that have been attempted in the American experiment at governance, and it seeks to evaluate their efficaciousness. Over the last two centuries, however, protections for freedom of conscience have become attenuated—indeed some have become corrupted—so that today, freedom of conscience in the American Republic no longer stands on as firm a ground as in the past. There is, from the lessons of American experience, no single formula of governance that can guarantee the right of conscience. But there are a number of factors that can conduce to its observance.

Key words: conscience, constitution, law, republican government, popular sovereignty

1 Introduction

Can a sovereign brook disobedience? Can a person, believing in utter confidence that he is in the right, claim an exemption from law that applies to everyone else? In theory, the answer has to be "No," for a sovereign that cannot apply its laws universally is no sovereign, and a state that rules only by sufferance of each individual person's consent does not govern by the rule of law.

Yet sovereign states do violate moral norms. Sovereign states do claim the obedience of subjects even when it goes against their deepest moral positions. How can an individual living by a well-informed conscience find his moral space in such a regime? And even if he could, how would one know whether an intensely held belief is the result of a truly disciplined conscience or only an emotional preference?

One option is to infuse the political sovereign with the normative underpinnings of its very existence. In other words, to arrive at a natural-law state. Such a state, almost by definition, would not interfere with the acts of an individual based upon a properly morally reasoned conscience.

A second option is to limit the sovereign's reach. Appropriate political mechanisms can hamstring the sovereign from doing harm. Dividing sovereignty between the center and the provinces or states is one option, as well as devices for internally checking the power of each government itself. Elections, freedom of the press, and, most importantly, the subsidiary activity of civic associations also help to prevent a government from intruding into the moral space of the individual. Further, a sovereign that affirms the existence of divine authority (but avoiding a theocratic alliance) thereby normatively limits its own reach.

A third option is to create regimes of rights, safe harbors for individuals. A general right of conscience is not protected thereby, but only particular exercises of conscience, such as free expression. But this requires, in the end, the agreement of the state. It also requires that the regime protect true rights, and not privileges of groups of people using the language of rights to impose their views upon others.

A fourth option is to leave religion, in particular, a limited self-governing independence from the political sovereign. Such a device does protect religiously based acts of conscience to a degree, but it leaves vulnerable individual acts of conscience based solely upon moral reasoning.

To some degree or another, at its founding, the American regime attempted all four mechanisms: (1) It established a Constitution, the positive law content of which was at least compatible with natural law principles, if not instantiating them; (2) It limited and divided political sovereignty; (3) It created rights within protected safe harbors; (4) It recognized the independence of religion to have its own limited but self-governing sphere within the polity, and to tie the protections of an individual's conscience to that self-governing sphere of organized religion.

In the brief summary that follows, I shall describe each of these options as attempted in the American experiment at governance, and I shall judge upon their efficaciousness. One can say, at this point, however, that over the last two centuries, these mechanisms have become attenuated—indeed some have become corrupted—so that today, freedom of conscience in the American republic no longer stands on as firm a ground as in the past.

2 Sovereignty

In his classic work on sovereignty,[1] Bertrand du Jouvenal points out that sovereignty is an ancient concept, but that in practice it meant that each station in society had a superior, and the superior possessed sufficient power consonant with and limited to his station. The modern notion of sovereignty, Jouvenal declares, comes with the monopolization of power.

Historians have recounted the many factors that led to the monopolization of power and the modern notion of the sovereign as unlimited in his rightful exercise of power. The plague of the 14th century undermined the manorial

1 Bertrand de Jouvenal, *Sovereignty* (Indianapolis: Liberty Fund, 2001).

economy; the Reformation shattered the Catholic confederacy under the Pope and left a vacuum that the secular power could fill; the development of military technology necessitated a greater concentration of resources to marshal them. In addition, philosophical justifications arose from authors such as Jean Bodin (1530–1596), Niccolo Machiavelli (1469–1527), and Baron von Puffendorf (1632–1694) that legitimated the concentration of power. Lastly, the religious wars of the era culminated in the Treaty of Westphalia (1648), which legally ratified the concentration of power in the hands of a sovereign.

Even in England, where Parliament had long resisted the like ambitions of England's kings, the resolution of the conflict in the Glorious Revolution of 1688 kept the idea of sovereignty, but lodged it in an ambiguous formulation of "The king in Parliament." By the time William Blackstone summarized the constitutional structure of England in his *Commentaries on the Law of England* (1765–1769), the idea of sovereignty remained that of power undiluted. "[I] is the very essence of law, that it be made by the supreme power," he declared.[2] "There must be in every government, however it began, or by whatsoever right it subsists, a supreme, irresistible, absolute, uncontrolled authority, in which the *jura summit imperii*, or the rights of sovereignty reside."[3]

3 The principles of the founding

In America's quest for independence from Great Britain, the colonials staked their moral position on three groundings, all of which were thought to be in utter harmony with one another: (1) divine sanction, (2) natural law, and (3) the "rights of Englishmen."[4] See, for example, the Resolves of the First Continental Congress, October 14, 1774, claiming rights derived from "the immutable laws of nature, the principles of the English constitution, and the several charters and compacts."[5]

2 William Blackstone, *Commentaries on the Law of England* (Indianapolis: Liberty Fund), sec. 46
<http://oll.libertyfund.org/titles/2140>

3 Blackstone, *Commentaries on the Law of England*, sec. 48.

4 See, for example, "Declaration and Resolves of the First Continental Congress," 14 October 1774, claiming rights derived from, in: *Colonies to Nation*, 1763–1789, ed. Jack P. Greene. (New York: Norton & Co., 1975).

5 "Declaration and Resolves of the First Continental Congress," in: *Colonies to Nation*, 1763–1789, ed. Jack P. Greene, (New York: Norton & Co., 1975), p. 244.

The problems with the mother country followed immediately after England's victory, in 1763, in the French and Indian War, known in Europe as the Seven Years' War. In order to finance its new empire in America taken from the French, Parliament imposed new taxes directly on the colonies. In response, the colonists asserted that Parliament had exceeded its constitutional powers. In 1764, in a pamphlet that would be reprinted throughout the American colonies garnering enthusiastic agreement among the Americans, James Otis decried against any right that Parliament had in fashioning laws that would deprive men of their property without their consent. But he grounded his argument in the relationship of the political state to God.

"The supreme power in a state," Otis declared, " is *jus dicere* only: – *jus dare*, strictly speaking, belongs alone to God. Parliaments are in all cases to declare what is for the good of the whole; but it is not the *declaration* of parliament that makes it so: There must be in every instance, a higher authority, *viz.* GOD. Should an act of parliament be against any of *his* natural laws, which are *immutably* true, *their* declaration would be contrary to eternal truth, equity and justice, and consequently void…"[6]

At the same time, Protestant ministers in America merged the law of God with the law of nature, and the two became a staple of their sermons of the era. Recall Thomas Jefferson's invocation of "the Laws of Nature and of Nature's God" in the Declaration of Independence. Of particular influence among the Protestant clergy was John Witherspoon, Presbyterian minister, President of the College of New Jersey (later Princeton), and a signer of the Declaration of Independence. In a sermon delivered on May 17, 1776, with the Revolutionary War well begun, Witherspoon merged the ideas of the Providence of God, the natural right to property and the connection between religion and public virtue.[7] "It would be a criminal inattention," he said, "not to observe the singular interposition of Providence hitherto, in behalf of the American colonies."[8] He declared that when the right to property is foregone, the rights of conscience fall into bondage.[9] And he extolled the degree of "public spirit" that had overcome jealousies and divisions.[10]

---

6 James Otis, "The Rights of the Colonies asserted and proved," in: Greene, *Declaration and Resolves of the First Continental Congress, p. 32 (emphases in original).*

7 John Witherspoon, "The Dominion of Providence over the Passions of Men," in: *Political Sermons of the American Founding Era, 1730–1805*, ed. Ellis Sandoz (Indianapolis: Liberty Press, 1991), pp. 531–558.

8 Witherspoon, "The Dominion of Providence over the Passions of Men," p. 546.

9 Witherspoon, "The Dominion of Providence over the Passions of Men," p. 549.

10 Witherspoon, "The Dominion of Providence over the Passions of Men," p. 551.

Whereas in Europe, the doctrine of natural rights often set itself against religion, in America rights were tied to religion in a way that harkened back to a medieval notion of rights as derivative from natural law obligations. Recall Jefferson's plaint about slavery in his 1774 *A Summary View of the Rights of British America.* "Can the liberties of a Nation be secure when we have removed a conviction that these liberties are the gift of God? Indeed I tremble for my country when I reflect that God is just and that his justice cannot sleep forever." Or, note in the justification for the existence and the founding of the government itself. "We hold these truths to be self-evident, that all men are created equal, that they are endowed by their Creator with certain unalienable rights, that among these are life, liberty and the pursuit of happiness. That to secure these rights, governments are instituted among men, deriving their just powers from the consent of the governed."[11]

4 Divided and limited sovereignty

Having called upon natural law or natural right principles in the struggle for independence, it was logical to assume that the Framers would have crafted the law of the Constitution to be in harmony—slavery excepted—with those principles. They held that sovereignty was no longer lodged in the King, or even in the "King in Parliament." Sovereignty was lodged in the people, not as a mystic whole, as the French would later have it. But rather sovereignty was lodged in the right of the people to come together from a state of nature to form structures of government. That was why James Wilson, in his influential work, *On Municipal Law* (1804) disputed Blackstone's definition of sovereignty as co-extensive with the legislative power. It was rather, consent of the person, that bound him, not the decree of the legislature standing above him as "sovereign." "*[C]onsent,* Wilson wrote, is the sole obligatory principle of human government and human laws."[12] It would follow from Wilson's logic that no man could be forced to consent to laws that intruded upon his conscience. As James Madison put it, "Before any man can be considered as a member of Civil Society, he must be considered as a subject of the Governor of the Universe."[13]

---

11 U.S. Declaration of Independence.

12 James Wilson, "On Municipal Law," in: *American Political Writing During the Founding Era,* 2 vols., ed. Charles S. Hyneman and Donald S. Lutz (Indianapolis: Liberty Fund, 1983), Vol. II, p. 1293 (emphasis in original).

13 James Madison, "Memorial and Remonstrance against Religious Assessments" (1785) <http://press-pubs.uchicago.edu/founders/documents/amendI_religions43.html>

When it came to structure of the Constitution itself, which they expected would endure for the sake of their "posterity," the Framers of that document also did something that had more of a medieval ring than a modern one. They divided sovereignty into multiple nodes. As Justice Anthony Kennedy put it, "The Framers split the atom of sovereignty. It was the genius of their idea that our citizens would have two political capacities, one state and one federal, each protected from incursion by the other. The resulting Constitution created a legal system unprecedented in form and design, establishing two orders of government, each with its own direct relationship, its own privity, its own set of mutual rights and obligations to the people who sustain it and are governed by it."[14]

At the time of framing, Madison described how the mechanism of the new government would work.

"In a single republic, all the power surrendered by the people is submitted to the administration of a single government; and the usurpations are guarded against by a division of the government into distinct and separate departments. In the compound republic of America, the power surrendered by the people is first divided between two distinct governments, and then the portion allotted to each subdivided among distinct and separate departments. Hence a double security arises to the rights of the people. The different governments will control each other, at the same time that each will be controlled by itself."[15]

When the delegates to the Constitutional Convention met in Philadelphia in 1787, the Virginia delegation came with a plan for a rather centralized government. The states would continue to exist, but the national legislature would have jurisdiction to legislate in all cases where "the separate States are incompetent, or in which the harmony of the United States may be interrupted by the exercise of individual Legislation." The national legislature would also have had the power to veto state laws and to call out the army against any state that failed "in its duties" under the articles of the Constitution.[16] It was a formula to make the state prefectures. It was also a recipe for civil war.

As the convention proceeded, however, the delegates came to a different insight and an entirely different structure. They decided to protect state sovereignty first, by limiting the substantive areas over which the national Congress could legislate, leaving the entire residue to the states; second, by preventing

---

14 U.S. Term Limits, Inc. v. Thornton, 514 U.S. 779, 838 (1995) (Kennedy, J., concurring).

15 Federalist 51

16 Gaillard Hunt and James B. Scott, eds., *Debates in the Federal Convention of 1787 Reported by James Madison* (New York, 1920), pp. 23–26.

Congress from favoring any one section of the Union over another; and, third, by integrating the states as constituent elements of the national government.

Thus, under the United States Constitution, "All legislative Powers *herein granted* shall be vested in a Congress of the United States..."[17] All the remainder of governmental powers were left to the states. Congress does possess extensive powers, but they must ultimately be derived from a positive grant of power listed in the Constitution, primarily in Article I, Section 8. The bifurcation of sovereignty was confirmed in the Tenth Amendment: "The powers not delegated to the United States by the Constitution, nor prohibited by it to the States, are reserved to the States respectively, or to the people."[18]

The Constitution also prohibited Congress from preferring "the Ports of one State over those of another."[19] It required that federal monies had to be spent "for the general Welfare."[20] It guaranteed a republican government to each state.[21] It strongly indicated that new states would be admitted on the basis of equality with the existing states,[22] and it provided that each state had equal representation in the Senate.[23]

Moreover, the states as political actors were integrated into the governance of the union. Those persons who were qualified to vote for members of the House of Representatives were determined by what each state set as requirements for those who could vote for the state's most numerous branch of its legislature.[24] The members of the Senate were chosen by each state's legislature.[25] The states had the initial power of setting the rules for the election of members of Congress,[26] and three-fourths of them had to approve any proposed amendment to the Constitution for it to go into effect.[27] In 1789, the Bill of Rights was passed by Congress and sent to the states, entirely designed to limit the federal government further.

---

17 U.S. Constitution, Article I, Sec. 1. Emphasis added.
18 U.S. Const., Amend. X.
19 U.S. Const., Article I, Sec 9.
20 U.S. Const., Article I, Sec. 8.
21 U.S. Const., Article IV, Sec. 4.
22 U.S. Const., Article IV, Sec. 3.
23 U.S. Const., Article I, Sec. 3.
24 U.S. Const., Art I, Sec. 2.
25 U.S. Const., Article I, Sec. 3.
26 U.S. Const., Article I, Sec. 4.
27 U.S. Const., Article V.

With the central government limited, and the state governments also limited by their constitutions and their own limited political norms, the divided sovereignty left open a vast social space where people, free of encumbering positive law, could live by their own voluntary societies. What would later be termed "civic associations" governed Americans in the 19th century. Primary among these self-governing institutions was the family and the church. Throughout the 19th century, the influence of religion grew and greater proportions of Americans became formally attached to a church. As de Tocqueville noted, religion prospered in the new country, and neither religion nor the state viewed the other as an enemy. For example, he observed, "Religion in America takes no direct part in the government of society. But it must be regarded as the first of their political institutions."[28] And while religion supported the democratic state, the state acknowledged the authority of religion over men's souls and minds.

5 Extrinsic restraints

In 1789, the Bill of Rights was appended to the Constitution. It contained two clauses dealing with religion: "Congress shall pass no law respecting an establishment of religion or prohibiting the free exercise thereof."[29] It was clear that the country wanted no formal established church, as the Anglican Church was established in England. Nor did the Congress wish to stifle official affirmation for the good of religion. In fact, subsequent to the drafting of what came to be the First Amendment, Congress quickly asked the country for days of prayer and thanksgiving, established chaplains for itself and for the army, held church services in the House of Representatives, and paid missionaries to convert the Indians.

Many scholars are now certain from the debates surrounding the drafting of the First Amendment that it was also designed affirmatively to protect those states that wished to have an established religion.[30] At the time, six states had such establishments, consisting mostly in collecting taxes form the support of clergy.

---

28 Alexis de Tocqueville, *Democracy in America* (New York: Random House, 1945), Vol. I, p. 316.

29 U.S. Const. Amend I.

30 See, e.g., Vincent P. Muñoz, "The Original Meaning of the Establishment Clause and the Impossibility of Its Incorporation," *University of Pennsylvania Journal of Constitutional Law*, Vol. 8 (2006), pp. 585, 605. <https://www.law.upenn.edu/journals/conlaw/articles/volume8/issue4/Munoz8U.Pa.J.Const.L.585(2006).pdf>

Nonetheless, two centuries after its founding, the United States Constitution has been modified—by amendment, judicial interpretation, and political practice. The power of the central government over society has vastly increased, while the states have become enablers of federal programs. Beginning in the 1940s, judicial decisions have placed religion and the state at odds with one another, and today, church organizations themselves are being directed to act at the behest of state, even if it offends the religion's own mores.

The Free Exercise Clause of the First Amendment has not been of much support to the rights of conscience. It is curious that in the draft of that amendment that the House of Representatives approved and sent to the Senate, the right of conscience was affirmed: "Congress shall make no law establishing religion or prohibiting the free exercise thereof, not shall the rights of Conscience be infringed."[31] Yet, when a different version was returned by the Senate, the mention of conscience was deleted, as was the final draft worked out between Senate and House of Representative committee members.

There is no contemporaneous record attesting to why the protection of conscience was deleted. Certainly, no one thought that Congress possessed any right to interfere with conscience. It may have been dropped because the protection of free exercise includes within it the protection of conscience.

Nonetheless, the impact of the free exercise clause has not been great as a limit on government. There was a period in the late 20th century, when the Supreme Court subjected laws impacting on the free exercise of religion to a high level of scrutiny.[32]

But the Court made so many exceptions that the body of law protecting religion practice became incoherent. Finally, in 1990, the Court withdrew from protecting most acts of free exercise by declaring that generally applicable laws that do not single out religion will be held valid.[33]

Of all the devices, therefore, that can be utilized to protect freedom of conscience, those creating a safe harbor for conscience have, in the American experience, been the weakest. Conscience has prospered more from a Constitution that limits the reach of government and where government acknowledges the limited self-governing nature of religion.

---

31 Neil H. Cogan, ed., *The Complete Bill of Rights* (New York: Oxford University Press, 1997), p. 3.

32 Sherbert v. Verner, 374 U.S. 398 (1963).

33 Employment Div., Dept. of Human Resources of Oregon v. Smith, 494 U.S. 872 (1990).

6 Conscience and the republic

Even though the Supreme Court has set up a false dichotomy between the state and religion, the official acknowledgement of divine authority still abounds in American political discourse. A republic, that is, a true republic, respects religiously based conscience because it represents a different authority from governing power and hence affirms the limited nature of the governing power. It avows, by explicit reference, that the government is not the only authority over the person. The religious sense that a republic respects can be evidenced in the very source of the right to govern, in the deliberative process, or spoken by the public authority itself. The public references to God as judge, or as helper, or as protector, are the chorus in our republican Greek play. They are the slave holding the garland of laurel over the head of the triumphant returning Roman General while intoning, "Remember that thou art only mortal."[34] The iconic phrases that swirl about Americans in motto, oath, and Presidential statement have the salutary lesson of warning the state of the danger of political hubris—that is, the conceit that it is only through government and the political process that social and moral problems can be addressed. They signal that, for the sake of liberty, there are limits to what government can do. Here are some examples.

Washington, to whom all looked to for example, and whose practice shaped our mode of constitutional governance, declared as part of his "first official act," his "fervent supplications to the … Almighty Being who rules over the Universe … that his benediction may consecrate to the liberties and happiness of the People of the United States, a Government instituted by themselves."[35] And in his Thanksgiving Proclamation, he offered a prayer to God "to enable us all, whether in public or private stations, to perform our several and relative duties properly and punctually; to render our National Government a blessing to all the people by constantly being a Government of wise, just, and constitutional laws, discreetly and faithfully executed and obeyed."[36] In his farewell address he charged, "Whatever may be conceded to the influence of refined education on minds of

---

34 Some of the phrasing in this section of the essay is drawn from David F. Forte, "Religion and the Republic", Public Discourse blog, the Witherspoon Institute, 6 July 2015 http://www.thepublicdiscourse.com.

35 George Washington, "Thanksgiving Proclamation Washington's Inaugural Address of 1789"
http://www.archives.gov/exhibits/american_originals/inaugtxt.html .

36 George Washington, "Thanksgiving Proclamation" <http://lcweb2.loc.gov/ammem/GW/gw004.html>

peculiar structure, reason and experience both forbid us to expect that national morality can prevail in exclusion of religious principle."[37]

Lincoln too called upon God to provide the wisdom by which the nation could possess good laws: "With malice toward none; with charity for all; with firmness in the right, as God gives us to see the right." And when national morality breaks down, then the judgment of that beneficent Governor of the Universe can be terrible indeed. Lincoln intoned: "Fondly do we hope fervently do we pray that this mighty scourge of war may speedily pass away. Yet, if God wills that it continue until all the wealth piled by the bondsman's two hundred and fifty years of unrequited toil shall be sunk, and until every drop of blood drawn by the lash shall be paid by another drawn with the sword, as was said three thousand years ago, so still it must be said, 'The judgments of the Lord are true and righteous altogether.'"[38]

Today, when government officials take an oath, they call upon God to help them fulfill it. In the State of Ohio, the standard "So help me God" is replaced by the more formidable "And so shall I answer unto God." Americans have added to the Pledge of Allegiance the declaration that we are "a republic, under God." They have adopted as the national motto, "In God we trust." None of these are instances of empty "ceremonial deism," as one secularist Supreme Court justice put it. On the contrary, they are explicit affirmations of the necessity of a divine authority that is the ultimate source of rights, of guidance for public policy, and of judgment.

The very nature of a republican limited government, therefore, is grounded in the acknowledgement of the presence of another, higher sovereign, to whom individuals owe their loyalty and into which loyalty the government has not a right to intrude.

Therefore, from the lessons of American experience, there is no single formula of governance that can guarantee the right of conscience. But we have found that a number of factors conduce to its observance.

1) A sense that sovereignty resides in the people.
2) That the authority of God precedes that of the civil state.
3) That the state is created to protect liberty.

---

37 George Washington, "Farewell Address" <http://avalon.law.yale.edu/18th_century/washing.asp>

38 Abraham Lincoln, "Second Inaugural Address" <http://avalon.law.yale.edu/19th_century/lincoln2.asp>

4) That governments should be constitutionally limited in the powers they can rightly exercise.
5) That affirmative guarantees protecting conscience are in the positive law.
6) That a limited range of self-government should be accorded religion and other civic associations.
7) That government should by symbolic acts acknowledge its own limited nature.

In the end, the struggle for rights of conscience is a struggle to affirm the nature of the human person, his reason, and his liberty.

David Thunder

The Place of Conscience-Based Exemptions in the Struggle Against Injustice

Abstract: The chapter presents a balanced assessment of the merits of seeking conscience-based exemptions to general legal obligations as a strategy for fighting injustice when one happens to find oneself in a community that dissents from the conventions and practices of the majority or ruling party. Dissenting communities, in cases where they face intransigent majorities or powerful and stubborn ruling elites, may find themselves compelled to seek out responses to injustice that fall short of full-scale social reform. Among these second-best responses are measures that reduce the costs of dissent from injustice. In this category, it is preferable to secure the liberty of all from any obligation to act unjustly than to seek special conscience-based exemptions from a requirement to engage in unjust conduct, since the former is less burdensome on dissenters and more consistent with the rule of law than the latter. Some of these second-best responses to injustice may tempt dissenters to put their own security or immunity from prosecution ahead of the imperative to bring an end to grave injustices in their society, and may encourage the wider society to view dissenters as harmless sects to be tolerated rather than serious interlocutors who deserve to be listened to. In conclusion, more direct and confrontational style of engagement, even in a politically unfavorable climate, may be more effective than the pursuit of conscience-based exemptions at making an injustice socially conspicuous.

Keywords: community, conscience, injustice, personal freedom

1 Introduction

The question of freedom of conscience come center stage in the United States in 2010 due to the US government's decision to require, under the auspices of its *Patient Protection and Affordable Care Act*[1] (otherwise known as "Obamacare"), that companies with 50 or more employees provide health insurance that includes coverage for contraceptive drugs and devices, including

1 Signed into law by President Obama on March 23, 2010. What later became known as the "HHS mandate" was the requirement that medium and large scale companies provide health insurance, including coverage for "preventive care," to all employees. What made the mandate especially controversial was the US Department of Health and Human Services' decision to include contraceptives under the category of mandatory "preventive care" coverage.

contraceptive drugs that act as abortifacients.[2] Although the bill exempted certain religious organizations such as churches, many religious organizations such as Little Sisters of the Poor, as well as for-profit companies with a Christian ethos, such as Hobby Lobby, were not exempted from the requirement. Hobby Lobby, a private, family-owned arts and craft corporation, challenged the bill, which would have cost them millions of dollars in annual fines, on the grounds that compliance with the mandate would violate the Christian owners' conscientiously held religious opposition to what they considered as "potentially life-terminating drugs and devices"[3], including abortifacients. The United States Supreme Court found that the bill was illegal, since it violated the Religious Freedom Restoration Act inasmuch as it substantially burdened the owners' religious beliefs and was not the "least restrictive means" of furthering compelling government interests.[4]

Although the details of the Hobby Lobby religious freedom victory need not concern us here,[5] the stand-off it generated is illustrative of a long history

---

2 In particular, Plan B (the morning after pill) and Ella (the week after pill). The bill authorized the Department of Health and Human Services to determine which "preventive" services would be mandated in employers' health insurance. Controversy erupted when the Department of Health and Human Services decided to include a number of contraceptive drugs and devices, including Plan B and Ella, under the broad umbrella of "preventive services" mandated in employee health insurance schemes.

3 See <http://www.hobbylobbycase.com/the-case/the-decision, where Hobby Lobby lays out the details of the case.>

4 The Religious Freedom Restoration Act was passed by the federal government in 1993 to restore the so-called "Sherbert test" established by Sherbert vs. Verner (1963) and Wisconsin vs. Yoder (1972) after that test had been struck down by the US Supreme Court in Employment Division vs. Smith (1990). The Sherbert test as set out in the Religious Freedom Restoration Act provides that the "Government shall not substantially burden a person's exercise of religion even if the burden results from a rule of general applicability." This prohibition can only be disregarded in case two conditions are met: first, the burden must be necessary to further a "compelling government interest," not just routine policymaking. Second, the rule must be the least restrictive way in which to further the government interest in question. It was not deemed necessary by the judges in the Hobby Lobby case to inquire into the question whether or not the government interests at issue were "compelling," since even conceding that they were, the judges did not consider the means employed to advance them to be the least restrictive available.

5 However, for a useful discussion that puts the case in a broader context, see Matthew J. Franck, "After Hobby Lobby, the Struggle for Religious Freedom Continues," *Public Discourse*
<http://www.thepublicdiscourse.com/2014/07/13418>

of conflict between political rulers and citizens of faith, not only in the United States but in many other parts of the world. What is especially striking about these conflicts is that they need not be occasioned by a political campaign of persecution or anti-religious zeal. They may simply arise from the fact that political rulers, for whatever reason, impose requirements upon citizens that they for their part cannot in good conscience submit to. In societies becoming progressively more divided on moral questions, such as the United States and Europe, these sorts of disputes are likely to become more frequent, not only in connection with communities of faith, but in connection with any community that dissents from the values of majorities or ruling parties. Now is therefore a good time to reflect on the value of acting according to conscience, and to consider the comparative merits of diverse strategies dissenting communities might embrace in order to resist laws and social practices they view as morally pernicious or unjust.

It is perfectly possible that members of a minority community may find that majority norms require them to violate conscientious commitments, not because they are fundamentally opposed to those norms *in general*, but simply because, on account of their own distinctive religious or moral commitments, they themselves cannot comply in good conscience with the said norms. *Wisconsin vs. Yoder*,[6] is a case in point: The Amish community challenged a state law imposing mandatory education up to the age of 16, because it interfered with their ability to give their own children a particular kind of education, sheltered from the influences of the wider culture, in order to preserve their way of life. They insisted on giving their own style of education to their children past the eighth grade (typically age 13–14). But they did not condemn *other* families for educating their children up to the age of 16 in public schools, nor did they even condemn the state for requiring formal education up to the age of 16 for citizens outside the Amish community. Rather, they asked to be exempted from the general requirement, so that they themselves could live up to the ideals of their own community. In this case, the threat to the moral integrity of the Amish community could be neutralized, so to speak, by simply carving out an exception to the law.[7]

What interests me in this chapter is not conscientious dissent *in general*, but a particular type of conscientious dissent, one which not only speaks in the name of a dissenting community's core values, but claims to speak in the name

6 *Wisconsin v. Yoder*, 406 U.S. 205 (1972).

7 Indeed, the relative harmlessness to the wider community of granting this exemption was one of the reasons the US Supreme Court ultimately found in the Amish community's favor.

of core values relevant and binding in the wider society. This type of dissent questions the justice of a general law or social practice beyond the boundaries of the dissenting community, and naturally carries the dissenter not only to refuse complicity with the perceived injustice, but to *actively work to bring an end to the injustice* in question. A conscientious dissenter of this type, such as Martin Luther King, cannot salve his conscience with the thought that he himself has been formally exempted from actively collaborating with an evil or unjust law. He feels a responsibility, insofar as it lies within his power, to fight against an injustice, on pain of being found guilty of the complicity of the silent bystander. Even if citizens of Nazi Germany with refined moral sensibilities had secured special exemptions from being compelled to collaborate with the Nazi agenda, this would not have excused them from the duty of actively resisting Nazi efforts to demolish the rights, and ultimately destroy the lives, of Jewish residents and citizens of Germany.

At times there is a tendency to speak about conscience and conscientious commitments as if they were a very special phenomenon, associated with private life, rather than a phenomenon tied up with being a responsible member of a community. But there is a respected tradition of thought, which includes authors such as Mahatma Gandhi and Martin Luther King, that views any grave injustice unfolding before our eyes, especially injustices inflicted by or against our neighbors, as an affront to our conscience, *even one in which we are not actively complicit*. Each one of us, on this view, bears some responsibility for what happens to our neighbors and fellow citizens "on our watch," and each one of us ought to examine his or her conscience to determine whether or not he or she is doing enough to defend their rights in the community. After all, as the old adage goes, "the only thing necessary for the triumph of evil is that good men should do nothing." This essay takes its bearings from this tradition of thought, and therefore views the claims of conscience not primarily as revelations of the inner state of mind of the agent ("let me tell you what my conscience says"), or even about the inviolability of his own conscience ("do not make me act against my conscience"), but about injustices in the community that the agent perceives, in good faith, as sufficiently grave that they cry out for legal or social redress. In short, in this essay, I view conscience as a catalyst for the struggle against injustice. As such, I would like to explore what role, if any, conscience-based exemptions from general legal requirements could or ought to play in a dissenting community's efforts to combat what they in good faith take to be injustices perpetrated in the wider community.

The argument proceeds in two steps. First, I offer a few remarks on the meaning and value of conscientious action, and its connection with the pursuit of justice. Second, I examine the merits of (1) conscience-based exemptions as a tool for resisting gravely unjust social practices, when compared with two alternative strategies, namely, (2) the creation of a generic liberty of action, and (3) the root-and-branch reform of the offending practice. On my analysis, appeals to freedom of conscience, whether defended through conscience-based exemptions or through generic spheres of liberty from legal compulsion, while they may be strategically necessary to defend minority interests and rights, should be used sparingly and should not be allowed to distract dissenters from the main task at hand, the reform of unjust laws and practices, the creation of a better and more just society.

2 Conscientious action and the pursuit of justice

One of the most remarkable features of the experience of being human is the realization that we are, in some profound sense, free to determine our own destinies. When we make a choice, whether large or small, we realize that we *could have* done otherwise, we were not fore-ordained to do *this*. Of course, our actions are constrained in many respects – we are not Supermen or Superwomen; on the contrary, we are weak, vulnerable, and dependent creatures. But so are other animals, yet we do not have reports of dogs or monkeys introspecting and coming to a realization of their own freedom to shape their own futures. This sense of freedom is accompanied by a sense that our choices are charged with meaning and value, and that we bear personal responsibility for them, for the way they shape our lives, and for the impact they have on other persons. To be *responsible* is to be somehow *answerable* for what one does, to be liable for our actions, or submit them to judgment, whether we understand the judge of our actions to be our "better self," an imagined impartial spectator, the community and its representatives, or God almighty.

There are two features of this sense of responsibility that I would like to underline: first, it is not an attitude that we assume by choice. Rather, it is a keen awareness that *like it or not*, we must answer, sooner or later, for the quality of our choices. Secondly, we are not just answerable for this or that discrete choice, but for the cumulative effect of our choices on our own personality and life taken as a whole, and on the personalities and lives of those around us. Although this responsibility must be qualified by the fact that many aspects of our lives are beyond our control, we do have a significant degree of control over how we *respond* to those restrictions, just as a football player, though he is not responsible for the rules of the game, he is in control of how he personally uses those rules to win or lose a game.

The sense of personal freedom and responsibility is not equally developed or present in everyone. In some it may be highly developed, in others muted or partially silenced. Be that as it may, insofar as we *take ourselves seriously* and come to terms with the fact that we bear responsibility for how we choose to live (or not to live), then we will take care to choose wisely.[8] Rather than mindlessly floating through life, nonchalantly taking the path of least resistance, or merely satisfying short-term desires with no thought for their lasting value, the serious person makes a good faith effort, proportionate to the values at stake, to direct his choices aright, to shape his life according to sound criteria rather than passing whims. We could say that the serious person acts *conscientiously*, rather than frivolously. That is because he recognizes that the "business of living" is not a small matter, but a matter worthy of serious attention, concern, and effort. Conscientious action is not only something the serious agent demands of himself in the interests of living a successful or worthy life; it is also something that can enhance the life and happiness of his associates, peers, friends and family, insofar as they benefit from his efforts to live a worthy life.

So far, I have described conscientious action as action inspired by an attitude of *seriousness* in relation to the business of living, an attitude that marks off the serious person from the frivolous one. I have not proven that the serious person is morally superior, all things considered, to the frivolous person, or more worthy of our emulation. However, I think it is safe to assume that many readers will accept that seriousness and not frivolity, as a general attitude toward life, is worthy of our admiration and emulation. If this is indeed the case, then conscientious action has a special value that other exercises of freedom do not necessarily possess.

Free acts may be frivolous, thoughtless, and superficial, whereas only a special subclass of free acts, namely, *conscientious* acts, are thoughtful, deliberate, and reflective. Furthermore, philosophers have argued, quite plausibly in my view, that an agent is duty-bound to follow the dictates of his own conscientious judgments about how to act (which, for present purposes, I will consider as his *conscience*), on pain of failing in the business of living. Even if his conscience turns out to be mistaken, once he has employed due diligence in seeking out the truth of the matter, there is nothing more he can reasonably be expected to do to discover his error. I would go so far as to suggest, following St Thomas Aquinas

8 This notion of "taking ourselves' seriously" as integral to a life we can take pride in or embrace wholeheartedly, is developed at much greater length in Harry Frankfurt, Taking Ourselves Seriously and Getting It Right (Stanford, California: Stanford University Press, 2006).

and St Thomas More, that a person's conscientious, reflective judgment about the right thing to do is binding upon him even if his judgment turns out to be objectively mistaken.[9]

Among those acts that are conscientiously undertaken, some are deemed by the agent to be morally recommended, while others are judged by the agent as *imperative* or necessary on pain of doing evil, or forfeiting the integrity of his character. An agent may, for example, act conscientiously when he leaves a tip for the waiter, but that does not mean that he feels he *must* leave a tip on pain of forfeiting his integrity, or that he feels not leaving a tip would be a wicked action. Contrast this with the attitude of a Jehovah's witness toward the prospect of accepting a blood transfusion. A Jehovah's witness may be firmly convinced that accepting a blood transfusion is tantamount to committing an evil action, and in that sense, a particular course of action, refusing the blood transfusion, is *strictly demanded* by his conscience. It is particularly when an agent feels bound by his conscientiously formed judgment to undertake or refrain from a particular course of action that potential legal and social conflicts may arise.[10]

9 Thomas More's life and death are a moving testament to the sacredness of conscience, though More was careful to insist that a conscience must be well informed and open to the wisdom and correction of the wise. More's firm but sophisticated view of the bindingness of conscientiously formed judgments is explained and elaborated on in his letters from the tower (see Thomas More, *The Last Letters of Thomas More* (Grand Rapids, Michigan and Cambridge, England: William B. Eerdmans Publishing Company, 2000)). Thomas Aquinas takes a similar view, maintaining unequivocally that a person's conscientious judgments about good and evil are binding upon him even if he is objectively in error. See *Quaestiones de duodecim quodlibet*, Quodlibet III, q. 12, a. 2 [27]: "Et ideo dicendum est quod omnis consciencia, si recta sive erronea, sive in per se malis sive in indifferentibus, est obligatoria, ita quod qui contra conscienciam facit, peccat" ("[...] every conscience, whether correct or erroneous, whether about things evil in themselves or things indifferent, is binding, from which it follows that he who acts against his conscience, sins").

10 This is intended as a rough statement of the special value of conscientious attitudes and action in the moral life. For more exhaustive treatments of the subject, see, inter alia, Robert K. Vischer, *Conscience and the Common Good: Reclaiming the Space Between Person and State* (Cambridge: Cambridge University Press, 2009); Kent Greenawalt, *Private Consciences and Public Reasons* (New York: Oxford University Press, 1995); Ian Shapiro and Robert Adams, *Integrity and Conscience* (New York: NYU Press, 1998); A. Campbell Garnett, "Conscience and Conscientiousness" and C.D. Broad, "Conscience and Conscientious Action," in: Moral Concepts, ed. Joel Feinberg (Oxford: Oxford University Press, 1970).

Conscientious judgments and the actions that flow from them cannot be isolated within the "private" sphere or separated from the public life of a community. We make conscientious judgments, for example, about whether or not the laws passed in our name are legitimate or binding; whether or not certain persons and groups in the community are being treated fairly; and whether or not to resist injustice by engaging in acts of civil disobedience. Those who sheltered Jews in Nazi Germany, at great personal risk, conscientiously judged that this was the right thing to do under the circumstances, that the risk was justified by the imperative to rescue their neighbors from imprisonment, persecution, torture, or death. Martin Luther King conscientiously reached the conclusion that a campaign of civil disobedience, and the public disorder that would result from it, was justified insofar as it was the only way to awaken the white man's conscience to the evils of racism. Although some instances of conscientious commitment and action, such as the commitment of a Jew to observe a kosher diet, only directly concern the behavior of a particular religious group, many conscientious commitments, such as King's commitment to racial equality, are oriented toward the root-and-branch reform of unjust social practices, and in that sense are anything *but* private in character.

3 The place of freedom of conscience in the fight against injustice

For the purposes of the present inquiry, let us set aside the special case of conscientious objections based exclusively on the special impact of some law or practice on a *particular person or group of persons* and their way of life[11], and focus instead on the case of conscientious objections motivated by larger questions of justice implicating the morality and way of life of the wider community. In this context, it seems to me that it is worth posing the following question, given the recent proliferation of conscience legislation and jurisprudence: *what role ought the value of freedom of conscience and its legal protection play in a dissenting community's fight against unjust social practices?* Is it the "weapon of choice" or is it the weapon of last resort? Do appeals to freedom of conscience carry any significant risks if viewed as part of a larger campaign to dismantle

11 An obvious example would be *Wisconsin vs. Yoder* (1972), in which the Amish community argued that their way of life and its underlying values required that their members receive a particular sort of education, which compulsory school attendance beyond the age of 16 did not permit.

systemic injustices? We might approach One way to approach these questions by considering the comparative merits of (1) conscientious exemptions to general laws, (2) unqualified freedom under the law to withhold one's cooperation from unjust social practices; and (3) a root-and-branch reform of the offending law or practice.

Let us begin by considering the first two strategies mentioned above, namely (1) seeking out conscience-based exemptions to general laws and (2) ensuring that cooperation with injustice is optional and not required by law. What both of these strategies have in common is that they seek to reduce the cost of dissent. The first seeks to lower the cost of dissent by introducing conscience-based exemptions to general obligations, while the second does so by creating a general liberty to withhold cooperation from objectionable practices. The second approach does not need to invoke the value of conscience directly within the law. Rather, legal regulations would be drafted in such a way as to leave certain actions deemed unjust by a dissenting individual or community entirely at the agent's discretion, whether by remaining silent[12] or granting an explicit liberty from coercion within some domain of action to all similarly situated subjects without regard to their deeper motivation. For example, a Catholic community opposed to abortion and same-sex marriage could campaign for a legal arrangement in which there is no general legal obligation to participate in abortion procedures, and no general legal obligation to provide wedding services to gay couples. A law along these lines would extend the same liberty to all, irrespective of the conscientious beliefs people happen to have.

To the extent that individuals are granted a generous latitude to determine the course of their own lives, they will have a space of uncoerced choice, and within this space, they may act as their conscience dictates without suffering significant legal or social penalties. For example, in modern Western societies people are relatively free to marry whom they will, free to choose a profession, free to choose which religion to practice, and so forth. Here, the law honors and protects the value of conscientious action, but only indirectly, since the only value it explicitly protects is the value of *individual liberty*, guaranteed in areas of behavior that legislators and policymakers have good reason to believe are

12 Cf. Thomas Hobbes's claim that "[t]he liberty of a subject lieth [...] only in those things which, in regulating their actions, the sovereign hath praetermitted" (Thomas Hobbes, *Leviathan* (Indianapolis and Cambridge: Hackett Publishing Company, 1994), chap. xxi, "Of the Liberty of Subjects," p. 138).

especially ethically sensitive, *whether or not that liberty happens to be exercised conscientiously.*

Extending freedom to all uniformly with regard to ethically sensitive decisions has a number of obvious advantages when compared with giving special treatment to conscientious action as a special class of action. First, it seems to favour the consistent application of the law, since the same liberty of action is extended to all without exception. Second, it favours the transparency and predictability of the law, since people know in advance, broadly speaking, the meaning and likely impact of the law, rather than having to await the results of complicated court battles or subtle tests to determine which actions count as conscientious and which do not. Third, it creates a climate that is especially favorable to conscientious action, since the freedom to act conscientiously is guaranteed in advance rather than based on the need to prove oneself eligible for an exemption from a generally applicable law.

On the other hand, securing a uniform liberty to withhold one's cooperation from unjust practices is a far cry from bringing an end to the injustices in question. While a dissenting community may find some relief in the fact that it is not compelled to implicate itself directly in grave injustices, and in the fact that nobody else is so compelled, this is hardly a cause for celebration, given that the grave injustice remains in place. Even if some will not defile their consciences, others will. Thus, securing "freedom from" injustice is tantamount to coexisting with injustice, or being an innocent bystander who witnesses but will not condone an unfolding injustice. The person who keeps his hands "clean" might reasonably ask himself the question, "could I have done something more to protect the victims of this injustice than keep my hands clean?" In short, reducing the costs of dissent by enlarging individual liberties does not seem to amount to a satisfactory response to a grave injustice.

There is another way to reduce the costs of dissenting from an unjust law or social practice, namely carving out explicit *conscience-based exemptions* to generally applicable legal or institutional obligations. Efforts to render direct cooperation with unjust social practices entirely optional may break down in cases where the majority or ruling party is convinced that a particular legal or institutional requirement, notwithstanding the controversy that surrounds it, is a basic demand of justice or required by the common good. In such a case, a liberty-based approach may fail to obtain the required concessions for conscientious dissenters, since the majority or ruling party may not be willing to set aside what they judge to be basic requirements of justice. Yet they may be willing, for the sake of social peace or out of respect for the claims of conscience, to exempt a *limited section of the population* from a principle on the grounds that it conflicts with their conscientiously held moral or religious convictions.[13]

Conscience-based exemptions, however, are not without their drawbacks. First, at the level of the overall legal regime, granting a limited number of conscience-based opt-outs invites a multiplication of conscientious objections, which may, over time, hollow out the force of the law, or undermine its credibility as a general rule regulating the life of the community. After all, if the rationale for such exemptions is that they violate some person's or community's conscientious commitments, then there is no principled way to prevent an eruption of conscience-based objections to the law, motivated by a host of different moral and philosophical beliefs.[14] In addition, where conscientious objections implicate principles of basic justice, they risk splintering a society presumed to be united by a core set of values into many different communities oriented toward diverse and incompatible values, as might occur, for example, with the emergence of special rights and obligations under Islamic (sharia) law, were Western nations to extend toleration to Islamic legal regimes in their midst.[15]

---

13 It is important to note that the rights of conscience cannot be absolute in any functional legal order. It is naturally qualified by the requirement that conscientious behavior meets some minimal threshold of reasonableness or justice. The burdens placed upon a person's conscience must be balanced against the corresponding burdens placed upon basic communal goods, such as justice and security. Someone may be safely exempted from a minor regulation like a dress-code in order to comply with their conscience, but someone may not be exempted from a law against murder or theft to comply with their conscience, insofar as the latter prohibitions protect goods that are part of the bedrock of a decent social order.

14 Judges and legislators may attempt to restrict this proliferation of conscientious objections by defining conscientious objection more narrowly, or introducing tests of sincerity and conscientiousness. The application of some such test could reveal that two actions that are materially identical may be classified in one case as an ordinary exercise of freedom, and in another case as a choice strictly demanded by the agent's best judgment about his moral or religious duties. It is the apparent arbitrariness of distinctions of this sort, at least when issued by political rulers and judges (what judge besides God and perhaps a person's confessor, spiritual director, or intimate confidant is truly competent to distinguish between superficially and conscientiously motivated behavior?), that would cast serious doubts over attempts of this sort to privilege the claims of some conscientious objectors over those of others.

15 The possibility of the creation of local pockets of sharia law has been the subject of public debate within the United Kingdom. See, for example, the Archbishop of Canterbury's speech (given on February 7, 2008) fielding the possibility of the tolerance of some elements of Sharia law within British society even if they are in tension with national laws: <http://rowanwilliams.archbishopofcanterbury.org/articles.php/1137/archbishops-lecture-civil-and-religious-law-in-england-a-religious-perspective>

From the perspective of minorities seeking to promote their vision of justice in society at large, the short- and medium-term gains for their communities – namely, a wider sphere of freedom to pursue the values and lifestyles they see as worthy of their allegiance – may be offset by some significant losses. First of all, conscience-based exemptions to generally applicable laws may provide spotty and unreliable protection for conscientious action, since (1) the full reach of exemptions may be difficult to anticipate, given the grey area between conscientious convictions and mere preferences, and given the uncertain application of conscience rights to corporate entities; and (2) exemption-based protections typically place the onus on the exempted to show that they qualify for the exemption to an otherwise binding law.

Secondly, the introduction of exemptions to laws perceived by a minority as gravely unjust may weaken the power of dissenting communities to witness against injustice and to participate credibly in mainstream debates about justice. After all, insofar as conscience-based exemptions are geared toward the collective toleration of dissenting behavior rather than toward the comprehensive reform of behavior and institutions, laws either permitting or mandating injustice may remain substantially intact *even after dissenters' hard-fought liberties have been secured.* Indeed, dissenters who have fought long and hard to be tolerated by the wider community and not legally required to defile their consciences may think twice before risking this hard-won victory by fighting to abolish the unjust practices they object to. Concomitantly, majorities, once they perceive that dissenters' campaigns have shifted away from a far-reaching critique of mainstream practices toward special accommodations for conscientious objectors, may be encouraged to view dissenting communities as idiosyncratic sects to be *tolerated* within a circumscribed domain, rather than equal conversation partners to be seriously engaged in the debate over how the political community as a whole should be governed. After all, dissenters may be granted certain liberties and immunities without seriously endangering mainstream values and practices.[16] In short, the net effect of strategies focused on reducing the cost of dissent may well be to further entrench contested majority views, weaken the political influence of minorities in the wider culture, and discourage minority

16 Imagine if the white allies of Martin Luther King's civil rights movement had sought conscience-based exemptions to racially discriminatory laws, rather than condemning the injustice of racism head-on and advocating a radical reform of the laws in question. They would hardly have added much to the civil rights movement when compared with King's tactics of public protest and civil disobedience.

and majority parties from engaging with each other in a serious way about basic principles of justice.

Dissenting communities may decide to embark on a more traditional path in the fight against unjust practices, namely, the path of active, head-on resistance to the offending law or practice. Dissenters may actively campaign against unjust laws and practices in the public square, contesting them on their merits, protesting against them, demonstrating the dissenting community' resolve to stand against injustice no matter the cost, and even engaging in acts of civil disobedience to draw the attention of the wider community to the gravity of the injustice they are protesting. Even if the dissenting community is vastly outnumbered or out-gunned, the advantage of this direct, confrontational style is that it brings visibility to the cause the dissenters' represent, and leaves no shadow of doubt in onlookers' minds that the dissenters are not merely pleading for special exemptions or campaigning for the survival of their way of life, but fighting for what they take to be *basic principles of justice relevant to the wider society*. This style of engagement sets the bar of success much higher than a campaign aimed at protecting the rights of conscience. It says to the world, "we will not pack up and go home until this injustice is rectified." A dissenting community with that spirit is a force to be reckoned with, and not one that can easily be dismissed or bought off with some local concessions.

A large part of the reason dissenters of this sort pose a greater threat to the practices they are protesting against than they might were they merely to seek conscience-based exemptions, is that by demanding the wholesale reform of those practices (rather than just controlling some of their effects), and making themselves a "thorn in the side" of the broader community, refusing to rest content with local concessions, they generate a tension in the wider society that becomes painful for those involved and demands to be resolved. I am not referring here to the tension generated by threats of violence and intimidation, but by the tension generated by those who are willing to stand up against established practices they conscientiously judge to be unjust and to suffer the consequences of their opposition in a peaceful, civil, and public manner. Their accusations, amplified through peaceful protest, public debates, advertising campaigns, and acts of civil disobedience, may strike a cord with their audiences, and may eventually begin to penetrate their complacency and make them wonder if practices they had until then accepted as "civilized" and "perfectly normal" are in fact as innocent as they had liked to think until then. The evident disharmony between moral opinions of different sections of the community becomes a serious problem that demands the attention of the society as a whole. Martin Luther King described this as "creative tension," and believed that nonviolent resistance, including civil disobedience, could generate such a tension in the wider society, and eventually shake people out of their moral complacency.[17]

4 How to reduce the costs of dissent

Now, let us recall the central point of this discussion: efforts to reduce the cost of dissent, whether through conscience-based exemptions or generic liberties to refrain from engaging in unjust practices, are not the only weapons in the fight against injustice, and there are good reasons for preferring other weapons, in particular campaigns aimed at full-scale reform, where conditions permit. Admittedly, the weapons of conscience-based exemptions, universal liberty, and far-reaching reform, are not mutually exclusive. They could very well constitute a multi-pronged campaign against injustice. However, dissenting communities should be aware that efforts employed to reduce the personal and communal costs of dissent, *while simultaneously* fighting aggressive campaigns for social and legal reform, may be sending mixed signals to their adversaries and to the general public. Seeking generic or conscience-based liberties to withhold cooperation from unjust laws seems to send the signal that we object to an activity *because we have idiosyncratic moral beliefs and find this activity personally offensive*. It seems to convey the message "Whatever you ask of other people, leave me alone to follow my conscience." Whereas fighting unjust laws and practices on their merits seems to send a clear signal that the dissenter objects to an activity *because it is wrong and unjust, period, not just wrong for me but wrong for any human being*. While these two messages are logically reconcilable, conveying them *both* simultaneously, particularly in a culture under the sway of relativistic principles, is likely to lead to considerable confusion, since a relativistic mindset will likely interpret a conscientious objection as motivated by a desire for subjective wholeness or inner coherence or peace, rather than as a desire to see justice done in the wider political community.

17 See Martin Luther King, Jr., "Letter from Birmingham Jail," in: *Why We Can't Wait* (Signet Classics, 2000). Tactics of this sort were used, in some cases with great success, in the campaign for the abolition of slavery in the United States and Britain, in the independence movement in India, and in various civil rights movements around the world over the course of the twentieth century. Resistance to communism in Poland and other Soviet-occupied countries was spearheaded by public denunciations of Communist policies and principles, combined with the willingness of some social and religious leaders to risk imprisonment, torture, or death for their opposition to the Communist regime.

5 Conclusion

I have done my best to present a balanced assessment of the merits of seeking conscience-based exemptions to general legal obligations as a strategy for fighting injustice when one happens to find oneself in a community that dissents from the conventions and practices of the majority or ruling party. I have suggested that dissenting communities, in cases where they face intransigent majorities or powerful and stubborn ruling elites, may find themselves compelled to seek out responses to injustice that fall short of full-scale social reform. Among these second-best responses are measures that reduce the costs of dissent from injustice. I have further argued that within this category, it is preferable to secure the liberty of *all* from any obligation to act unjustly than to seek special conscience-based exemptions from a requirement to engage in unjust conduct, since the former is less burdensome on dissenters and more consistent with the rule of law than the latter. But I have also suggested that either of these strategies may tempt dissenters to put their own security or immunity from prosecution ahead of the imperative to bring an end to grave injustices in their society, and may encourage the wider society to view dissenters as harmless sects to be tolerated rather than serious interlocutors who deserve to be listened to. Finally, I have pointed out that a more direct and confrontational style of engagement, even in a politically unfavorable climate, may be more effective than the pursuit of conscience-based exemptions at making a problem socially conspicuous and generating the sort of "creative tension" that Gandhi and King sought to induce in their campaigns against injustice.

Let me conclude by underlining that it is not my intention to delegitimize or condemn efforts by dissenting communities to secure opt-out rights for those who are vulnerable to legal obligations to engage in what they judge to be unjust conduct. Rather, I simply wish to remind advocates of freedom of conscience of the costs this strategy can incur, especially when pursued as an alternative to more far-reaching campaigns against injustice. A fundamentally unjust legal and social arrangement that extends conscience-based exemptions to dissenters is liable to impose special legal burdens on dissenting communities, to "ghettoize" society into a plethora of diverse communities whose views of justice and rights diverge radically, and to reduce the public standing of dissenters to that of a benignly tolerated sect, rather than a serious moral and political force to be reckoned with. To keep these costs to a minimum, advocates of freedom of conscience ought to resist the temptation to abandon more ambitious and transformative tactics in the fight against injustice. They ought to see exemptions not as permanent settlements, but as lesser evils, halfway houses to full legal and social reform. More traditional strategies of combatting injustice, such as political advocacy, public education campaigns, lobbying, and civil disobedience, should be employed both during and after campaigns for conscience-based exemptions. In this way, dissenting minorities will remain dynamic forces for social reform rather than collapsing into the equivalent of self-contained Amish communities, relatively harmless to the wider culture.

Jakob Cornides

Freedom of Conscience – A Basic Human Right?

Abstract: *Medical ethics as we used to know them are undermined by new laws, resulting in acute ethical dilemmas for a growing number of professionals. As a counter-strategy, "freedom of religion and conscience" is invoked as a justification for disrespecting controversial statutory provisions, and to do so with impunity. In this contribution I argue that the freedom of religion and conscience be interpreted to confer to religious believers (or secularists) a general right to disobey the law with impunity based on their own moral convictions. Moreover, "freedom of conscience" is unlikely to be a winning strategy in public discourse. Instead, it seems advisable to invoke freedoms that are appealing also to non-believers - in particular, the freedom of contract being an aspect of the "right to respect for one's private life", which is protected under Article 8 of the ECHR.*

Keywords: freedom of religion and conscience, human rights, freedom of contract, unjust law.

1 Introduction

In many countries, the legal order is currently being transformed in a way that makes it difficult for Christians, and not only for them, to live and act according to their consciences. As the recent case of Prof. Bogdan Chazan evidences, Poland is no exception although the situation is certainly far worse in other countries.

Abortion, euthanasia, the fabrication of human beings in vitro, organ transplantation, and so on are gradually undermining the code of medical ethics as we knew it; the medical professions are thus more than any other group of professionals exposed to acute ethical dilemmas. But, of course, it doesn't stop here. The current trend among European law-makers to legally recognize same-sex "marriages" creates problems for those who believe these "marriages" to be unacceptable celebrations of sexual indecency and moral decadence. There are cases of public servants who do not want to be involved in the registration of such "marriages",[1] and there are countless cases of bakers,[2]

1 e.g., US District Court for the Eastern District of Kentucky, *Miller v. Davis*, 12 August 2015.

2 e.g., US Supreme Court, *Masterpiece Cakeshop v. Colorado Civil Rights Commission*, No. 16-111 – case pending.

florists,[3] musicians, and photographers,[4] who have been punished for refusing to prepare or embellish such celebrations. The legal basis for such sanctions are usually found in rather far-reaching "equality" or "anti-discrimination" laws, which curtail the freedom of contract in the sense that they oblige professionals to sell their goods and services to whoever demands them, thus prohibiting any "discrimination" on the basis of race, sex, age, religion, religious belief, and so on.

At the same time, religion and conscience are invoked not only by Christians wishing to live in conformity with Christian teachings (or rather, as they would claim, with Natural Law), but also by others. In the United States, some years ago, the Supreme Court decided that a ban on drug use did not violate the right to religious freedom of the members of several Indian tribes who smoke a drug called Peyote as part of their pre-Christian rituals.[5] As a reaction, Congress adopted a new law, the Religious Freedom Restoration Act of 1993 (RFRA),[6] in order to allow such drug use if it was for religious purposes. It is quite ironic that those who once voted in favour of the RFRA – that is, the political left – are now pushing for its abrogation (and inversely, those who once were against – that is, the political right – are now defending it) because word has gone round that it could be used by Christians who oppose abortion and same-sex "marriage".[7] So freedom of religion apparently is a legitimate reason for using drugs, but not for refusing to partake in abortions or in the celebration of homosexuality.

Another remarkable case is the recent decision by a Cologne law court to treat as a criminal offense the circumcision of male infants.[8] Seventy years after the Nazi Holocaust, Jewish religion and culture was again outlawed, and Islam

3 e.g., Supreme Court of Washington, *Ingersoll v. Arlene's Flowers* and *State of Washington v. Arlene's Flowers* - petition for writ of certoriari filed with US Supreme Court.

4 New Mexico Supreme Court, *Elane Photography v. Willock.*

5 US Supreme Court, *Employment Division, Department of Human Resources of the State of Oregon, et al. v. Alfred Smith*, 494 U.S. 872 (1990).

6 Religious Freedom Restoration Act of 1993, Pub. L. No. 103–141, 107 Stat. 1488 (November 16, 1993).

7 The most recent of these controversies concerned Indiana Senate Bill 101, titled the Religious Freedom Restoration Act, which was signed into law by Governor Mark Pence on 26 March 2015. Political activists opposing the measure called for an economic boycott of the State of Indiana. Some boycott measures were indeed adopted by States and cities governed by politicians of the Democratic Party, but most of these were lifted later on.

8 LG Köln, 7.5.2012 - 151 Ns 169/11. For a detailed analysis see: Julian Krüper, "Religionstradition und Rechtskonvention: Die Unzulässigkeit religiöser Knabenbeschneidung," *ZJS* (2012), pp. 547–552.

(where circumcision also is a key initiation ritual) with it. Of course, completely unacceptable in a society that takes pride in its multi-culturalism, so the German Federal Diet swiftly introduced a new provision into the Civil Code to clarify that circumcision was not a crime[9] – even if indeed it might be viewed as violating the bodily integrity of someone who hasn't asked for it.

2 Freedom of thought, religion and conscience

As it appears, a venerable religious tradition can have precedence over a basic provision in criminal law. And what makes this case particularly noteworthy is the fact that what we are speaking about here really is a purely religious ritual (which to skip, however, would certainly create conflicts of conscience for those involved), rather than a fundamental moral issue that may affect believers and non-believers in the exactly same way. That is precisely the difference between "religious freedom", which relates to religious faith and worship, and "freedom of conscience", which relates more broadly to the right of everyone, believers and non-believers alike, to act in accordance with his or her conscience.

As a reaction to laws legalizing abortion, or recognizing same-sex "marriages", there are nowadays many who place high hopes in what they believe to be a panacea. They point to Article 18 of the Universal Declaration of Human Rights (UDHR), which provides:

"Everyone has the right to freedom of thought, conscience and religion; this right includes freedom to change his religion or belief, and freedom, either alone or in community with others and in public or private, to manifest his religion or belief in teaching, practice, worship and observance."

Article 9 of the European Convention on Human Rights (ECHR) provides likewise:

> "1. Everyone has the right to freedom of thought, conscience and religion; this right includes freedom to change his religion or belief and freedom, either alone or in community with others and in public or private, to manifest his religion or belief, in worship, teaching, practice and observance.
> 2. Freedom to manifest one's religion or beliefs shall be subject only to such limitations as are prescribed by law and are necessary in a democratic society in the interests of public safety, for the protection of public order, health or morals, or for the protection of the rights and freedoms of others."

As one quickly understands, the law makes no distinction between thought, conscience and religion. However, what is important here is that it includes the right

9 Bürgerliches Gesetzbuch (BGB), § 1631d - Beschneidung des männlichen Kindes.

to manifest one's belief (or thought, or moral stance) in practice, that is to live and act according to it. At the same time, however, Article 9 (2) of the ECHR provides for an important restriction of that right: it can be limited through laws that are necessary in a democratic society. So, which limitations to the freedom of conscience are necessary in a democratic society?

3 Possible development

It is all, of course, a matter of interpretation, but recent developments in the ECtHR's case law provide no reasons for great optimism. In the case of abortion, for example, the Court has never said that there is such a thing as a "right to abortion", but it has issued several rulings that may be interpreted as meaning that wherever and whenever abortion is "legal" (in the sense of "not punishable") in a country, the state *must guarantee* its factual availability even at the expense of the freedom of conscience of doctors and other medical staff.[10] Assuredly, this case law seems quite ill-founded, as it transforms the state's decision to *abstain from punishing a given act* into *a legal obligation* to make that act possible, which to all friends of logical thinking must be a clear case of *non sequitur*.[11] However, for reasons of "consistency" we may expect that a similar approach will be taken in cases concerning euthanasia, assisted procreation, pre-natal selection, and so on. The ECtHR's "consistency" very often means that it will remain consistent in its errors, especially when those errors are part of a fashionable ideology.

With regard to same-sex "marriage" and its imposition on dissenters through "anti-discrimination" laws, I am not aware of any ECtHR case law. There is, however, the case of *McFarlane vs. UK* in which the Court decided that a therapist who lost his employment because he did not want to counsel homosexual couples how they could have a more gratifying (homosexual) sex life could not rely on his freedom of conscience.[12]

---

10 See in particular *Tysiąc v. Poland* (Application no. 5410/03), *R. R. v. Poland* (no. 27617/04), *A. B. & C. v. Ireland,* (G.C., no. 25579/05). A similar view was expressed by the EU Network of Independent Experts on Fundamental Rights, an advisory body of the EU that existed between 2002 and 2006, in its controversial Opinion no. 4.2005 on "The right to conscientious objection and the conclusion by EU Member States of concordats with the Holy See".

11 For a more exhaustive analysis, see Jakob Cornides, "Human Rights Pitted Against Man," *International Journal of Human Rights,* Vol. 12, No.1 (2008), pp. 107–134.

12 *McFarlane v. United Kingdom* (no. 36516/10)

On the other hand, the Court did censure Armenia for not having provided for an alternative to compulsory military service for those who claim that it is against their conscience to serve in the armed forces.[13] Thus, it appears that for the ECtHR "freedom of conscience" exists with regard to making a contribution to the defence of one's countries, but it does not exist with regard to abortion, the public celebration of sodomy, and other achievements of the enlightened post-1968 society.

Whatever one may think of this paradoxical situation, one certainly has reason to doubt that "freedom of conscience" can entail a sweeping "right" to disrespect positive law and to violate it with impunity.

4 Is that what we need?

From a purely legal point of view, such a "right" to violate every law that one happens to consider unjust makes no sense at all: if taken at face value, it would simply mean that, having lost its binding force, the law is not the law any more. Freedom of religion and conscience cannot be unlimited. If it were, what would be our answer to people who claim that they have converted back to the religion of the old Aztecs, and therefore must be given leave to perform human sacrifices? What would be our answer to Muslims who want to practice polygamy, to African immigrants who claim a right to practice female genital mutilation, to Kosovars and Albanians who practice blood vengeance, or to Kurdish families who preserve their set of traditional values through "honour killings"? Not in all, but certainly in many of these cases the delinquents are driven by a sincere sense of duty and obligation – but does that mean that society must tolerate what they are doing?

Obviously not. But if this is so, then it follows that "freedom of religion and conscience" cannot simply be the right to disobey the law with impunity. In this context it is noteworthy that up until the second Vatican Council the Catholic Church vehemently opposed – on the religious/philosophical level the notion of "freedom of religion and conscience". As it appears, it did so for good reasons. Philosophically speaking, what sets man apart from all other species is his moral capacity, that is the ability to understand the difference, and indeed to choose, between good and evil. But the ability to choose between good and evil, which we may call a "freedom", is a *faculty*, not a right. We *can* choose evil, but we are

13 *Bayatyan v. Armenia* (no. 23459/03)

under a strict moral obligation to not to choose it. Thus, there is no "right to do wrong" while there is, of course, every right to do what is right.

The traditional stance of the Catholic Church with regard to other religions therefore was not to say that they enjoyed "freedom of religion"; instead, it consisted in showing a certain amount of tolerance.[14] But that was, of course, a moral/philosophical stance, not a purely legal one. There is in principle nothing wrong in saying that "tolerance" can consist in granting to somebody something that in the language of law is termed a "right", even though, morally speaking, it isn't one.

However, what we are discussing today is not the freedom of conscience of those who want to do what seems evil, but the freedom of those who want *to abstain* from doing evil. Indeed, what we are saying when we invoke our freedom of conscience is that any laws against which we invoke it are inherently and manifestly unjust. The claim is that they are "injustice disguised as law", and therefore lose their binding force as laws.

But which state can be expected to regard its own laws as "injustice disguised as laws"? It is no surprise, therefore, that specific "conscience clauses" are a rare phenomenon in the positive legal order. They exist predominantly in the contexts of compulsory military service, abortion, and euthanasia, casting a shadow of moral doubt on the matter that is being regulated. In the case of military service, this shadow of doubt is the political achievement of the (Western European, but mainly Soviet-sponsored) peace movement, whereas in the case of abortion and euthanasia it can be seen as a clear indicator that there is something substantially wrong with the laws that legalize such actions. Pro-abortionists are, of course, painfully aware of this – and this, more than any practical reasons, explains why they are so assiduously pressing for the removal of so-called "conscience clauses".

For those believing that abortion violates the sanctity of human life, a "conscience clause" that protects doctors and nurses who do not want to perform abortions can only alleviate, but not solve the problem. To them, the true problem is not the lack of conscience clauses, but the fact that a law legalizing abortion or similar practices is in and by itself a monstrosity. Where such laws exist they will call for their abrogation, not for less. If their opponents seek to appease them with conscience clauses, they may, of course, accept the offer – but never should

14 As late as 1953 Pope Pius XII said as much in an allocution, entitled *Ci riesce*, addressed to the Association of Catholic Lawyers in Italy: *"First: that which does not correspond to truth or to the norm of morality objectively has no right to exist, to be spread or to be activated. Secondly: failure to impede this with civil laws and coercive measures can nevertheless be justified in the interests of a higher and more general good."*

this prevent them from working towards a full realization of their true objective, the removal of apparently unjust laws.

In the same vein, they may feel entitled, and even obliged, to disobey manifestly unjust laws even where there is no "conscience clause" to protect them. But this means that they will also have to put up with the unpleasant consequences of such disobedience. This may require a great deal of courage and a spirit of self-sacrifice – and one should not condemn those who are lacking the one or the other. Nevertheless, it is clear that injustice can ultimately be overcome only through such courage and sacrifice. If noone is willing to make sacrifices, then the makers of the new moral order will find it easy to impose their ways. If, by contrast, someone really wants to resist them, he will need some courage.

It is clear then that "freedom of conscience" is not simply a "right" in the legal sense of the term. Rather, it is a moral right that transcends and supersedes the positive legal order. Obviously, this is the same for the doctor who refuses to perform abortions as for the Kurdish family father who kills his daughter to preserve his family's "honour". The difference however is not only that in the latter case there is violence whereas in the first there is abstention of violence, but also that in the first case the disobedience against positive law is based on sound moral principles whereas in the latter case it isn't. Freedom of conscience comprises not only the obligation to follow one's conscience, but also to educate and form it in the right way.

5 A final remark

Supporters of abortion, euthanasia, homosexual "marriages", and so on often argue that opposition against their agenda is – and can only be – driven by "religious beliefs", which they believe can be dismissed as "irrational" without further argument. This is for them an easy stratagem to cut short a critical discussion, which, if it were allowed to take place, would quickly reveal that rationality is not on their side. Those, however, who for very sound and rational reasons oppose abortion, euthanasia, and so on, should be aware of this discourse strategy – and of the fact that invoking "freedom of religion and belief" plays into the hands of the other side, seemingly lending support to their view that religion is some kind of escape from rational argument. The invocation of "freedom of conscience" is therefore unlikely to be a winning strategy in public discourse. Rather, prolifers would be well advised to invoke freedoms that are appealing also to nonbelievers. This applies in particular to the freedom of contract, which plays a role both in the case of a doctor not wishing to perform an abortion and in the cases of bakers and florists refusing to be involved in the celebration of same-sex "marriages". Without doubt, the freedom of contract, also known as "private autonomy", is an important aspect of the "right to respect for one's private life", which is protected under Article 8 of the ECHR. But while the ECtHR interprets Article 9 of the Convention restrictively, its recent case law has provided for astonishingly expansive interpretations of Article 8. There is no doubt that the conclusion of contracts is, besides the mere exchange of words, one of the most important means of social interaction, and that therefore the freedom of contract is one of the most important freedoms. This does not mean that it cannot be restricted, but clearly the burden of proof for the necessity of such restrictions lies with the state.

To summarize, it seems to me that "freedom of religion and conscience" is a relatively weak argument, and probably not one that wins many sympathies. If they want to win today's culture wars, social conservatives should try to find alternative ways of defending their causes.

Jakub Pawlikowski

Conscientious Objection and the Goals of Medicine

Abstract: In the chapter author distinguishes conscientious objection from conscience clause. He argues that the main cause of the problem of conscientious objection in medical practice is not the scope of the conscience clause, but the scope of duties imposed on medical workers. The problem should be analyzed from the perspective of teleology and axiology of medicine: can the duties imposed on medical personnel be objectively justified based on medicine's purposes and values? Duties arising from internal goals and most of external goals are justifiable. However, several obligations arising from external goals conflict with medicine's purposes and fundamental norms of medical ethics such as respect for life or non-maleficence principle. Attempts should be made to limit the scope of guaranteed health services to procedure that do not violate medicine's essence, its internal goals and fundamental ethical principles.

Keywords: conscientious objection, freedom of conscience, goals of medicine, medical practice

1 Introduction

Conscience, reason and freedom are the most fundamental features signifying human nature's uniqueness and, in particular, its dignity, which is the foundation of any system of positive law. The Universal Declaration of Human Rights (UDHR) underlines in Article 1 that all human beings are "endowed with reason and conscience and should act towards one another in a spirit of brotherhood."[1] Freedom of conscience occupies a special place among the fundamental human rights and freedoms, and is a necessary condition for the development of every human person and a responsible democratic society capable of creating a state based on justice and the moral integrity of its citizens.[2] Freedom of conscience is not only the right to create and possess one's own beliefs (*forum internum*), but also the right to manifest one's own beliefs, act according to these beliefs and refuse to act in a manner that contradicts them (*forum externum*). Consequently,

1 The Universal Declaration of Human Rights proclaimed by the United Nations General Assembly in Paris on 10 December 1948 (General Assembly resolution 217 A): 2 Feb. 2018 <http://www.un.org/en/universal-declaration-human-rights/>

2 Dan P. Sulmasy, "What is conscience and why is respect for it so important?" *Theoretical Medicine Bioethics*, Vol. 29 (2008), pp. 135–149.

the right to conscientious objection originates directly from freedom of conscience.[3]

Freedom of conscience is protected in democratic societies by constitutional provisions and international agreements (Article 18 of the International Covenant on Civil and Political Rights; – ICCPR Article 10 of the Charter of Fundamental Rights of the European Union;[4] Article 18 of the Universal Declaration of Human Rights of the United Nations). This fundamental freedom can only be limited by an enactment of law (it could, for example, be included in conscience clauses), and only if this is necessary for the protection of the fundamental rights and freedoms of others, ensuring public safety, order, health and morality (Article 18 of the ICCPR). The imposition of such restrictions cannot violate the principle of equality or non-discrimination, or the ideological impartiality of the public authorities and should also respect the nature and goals of a concrete particular sector of public life.

Conscientious objection should not be confused with the conscience clause. Conscientious objection should be understood as a manifestation of moral attitudes (such as those presented in Sophocles' *Antigone*), whereas a conscience clause codifies the expression of conscientious objection. Conscientious objection in its broadest sense (e.g., in the form of civil disobedience) can be independent of the existence of the legal codification of refusals. Instead, the conscience clause contains regulations that mainly limit freedom of conscience or religion (limiting also conscientious objection) due to other important values such as public safety and order or the life or health of a patient. The conscience clause creates a legal opportunity for refusing to perform legally imposed obligations because they conflict with religious beliefs, personal convictions and moral values, and can also indicate other, substitutive forms of fulfilling these obligations (e.g., in many military conscience clauses, objectors can work at a charitable institution instead of performing military service). In legal doctrine, we can distinguish a broad and narrow understanding of conscientious objection. The former applies in cases relating to both action and lack of action whereas the second only applies to the refusal to perform certain legalized obligations on the basis of religious, ethical and philosophical premises.[5]

---

3 Carolyn Evans, *Freedom of Religion under the European Convention on Human Rights* (New York: Oxford University Press, 2003), pp. 133–166.

4 Translation included in the *European Journal of Laws* of 2010, C. 83, p. 389, last access: 11 November 2015 <http://eur-lex.europa.eu/LexUriServ/LexUriServ.do?uri=OJ:C:2010:083:0389:0403:PL:PDF>

5 Evans, *Freedom of Religion under the European Convention on Human Rights*, pp. 145–156; Jakub Pawlikowski, "Spór o klauzulę sumienia z perspektywy celów medycyny i

The right to conscientious objection is always associated with a legal obligation or duty. The conscience clause provides a special exemption to such a duty. Consequently, in a debate over the right to conscientious objection, we should not only be focusing on the issue of legal limitations of freedom of conscience or religion. We should, above all, be analysing the scope, necessity, purposefulness, appropriateness and justifiability of that imposed obligation or duty. This is particularly essential within the context of conscientious objection in health care. The primary questions that need to be asked should relate to the purposes of medicine and the values of medical ethics connected with these purposes. These objectives should delineate the scope, necessity, appropriateness and justifiability of the duty imposed on healthcare workers. If we fail to question the reasoning behind such duties, we are effectively permitting the legal authorities to establish a law in an arbitrary fashion. The main thesis of this chapter is the statement that the majority of the problems related to conscientious objection in medicine do not originate from conscience clause regulations per se. Instead, they mostly arise from the inappropriate, unnecessary and morally unjustifiable scope of duties imposed on healthcare workers, duties which in some areas are contrary to medicine's internal goals.

When analysing this problem, the first step should be to describe the circumstances of an objection and the second one to respond to the question of whether the procedures around which this objection appears should be a duty imposed on the physician. A response to this question can be found by examining the issues provoking the conscientious objection from the perspective of the teleology and axiology of the medical professions. In other words, an analysis should be undertaken of whether the imposed legal duties and social expectations accord with the essence of medicine, its purposes and fundamental principles of medical ethics such as respect for human life, the beneficence principle (*salus aegroti suprema lex esto*) or the principle of nonmaleficence (*primum non nocere*).

2 Conscientious objection in medical practice

The problem of the conscientious objection of healthcare workers has recently become a subject of interest from both the theoretical and practical perspectives. This has in turn resulted in the dynamic growth of scientific literature on this subject (more than 440 articles, over half of which date from the past 10 years, in the PubMed-Medline database), international resolutions (e.g., Resolution

---

etyki lekarskiej," in: *Sprzeciw sumienia w praktyce medycznej – aspekty etyczne i prawne*, eds. P. Stanisz, J. Pawlikowski, and M. Ordon (Lublin, 2014), pp. 145–170.

1763 of the Council of Europe, the Right to Conscientious Objection in Lawful Medical Care, 7 October 2010[6]), legislative initiatives, and court and international tribunal rulings (e.g., *P.S. v. Poland*,[7] *R.R. v. Poland*,[8] *Tysiac v. Poland*[9] cases examined by European Tribunal of Human Rights). The most important ruling on this matter in the Republic of Poland was made by the Constitutional Tribunal on 7 October 2015, a judgement that repealed some restrictions for physicians expressing conscientious objection (e.g., the duty to refer to another specialist).[10]

The subject of conscientious objection began to appear in the medical literature in 1953. However, the oldest articles do not refer to healthcare workers, but rather to the general requirement for children to be vaccinated and parental rights to evade this obligation.[11] Even today, the problem of parents/guardians objecting to some medical interventions is reported (e.g., vaccination, newborn screening tests).[12] In the 1970s and 1980s, the discussion focused more on the physicians' and other healthcare workers' refusal to perform certain procedures. This discussion coincided with the decriminalization and legalization of abortion and other procedures (euthanasia, assisted suicide) that could violate the principle of respect for human life. In the countries of Central and Eastern Europe, these discussions did not start until the 1990s, because in totalitarian regimes, freedom of conscience was not treated as the natural and fundamental

6 Council of Europe, Resolution 1763, *The right to conscientious objection in lawful medical care*, Assembly debate on 7 October 2010: 21 Feb 2018 <http://assembly.coe.int/nw/xml/XRef/Xref-XML2HTML-en.asp?fileid=17909&lang=en>; See also: Jakub Pawlikowski, "Prawo do sprzeciwu sumienia w ramach legalnej opieki medycznej. Rezolucja nr 1763 zgromadzenia Parlamentarnego Rady Europy z dnia 7 października 2010 roku [The right to the conscientious objection in lawful medical care. Resolution 1763 of the Parliamentary Assembly of the Council of Europe of 7 October 2010]," *Studia z Prawa Wyznaniowego*, Vol. 14 (2011), pp. 313–338.

7 P. S. v. Poland, No. 57375/08, 30 Oct 2012.

8 R. R. v. Poland, No. 27617/04, 28 Nov 2011.

9 Tysiac v. Poland, No 5410/03, 20 March 2007.

10 A ruling of the Constitutional Tribunal, 7 Oct 2015, No. K12/14 2015, OTK 9A, n. 143; Piotr Stanisz, Jakub Pawlikowski, "Il diritto dei medici all'obiezione di coscienza in Polonia: recenti sviluppi," Quaderni di diritto e politica ecclesiastica, Vol. 2 (2017), pp. 459–473.

11 A.V. Knack, "Compulsory vaccination with or without conscientious objection clause," *Hippokrates*, Vol. 24, No. 18 (1953), pp. 565–567.

12 Frank H. Beard, Brynley P. Hull, Julie Leask, Aditi Dey, Peter B. McIntyre, "Trends and patterns in vaccination objection, Australia, 2002–2013," *The Medical Journal of Australia*, Vol. 204, No. 7 (2016), p. 275.

right of every human being, but rather as a civil right, the scope of which had been authoritatively determined by the state.[13]

Globally, conscientious objection in medical practice can be provoked by a number of procedures related to both the initial period of human life (abortion, prenatal diagnosis, postcoital contraception, intrauterine devices, certain methods of assisted reproduction – particularly those that lead to the creation of supernumerary embryos and preimplantation selection) and the end of human life (euthanasia, medically assisted suicide, participating in the administration of the death penalty, brain death diagnosis), but can also apply to situations such as transplantation or blood transfusion in cases involving Jehovah's witnesses, refusal to withhold or the withdrawal of persistent or futile therapy, and the use of drugs and vaccines, which production is based on embryonic cells and fetal tissue.[14]

Conscientious objection can mainly be raised by physicians, but also affects nurses and midwives (e.g., refusing assistance in abortion), pharmacists (refusing to sell contraceptives, anti-implantation and abortive drugs) and laboratory

13 Oktawian Nawrot,, "Prawa człowieka, sprzeciw sumienia i państwo prawa," in: Sprzeciw sumienia w praktyce medycznej – aspekty etyczne i prawne, eds. P. Stanisz, J. Pawlikowski, and M. Ordon (Lublin, 2014), pp. 105–116.

14 Snyder L. Sulmasy, Paul S. Mueller, "Ethics and the Legalization of Physician-Assisted Suicide: An American College of Physicians Position Paper," *Annals of Internal Medicine*, Vol. 167, No. 8 (2017), pp. 576–578; R.D. Orr, "Autonomy, Conscience and Professional Obligation," *Virtual Mentor. American Medical Association Journal of Ethics,* No. 15 (2013), p. 245; F.A. Curlin, C. Nwodim, J.L. Vance, N.H. Chin, J.D. Lantos, "To Die, to Sleep: US Physicians, Religious and Other Objections to Physician-Assisted Suicide, Terminal Sedation, and Withdrawal of Life Support," *American Journal of Hospice and Palliative Care,* Vol. 25 (2008), pp. 112–120; L.H. Harris, A. Cooper, A. Rasinski, F.A. Curlin, A.D. Lyerly, "Obstetrician-gynecologists' objections to and willingness to help patients obtain an abortion," *Obstetrics and Gynecology*, Vol. 118 (2011), pp. 905–912; R.E. Lawrence, K.A. Rasinki, J.D. Yoon, F.A. Curlin, "Obstetrician-gynecologists' beliefs about assisted reproductive technologies," *Obstetrics and Gynecology,* Vol. 116 (2010), pp. 127–135; L. Ganzini, H. D. Nelson, M. A. Lee, D. F. Kraemer, T. A. Schmidt, M. A. Delorit, "Oregon Physicians' Attitudes About and Experiences With End-of-Life Care Since Passage of the Oregon Death with Dignity Act," *Journal of the American Medical Association,* Vol. 285 (2001), pp. 2363–2369; A. Gawande, "When law and ethics collide: why physicians participate in executions," *New England Journal of Medicine*, No. 354 (2006), pp. 1221–1229; Y. Kato, "Conscience in health care and the definitions of death," *Croatian Medical Journal*, Vol. 54, No. 1 (2013), pp. 75–77; Jakub Pawlikowski, Jarosław Sak, Krzysztof Marczewski. "Religijność lekarzy a kontrowersyjne moralnie procedury medyczne," *Wiadomości Lekarskie*, Vol. 5 (2010), pp. 5–16.

diagnostics (e.g., diagnostic actions in the in-vitro procedure).[15] In the literature, this issue also appears in relation to other non-medical staff members, for example, a driver and paramedics transporting a patient to an abortion clinic, administrative staff (preparing and issuing documents relating to the termination of a pregnancy) and even medical students (participating in an abortion, teaching physical examination of the opposite sex to Muslim students).[16] Conscientious objections can be raised by both non-religious and religious healthcare workers originating from different traditions such as the Christian, Jewish, Muslim, Buddhist traditions.[17]

When analysing the issue of conscientious objection, certain distinctions should be made. Conscientious objection should be distinguished from other refusal situations in medical practice. In the case of conscientious objection,

---

15 S. Davis, V. Schrader, M. J. Belcheir, "Influencers of ethical beliefs and the impact on moral distress and conscientious objection," *Nursing Ethics*, Vol. 9, No. 6 (2012), pp. 738–749; M.E. Duffy, "Good Medicine: Why Pharmacists Should Be Prescribed a Right of Conscience," Valparaiso University Law Review, Vol. 44 (2010), pp. 509–564; Dan W. Brock, "*Conscientious refusal by physicians and pharmacists: who is obligated to do what, and why*?" Theoretical Medicine and Bioethics, Vol. 28, No. 3 (2008), pp. 183–200;
J.E. Spreng, "Pharmacists and the 'Duty' To Dispense Emergency Contraceptives," Issues In Law & Medicine 2008, Vol. 23 (2008), pp. 215–277; Beata Dobrowolska, "Sprzeciw sumienia w zawodzie pielęgniarki i położnej – założenia i praktyka," in: Sprzeciw sumienia w praktyce medycznej – aspekty etyczne i prawne, eds. Piotr Stanisz, Jakub Pawlikowski, and Marta Ordon (Lublin: Wydawnictwo Naukowe KUL, 2014), pp. 197–209; Waldemar Głusiec, Elżbieta Puacz, "*Sprzeciw sumienia w zawodzie diagnosty laboratoryjnego*," in: *Sprzeciw sumienia w praktyce medycznej – aspekty etyczne i prawne*, eds. Piotr Stanisz, Jakub Pawlikowski, and Marta Ordon (Lublin: Wydawnictwo Naukowe KUL, 2014), pp. 227–234; Magdalena Prusak, Sprzeciw sumienia farmaceutów, (Kraków, 2015).

16 S.L.M. Strickland, "Conscientious Objection in Medical Students: a Questionnaire Survey," *Journal of Medical Ethics*, No. 38 (2012), p. 22; R.F. Card, "Is there no alternative? Conscientious objection by medical students," *Journal of Medical Ethics*, Vol. 38, No. 10 (2012), pp. 602–604.

17 R.E. Lawrence, F.A. Curlin, "Physicians' Beliefs About Conscience in Medicine: A National Survey," *Academic Medicine*, Vol. 84, No. 9 (2009), pp. 1276–1282; N.S. Wenger, S. Carmel, "Physicians' Religiosity and End-of-Life Care Attitudes and Behaviors," *The Mount Sinai Journal of Medicine*, Vol. 71, No. 5 (2004), pp. 335–343; D. Keown, "End of Life. The Buddhist View," *Lancet*, No. 366 (2005), p. 952; J.G. Schenker, "Assisted reproductive practice: religious perspectives," *Reproductive Biomedicine Online*, Vol. 10, No. 3 (2005), pp. 310–319; A. Sachedina, "End-of-life. The Islamic View," *Lancet*, No. 366 (2005), p. 778.

moral convictions or religious beliefs are raised by the objector. In other cases, healthcare workers can also refuse on the grounds of procedures being medically incorrect (e.g., antibiotics being used to treat viral infections), organizational restrictions (e.g., when the contract with the public funding body is exceeded) or ordinary difficulties in doctor-patient communication (e.g., about the treatment method), but the above situations are not typically regarded as conscientious objection.

First and foremost, however, a distinction should be made between, on the one hand, objection based on principles that are at the core of the professional ethics of a particular professional social group, and on the other, individual moral and religious sets of convictions that are derived from either personal reflection or the particular religious or ideological group to which that individual belongs. A situation of refusal arising from the evocation of widely accepted, or even universally adopted, principles rooted in professional ethics (e.g., nonmaleficence and respect for human life) is fundamentally different from any case in which the predominant reasoning stems from individual values and convictions that are independent of, and sometimes in accordance with, or sometimes even in conflict with, professional ethics. In the first case, the main moral principles are widely adopted (regardless of culture and religion) within a professional group and are transmitted from generation to generation, essentially unchanged (though they are adapted to meet the needs of particular situations). Such principles shape the social and professional identity of a group and its members over time through a process of identification. In the second case, reasons for refusals are derived from the subject's individual convictions, and it is easier to blame such situations of refusal on "the caprices" of personal conscience, which are not justified by deeper reasoning and more likely to swiftly and easily change since they are completely dependent on a personal decision.

It is also possible to distinguish between religious and moral motives of refusals. Religious motivations arise more directly from a/the religious doctrine (personal or communal) that is based on faith and transcends the natural reality processed by the intellect and senses, whereas moral motivations more often arise from the recognition of this natural reality (though they may be indirectly linked to religious beliefs) and are of a more universal nature.[18]

18 Jakub Pawlikowski, "Spór o klauzulę sumienia z perspektywy celów medycyny i etyki lekarskiej," in: *Sprzeciw sumienia w praktyce medycznej – aspekty etyczne i prawne*, eds. Piotr Stanisz, Jakub Pawlikowski, and Marta Ordon (Lublin: Wydawnictwo Naukowe KUL, 2014), pp. 145–170.

3 The internal and external goals of medicine

Any formulation of medicine's goals should be derived from an understanding of what its essence is, thus an attempt should be made to indicate the elements without which medicine would not be itself. Its essence contains its most important purposes which can be recognized as internal goals, in the sense that they immanently arise from its essence. From a phenomenological perspective, it can be seen that the essential elements determining medicine's identity are: (1) the fact of an illness (or other health problem) and (2) a relationship between: (2a) a person requiring help as the result of an illness or the threat it poses and (2b) a person who wishes and is able to provide this help. Illness and suffering are part of nature and human existence, so such fundamental goals are not conventionally established by a community or culture.[19]

During a debate on the goals of medicine that took place within medical circles several years ago, four basic goals were formulated for medicine, all of which are derived from medicine's essence: the care of those with a malady, treatment, prevention of diseases and alleviation of suffering.[20] Sometimes the avoidance of premature death is added to these goals.[21] Whereas some authors only regarded the first of these goals as fundamental, using it as a basis for deriving all the other goals, other authors treated all the goals as fundamental and made no attempt to hierarchize them. Advocates of the former stance include E. Pellegrino and L. Kass. Pellegrino believes that the fundamental goal of medicine should be to restore and improve the patient's health. When this is not possible, an attempt should be made to care for and assist the patient in such a way as to allow him or her to live with any disease-related pain, handicap or discomfort. However, the ultimate goal of the medical professions continues to be commitment to care arising from the relationship between the physician and his or her patient. If this

19 E. D. Pellegrino, "Toward a reconstruction of medical morality," *American Journal of Bioethics*, Vol. 6 (2006), pp. 65–71.

20 "The Goals of Medicine: Setting New Priorities: A Hasting Center Project Report," in: *Life Choices. A Hastings Center Introduction to Bioethics*, eds. J.H. Howell and W.F. Sale (Washington, 2000), p. 61; M.J. Hanson and D. Callahan, *The Goals of Medicine. The Forgotten Issues in Health Care Reform* (Washington, 2000).

21 M. Wicclair, "Is conscientious objection incompatible with a physician's professional obligations?" *Theoretical Medicine and Bioethics*, Vol. 29 (2008), pp. 171–185; F.G. Miller and H. Brody, "The internal morality of medicine: An evolutionary perspective," *Journal of Medicine and Philosophy*, Vol. 26, No. 6 (2001), pp. 581–599.

aspect were lost, medicine would cease to be medicine.[22] Much like the codes in many other countries, the current Polish Code of Medical Ethics formulates the medicine's fundamental tasks similarly: "The doctor's calling should comprise the protection of human life and health, prevention of disease, treatment of the sick and alleviation of suffering; the doctor cannot use his or her medical knowledge and skill for activities that conflict with this calling" (Article 2).[23]

The goals mentioned above (the protection of human life and health, prevention of disease, treatment of the sick and alleviation of suffering) are directly connected with the very essence of medicine, so may be termed "internal", "immanent" and "fundamental", or "medical" in the strict sense. They are not established on the basis of a social contract and do not arise from culture or legal regulations. In fact, a just law should create favourable conditions for their realization and safeguard medicine's autonomy.[24] There is no need to obligate healthcare workers to realize these goals, because they (goals) are naturally included in medical calling and the choice of the healthcare professions.

It is impossible in practice to realize medicine's essential (internal) goals without respecting the moral principle of respect for good of the patience, his/her life and health (*salus aegroti suprema lex*) and the nonmaleficence principle (*primum non nocere*), for it is from these that the duty arises to save lives, care for the health of others, prevent disease and strive to improve quality of life. Absolute respect for human life is expressed in the Hippocratic Oath ("I will neither give a deadly drug to anybody who asked for it, nor will I make a suggestion to this effect. Similarly I will not give to a woman an abortive remedy").[25] Similar goals and principles motivated the creators of modern deontological documents with a global reach that have been adopted as a moral template for the medical community. The Declaration of Geneva adopted in 1948 by the World Medical

---

22 E.D. Pellegrino, D.C. Thomas, *The Virtues in Medical Practice* (New York, 1993), pp. 53, 60; see also: T. Biesaga, "Właściwe i niewłaściwe cele medycyny," *Medycyna Praktyczna*, Vol. 5 (2004), pp. 1–5.

23 Code of Medical Ethics. Text dated 2 January 2004 containing amendments passed on 20 September 2003 by the Extraordinary 7th National Committee of Physicians, Warsaw, Supreme Chamber of Physicians.

24 R. Veatch, Veatch, "Internal and External Sources of Morality for Medicine," in: *The Health Care Professional as Friend and Healer*, eds. D.C. Thomasma and J.L. Kissel (Washington, 2000), p. 75.

25 Hippocratic Oath, Translation from the Greek by Ludwig Edelstein. From: Ludwig Edelstein, *The Hippocratic Oath: Text, Translation, and Interpretation* (Baltimore: Johns Hopkins Press, 1943), <http://www.pbs.org/wgbh/nova/body/hippocratic-oath-today.html> (last access: 14 February 2018)

Association emphasizes the physician's moral duty as follows: "I will maintain the utmost respect for human life from the time of conception; even under threat, I will not use my medical knowledge contrary to the laws of humanity," "The health of my patients will be my first consideration," or "I will practice my profession with conscience and dignity" (Declaration of Geneva, 1948).[26] Similarly, the International Code of Medical Ethics adopted by the Third General Assembly of the World Medical Association in London in October 1949 underlines: "Doctors must always bear in mind the obligation of preserving human life" (International Code of Medical Ethics, 1949).[27] These documents were a manifestation of a spontaneous moral response to the abuses of World War II, and later revisions to some of these provisions that aimed to relativize them are not able to erase the clear notion inspiring their first creators. The Polish Code of Medical Ethics also contains a set of articles enforcing absolute respect for human life. For example, Articles 30 and 31 obligate healthcare workers to provide humanitarian palliative care and prohibit them from performing euthanasia or assisting suicide. Moreover, when it comes to the process of providing care for pregnant women, the Code obligates physicians to care for both the mother and child, clearly emphasizing that "it is the physician's duty to endeavor to preserve the health and life of the child before its birth" (Article 39). State law also takes into consideration the above medical ethics standards. Article 4 of a Polish act relating to physicians explicitly obligates the doctor to provide health services that comply with the principles of professional ethics. References are also made in the jurisprudential practice of the Polish Constitutional Tribunal to deontological principles, for example, a judgement made on 15 January 1991, in which

26 World Medical Association, Declaration of Geneva, 1948, Adopted by the 2nd General Assembly of the World Medical Association, Geneva, Switzerland, September 1948 and amended by the 22nd World Medical Assembly, Sydney, Australia, August 1968 and the 35th World Medical Assembly, Venice, Italy, October 1983 and the 46th WMA General Assembly, Stockholm, Sweden, September 1994 and editorially revised by the 170th WMA Council Session, Divonne-les-Bains, France, May 2005 and the 173rd WMA Council Session, Divonne-les-Bains, France, May 2006: 21 Feb 2018 <https://www.wma.net/wp-content/uploads/2016/11/Decl-of-Geneva-v1948.pdf>

27 World Medical Association, International Code of Medical Ethics, 1949, Adopted by the 3rd General Assembly of the World Medical Association, London, England, October 1949 and amended by the 22nd World Medical Assembly, Sydney, Australia, August 1968 and the 35th World Medical Assembly, Venice, Italy, October 1983 and the 57th WMA General Assembly, Pilanesberg, South Africa, October 2006: 21 Feb 2018 <https://www.wma.net/wp-content/uploads/2016/11/Decl-of-Geneva-v1948.pdf>

the tribunal, referring to the deontological code, underlined that "the physician should refuse to perform actions that, according to his/her conviction and conscience, may be harmful or unethical."[28] This particularly applies to all actions that may violate the life or health of a human being at any stage of development.

The state authorities, legislators and society can, however, sometimes formulate additional goals for the medical community that are external to medicine's essence. Such external goals arise from needs that are not directly related to protection of human health and life but are solely based on medical personnel using their knowledge and skills. These may be termed "external", "non-medical" or "additional goals". For several decades, it has been clear to see that an increasing number of duties arising from external goals are being imposed on healthcare workers. This process is partially related to the substantial role of biopolitics in contemporary political ideology and practice.[29]

Such external goals can be either justifiable or unjustifiable depending on whether, on absorbing medical skills and knowledge, they respect medicine's essence (its purposes and fundamental values) or violate it. Justifiable non-medical goals can arise from economic, social, political and scientific needs, but the realization of these goals does not violate medicine's purposes and values. Two good examples of such goals would be the use of a physician's knowledge and skills for the objectives of forensic medicine (for investigation) or for social objectives (e.g., an insurance judicature and occupational medicine). The state authorities may obligate healthcare workers to realize justifiable non-medical goals, and the medical community may pursue them as part of the responsible performance of their civic duties. The imposition of such duties should of course be bound by rational limits, so as to ensure that they do not make it difficult for physicians to perform their core tasks.

However, when imposed duties or social expectations conflict with medicine's fundamental goals, they should be defined as unjustifiable non-medical goals. A good example of such actions would be obligating a physician to violate the principle of absolute respect for human health and life, for example, by inflicting torture and suffering during military service or selecting and eliminating weaker

28 The Decision of the Constitutional Tribunal of 15 January 1991, File No. U 8/90, OTK ZU 1991.

29 This state of affairs has many causes, but is undoubtedly the partial outcome of the processes whereby medical action is becoming increasingly bureaucratized and juridized, society is becoming medicalized, social insurance systems are developing, which are causing the physician to perform the role of a passive expert or consultant in matters not directly connected with health and life.

or sick human beings at various stages of their development, particularly during the prenatal or terminal stages. According to L. Kass, performing social, economic, or political tasks without caring about the patient's health is contrary to medicine's essence, even if some members of medical personnel may be undertaking such tasks due to their loyalty to the state authorities or having submitted to social pressure (L. Kass 1985).[30] In such circumstances, medicine becomes an instrument for the implementation of a particular biopolitical ideology, or a tool for satisfying the non-medical needs of certain groups of citizens.

4. The reason for conscientious objection in medicine: imposition of unjustifiable external medical goals

When observing and analysing the circumstances within which conscientious objection arises in medical practice, the conclusion may be drawn that the source of these problems is the imposition on medical personnel of duties that conflict with medicine's essence, that is its purposes and fundamental values. The content and form of the provisions of the conscience clause are of secondary importance. Such provisions must assume the existence of a specific duty and it should be demonstrated first that this duty is justified, in the sense that it is compatible with medical teleology and axiology.

Most procedures capable of provoking conscientious objection violate the principle of respect for human life at the prenatal (abortion, the destruction of supernumerary embryos, and anti-implantation or abortive drugs) or terminal (euthanasia, assisting suicide) stages. Being obligated to terminate the life of a sick child in the prenatal phase and at the same time being obligated to care for it in the postnatal stage can lead to moral ambivalence and individual and professional identity disintegration. This evokes an ethical dilemma how prenatal selection can be reconciled with postnatal solidarity and what reasoning could justify the imposition of the duty to terminate life on a physician whose calling is to protect it.

The scope of the duties binding the physician and other healthcare workers largely depends on the vision of medicine, its goals and the moral obligations derived from these goals. In the classic model alluding to the Hippocratic tradition, moral and legal duties are derived from medicine's very essence (its internal goals), which obligates healthcare workers to care for the patient's life, health and well-being and firmly object to any forms of destroying life. In other models of medicine, for example the contractual model, the primacy of medicine's

---

30 L.R. Kass, "The End of Medicine and the Pursuit of Health," in: *Toward a More Natural Science*, ed. L.R. Kass (New York, 1985), p. 160.

internal goals is not taken into account, and society or the patient have the right to impose other goals that are external to its essence. The relationship between the physician and his or her patient is more akin to that between the salesperson and the client and requires the physician to undertake the duty of performing all actions permitted by law on demand by the patient, even if they conflict with professional ethics, while the patient's requests are reinforced by reference to legal regulations (however, it should be noted that, in the case of a salesperson or contractor, it is difficult to point to regulations that would oblige him or her to perform actions against human life at a client's request).[31]

Another method expanding the scope of physicians' duties beyond the justified limits established by medicine's purposes is the broad interpretation of the right to privacy or the right to autonomy (*Roe v. Wade* 1973, *Tysiac v. Poland*). The Polish Constitutional Tribunal underlined in its ruling of 7 October 2015 that the right to privacy should be understood negatively, as freedom from interference or a guarantee of the inviolability of private life granted by the state authorities or other people. The reasoning that derives the physician's duty to take actions violating human life from the patients' right for their privacy to be protected should be regarded as faulty and a manifestation of the objective and patronizing treating of physicians.[32]

The final, but equally valid, reason for strengthening the duty derived from external unjustifiable goals is the predominance of the autonomy principle within medical ethics and medical law. The principle of respect for autonomy as the primary standard of medical ethics is further emphasized by the predominance in the bioethics debate of Tom Beauchamp's and James F. Childress' principlism model. However, it is worth noting that the model proposed by these authors does not include in its list of the fundamental principles of medical ethics (respect for autonomy, nonmaleficence, beneficence and justice), the principle of respect for human life (the impression may be gained that this principle is subsumed by the broadly conceived principle of respect for autonomy).[33] This model should, therefore, be regarded as inconsistent with classic medical ethics. Other models that are more compatible with medical experience and tradition incorporate the principle of caring for the patient's good as a medical ethics standard that gives rise in turn to other rules such as the

31 Jakub Pawlikowski, „Spór o klauzulę sumienia z perspektywy celów medycyny i etyki lekarskiej," pp. 145–170.

32 The Decision of the Constitutional tribunal of 7 October 2015, File No. K 12/14.

33 Tom L. Beauchamp and James F. Childress, *Principles of Biomedical Ethics*, 7th edition (Oxford University Press, 2013).

imperative to respect human life, the preservation of confidentiality or non-harm.[34] Absolutizing the patient's autonomy at the expense of the physician's conscience does not correspond to the nature of the relationship between the physician and patient and carries the threat of legislators or patients becoming paternalistic towards physicians. It should be added that excessive emphasizing the principle of respect for autonomy, while not giving due consideration to the patient's good and welfare, objectively conceived, may demotivate the physician from caring for the patient's health and life.

The methods of justification mentioned above fail to take into account medicine's purposes and diminish its fundamental moral principles, leading to an authoritarian broadening of the scope of the doctor's duties that overstep the boundaries of moral correctness and righteous law. However, the consequence of this is the degeneration of natural internal barriers within the medical community that protect against the further overstepping of boundaries destroying human dignity, especially if such actions are legally sanctioned or accepted by society. It should be stressed that not everything a physician may do needs to be a medical action, for this could lead to the position expressed by Eichmann's defense attorney during his case in Jerusalem in 1960, who said that forced sterilization and killing people in gas chambers was a medical issue, as all the preparations were being made by doctors.[35]

This begs the question of what a correct and justified range of duties for a physician should be. There is no doubt that physicians are mainly appointed to perform actions derived from medicine's internal goals and this should be required of them. Consequently, legal coercion obliging physicians to perform actions arising from medicine's internal goals and concomitant sanctions for failure to fulfill this duty can be regarded as justified. For example, a doctor may be obliged to dress a criminal's wounds even when such an action could cause emotional hesitation or assist a person whose life or health are threatened even if the treatment method is not compatible with the religion the physician practices (e.g., calling upon a physician who is a Jehovah's witness to perform a blood transfusion in a life-threatening situation). However, physicians refusing to provide services compatible with medicine's internal goals yet contrary to their religious beliefs is a marginal phenomenon, for such devout physicians will shape their career path in such a way as to avoid exposing themselves to such controversial

34 E. D. Pellegrino, *For the Patient's Good: The Restoration of Beneficence in Health Care* (New York: Oxford University Press, 1988).

35 H. Arendt, *The Origins of Totalitarism* (New York: A Harvest Book, 1973), p. 84.

situations on a continuous basis in their work. It should be stressed that the norms of professional deontology forbid the physician from refusing to assist in the event of a patient's life or health being threatened (Article 69 of the Polish Code of Medical Ethics).[36]

The question then arises of to what extent a physician can be obliged to realize external goals. A significant proportion of non-medical obligations are accepted from the point of view of medical ethics and, therefore, do not provoke any substantial moral dilemmas and are not a subject of controversy. However, those obligations that conflict with medicine's purposes and the fundamental values of medical ethics (e.g., causing harm or leading to the violation of human life at the prenatal or terminal stages) are the manifestation of unjustifiable law. Refusal in such circumstances is not akin to a recruit refusing to perform military service due to his subjective convictions. A more accurate analogy may be drawn with the situation of a soldier who refuses to carry out an order that conflicts with raison d'état or a policeman who refuses to shoot a citizen of his own country or a judge who excludes himself from passing an unjust sentence.

Some believe that a physician should not be forced into performing any non-therapeutic actions.[37] However, this postulate would appear to be too radical. It would suffice to ensure that a physician is not obligated to perform an action or cooperate in actions violating the life of another human being (with the exception of a situation when such action can be justified on the basis of the principle of double effect or proportionality of protected goods). This is a radical solution, but the only one that would make it possible to permanently resolve the problem of conscientious objection among healthcare workers and reduce difficulties interpreting the medical conscience clause. Such a solution need not be bound up with the penalization of these actions. It also does not seem to lead to the violation of the social order or discrimination against a particular group of people. Such an approach enables medicine's autonomy, the medical professions' ethos and the individual convictions of medical personnel to be respected to a greater extent

---

36 See also: Stance of the Presidium of the Supreme Medical Council No. 74/13/P-VI convened on 6 December 2013 on the issue of the conscience clause being used in medical practice: 21 Feb 2018 <http://www.nil.org.pl/aktualnosci/stanowiska-prezydium-nrl-z-dn.-6-grudnia-2013-r.>

37 Konstanty Radziwiłł, "Odmowa leczenia z perspektywy art. 7 Kodeksu Etyki Lekarskie,"" in: *Sprzeciw sumienia w praktyce medycznej – aspekty etyczne i prawne*, eds. Piotr Stanisz, Jakub Pawlikowski, and Marta Ordon (Lublin: Wydawnictwo Naukowe KUL, 2014), pp. 191–195.

without reducing healthcare workers to the role of tools facilitating the realization of biopolitics' ideological assumptions.

Finally, it should be emphasized that it is a misconception to label such varied activities as diagnosis, treatment, rehabilitation or the termination of a pregnancy (e.g., on the suspicion that the unborn child has a defect) as "medical services" or "medical procedures." The last one action differs markedly from the others in that it is not realizing a health-related goal. The conflicting goals integrated into health services or medical procedures being provided at the healthcare facilities of many developed countries are just one example of the defectiveness of the existing legislation and hinder the interpretation of the relevant regulations. The need has therefore arisen for a *de lege lata* and *de lege ferenda* limiting of the scope of guaranteed health services to actions that do not violate medicine's essence, its purposes and fundamental professional values. Legislative amendments that only relate to the provisions of the conscience clause will not be sufficient if no attempt is made to remove actions that arise from unjustifiable external medical goals from the catalog of guaranteed services. At a linguistic level, limiting the scope of guaranteed health services to activities focused on the patient's health and life would reduce the possibility of this category being used for the purposes of manipulation and adapt the relevant legal terms to more closely reflect the reality they actually describe.

5 Conclusion

To summarize, the main cause of the problem of conscientious objection in medical practice is the imposition of duties on medical personnel that conflict with medicine's internal teleology and axiology, while the content and form of the provisions of the conscience clause are of secondary importance. When analysing this problem, it should always be asked whether the duties being imposed on physicians can be objectively justified on the basis of medicine's internal aims and the values of medical ethics, or whether they are in fact nothing more than an arbitrary exercise of power of public authorities or society over healthcare workers. If legal regulations in the area of medical practice fail to follow these principles, they will do little more than contribute to the dramas of Antigone, Thomas Morus and other martyrs of conscience. Such a situation could also lead people who would pursue their vocation with complete devotion to resign from the profession. The most serious long-term consequence will be the erosion of the moral sensibilities of both individuals and collective medical personnel, while medicine based on law alone, rather than on conscience, could easily become a component in a totalitarian system.

When seeking a solution to this problem, calls should be made for the range of guaranteed health services to be limited to actions that do not violate the principle of respect for a human being's health and life. It can also be assumed that consciences formed from axiological foundations and bolstered by justified legal regulations will lead to actions being undertaken that are consistent with the patient's good and welfare. Such a solution would appear to be the only one that would guarantee the protection of patients' fundamental rights (i.e., the protection of life and health) as well as healthcare workers' freedom of conscience. Another benefit of such a solution would be that the scientific, political and social dispute over conscientious objection would not flare up to the extent it has in recent years.

Part II: European Perspective

Gregor Puppinck & Claire de La Hougue

Freedom of Conscience and Conscientious Objection in the Medical Area

Abstract: The chapter presents the thesis that freedom of conscience is at the very core of human rights. It is protected in all human rights instruments. Since the very nature of medicine was altered, the law provided conscience clauses to guarantee that medical staff would not be obliged to participate in those non-therapeutic activities. Strictly speaking, these clauses are not conscientious objection, because there is no legal obligation to participate in such non-therapeutic activities. However, some recent developments suggest that real medical conscientious objection will develop in Europe. The problem does not lie in the conscience of the objector, but in the act demanded, which falls out of the scope of medicine and contradicts human life or dignity.

Keywords: abortion, conscientious objection, discrimination, euthanasia, freedom of conscience, human rights

1 Freedom of conscience, a cornerstone of human rights

Freedom of conscience is at the very core of human rights. It is protected in all human rights instruments, especially in Article 18 of the International Covenant on Civil and Political Rights ("the Covenant") and Article 9 of the European Convention on Human Rights ("the Convention"), directly and/or through the prohibition of discrimination.

Its importance is underlined by the fact that, according to Article 4 of the Covenant, no derogation can be made to this right even "*in time of public emergency which threatens the life of the nation*". According to Article 9-2 of the European Convention (and Article 18-3 of the Covenant), limits can be brought only to the *manifestation* of religion or belief, under strict conditions, never on the substance of the right. The Strasbourg Court regularly asserts that "*As enshrined in Article 9, freedom of thought, conscience and religion is one of the foundations of a 'democratic society' within the meaning of the Convention*" and insists that "*it is also a precious asset for atheists, agnostics, sceptics and the unconcerned*" (*Kokkinakis v. Greece*, 14307/88, 25/05/1993 § 31).

Freedom of conscience has an internal dimension, the freedom to adhere or not to adhere to a belief, and an external dimension, the freedom to act "*in accordance with the dictates of his own conscience*" (Helsinki Final Act, Principle VII). This implies not only freedom *not to be prevented* from acting according to one's conscience (i.e., from manifesting one's belief) but also the right *not to be compelled* to act against one's conscience, as the Human Rights Committee recognised: *"while the right to manifest one's religion or belief does not as such imply the right to refuse all obligations imposed by law, it provides certain protection, consistent with Article 18, paragraph 3, against being forced to act against genuinely-held religious belief"* (*Yoon and Choi v. Republic of Korea*, 3rd November 2006, § 8.3).

2 Conscientious objection, a constitutive element of freedom of conscience

As human beings are endowed with conscience and able to make a moral judgement, conscientious objection is both a duty, enshrined in Principle IV of the Nuremberg Principles,[1] and a right. This is why it was already mentioned in the Convention and the Covenant. The development of international human rights law has led to recognise objection as an integral part of freedom of conscience.

2.1 The UN mechanism

In General Comment 22 (1993) on Article 18, the Human Rights Committee (HRC) stated that *"The Covenant does not explicitly refer to a right to conscientious objection, but the Committee believes that such a right can be derived from Article 18, inasmuch as the obligation to use lethal force may seriously conflict with the freedom of conscience and the right to manifest one's religion or belief."*

This led the Committee to find violations of Article 18 of the Covenant in countries that do not recognise conscientious objection: conscientious objection is an essential part of freedom of religion or belief. In the case *Jeong et al v. Republic of Korea* (communications 1642–1741/2007, 24 March 2011, § 7.3), the Human Rights Committee recognised that conscientious objection is not a mere manifestation of belief but a constituent element of freedom of conscience: *"The Committee recalls its General Comment No 22 where it has considered that the fundamental character of the freedoms enshrined in Article 18, paragraph 1 is reflected in the fact that this provision cannot be derogated from, even in time of public emergency, as*

1 "The fact that a person acted pursuant to order of his Government or of a superior does not relieve him from responsibility under international law, provided a moral choice was in fact possible to him"; on the duty to object, see also ECHR, *Polednova v. the Czech Republic*, 2615/10, June 21st 2011 and *K.-H. W. v Germany*, 37201/97, GC March 22nd 2001.

stated in Article 4, paragraph 2 of the Covenant. Although the Covenant does not explicitly refer to a right of conscientious objection, the Committee believes that such a right derives from Article 18, inasmuch as the obligation to be involved in the use of lethal force may seriously conflict with the freedom of conscience. The right to conscientious objection to military service inheres in the right to freedom of thought, conscience and religion. It entitles any individual to an exemption from compulsory military service if this cannot be reconciled with that individual's religion or beliefs. The right must not be impaired by coercion." The same paragraph is found in all subsequent cases on conscientious objection.

Freedom of conscience is not protected if people are obliged to act against the dictates of their conscience. For the Committee, it is clear that the right of objectors to refuse military service directly stems from the right to freedom of conscience (1st sentence of Article 18-1) therefore is not subject to limitations under Article 18-3. In the case of *Atasoy and Sarkut v. Turkey*, the Committee repeated *"that the right to conscientious objection to military service is inherent to the right to freedom of thought, conscience and religion"* (1853–1854/2008, 29 March 2012 § 10.4).

In the case of *Kim v. Republic of Korea* (1786/2008, 25 October 2012, § 7.3 7.4), the Human Rights Committee was even more precise: *"The Committee further notes that freedom of thought, conscience and religion embraces the right not to declare, as well as the right to declare, one's conscientiously held beliefs. Compulsory military service without possibility of alternative civilian service implies that a person may be put in a position in which he or she is deprived of the right to choose whether or not to declare his or her conscientiously held beliefs by being under a legal obligation, either to break the law or to act against those beliefs within a context in which it may be necessary to deprive another human being of life."*

2.2 The Council of Europe instruments

The European Court of Human Rights (ECHR) also *"considers that opposition to military service, where it is motivated by a serious and insurmountable conflict between the obligation to serve in the army and a person's conscience or his deeply and genuinely held religious or other beliefs, constitutes a conviction or belief of sufficient cogency, seriousness, cohesion and importance to attract the guarantees of Article 9"* (GC, 7 July 2011, *Bayatyan v. Armenia*, 23459/03, § 110) It must be noted that, for the ECHR, the objection itself is the belief that is protected by Article 9.

The Court concluded Armenia had violated Article 9, especially because the majority should not always impose their view in a democratic society: "The Court further reiterates that pluralism, tolerance and broadmindedness are hallmarks of a "democratic society". Although individual interests must on occasion be subordinated to those of a group, democracy does not simply mean that the views of a majority must always prevail: a balance must be achieved which ensures the fair and proper treatment of people from minorities and avoids any abuse of a dominant position (see Leyla Şahin, cited above, § 108). Thus, respect on the part of the State towards the beliefs of a minority religious group like the applicant's by providing them with the opportunity to serve society as dictated by their conscience might, far from creating unjust inequalities or discrimination as claimed by the Government, rather ensure cohesive and stable pluralism and promote religious harmony and tolerance in society." (Bayatyan, § 126)

Through this judgement, the Court rallied to the position of the Parliamentary Assembly of the Council of Europe (PACE), which had advocated conscientious objections for decades, since 1967. The Court expressly relied on the various PACE resolutions and recommendations (§ 51–53), beginning with Resolution 337 (1967):

"1. *Persons liable to conscription for military service who, for reasons of conscience or profound conviction arising from religious, ethical, moral, humanitarian, philosophical or similar motives, refuse to perform armed service shall enjoy a personal right to be released from the obligation to perform such service.*
2. *This right shall be regarded as deriving logically from the fundamental rights of the individual in democratic Rule of Law States which are guaranteed in Article 9 of the European Convention on Human Rights.*"

The Court further mentioned Recommendation 478 (1967), Recommendation 816 (1977) and Recommendation 1518 (2001) – which states that the right to conscientious objection is a "*fundamental aspect of the right to freedom of thought, conscience and religion*" **enshrined in** the Convention – and Recommendation 1742 (2006) concerning the human rights of members of the armed forces.

These PACE resolutions and recommendations manifest the consensus in Europe on conscientious objection, confirmed by Recommendations R(87)8 and CM/Rec(2010)4 of the Committee of Ministers, also mentioned in the *Bayatyan* judgement.

3 Conscientious objection in the workplace, especially in the medical area

Although the majority of the case law and documents on conscientious objection regards military service, objection is not limited to this area. It concerns every "*profound conviction arising from religious, ethical, moral, humanitarian, philosophical or similar motives*" (APCE Resolution 337 (1967)), especially "*within a context in which it may be necessary to deprive another human being of life*" (HRC *Kim v. Korea* § 7.3).

Normally, conscientious objection should not apply in the medical area: the aim of medicine is to cure, and no one, in conscience, may refuse to cure. However, the scope of medical action has changed in the past decades. Various actions that are not meant to cure have been included in medical activities. This began with contraception, developing with other non-therapeutic activities such as plastic surgery or sterilisation, eventually encompassing abortion and euthanasia.

Since the very nature of medicine was altered, the law provided conscience clauses to guarantee that medical staff would not be obliged to participate in those non-therapeutic activities. Strictly speaking, these clauses are not conscientious objection, because there is no legal obligation to participate in such non-therapeutic activities. However, some recent developments suggest that real medical conscientious objection will develop in Europe. The problem does not lie in the conscience of the objector, but in the act demanded, which falls out of the scope of medicine and contradicts human life or dignity.

Where human life, and possibly human nature, is at stake, it is certain that conscientious objection applies to medical acts. There is not only a right but also a duty to object to an injunction to kill, at any stage of life. Human life is a continuum from the moment of fertilisation, as recalled by the Court of Justice of the European Union in the case of *Oliver Brüstle v Greenpeace e.V* (C-34/10, 18 October 2011, § 35).

The European Court of Human Right has also recently confirmed that "*human embryos cannot be reduced to 'possessions'* " (*Parrillo c. Italy*, 46470/11, GC 27 August 2015, § 215). Since Roman law, only two categories exist, therefore, it can safely be deduced that if embryos do not belong to the category of things, they necessarily belong to that of persons. The Court had already stated that "*it may be regarded as common ground between States that the embryo/foetus belongs to the human race. The potentiality of that being and its capacity to become a person [...] require protection in the name of human dignity*" (*Vo v. France*, 53924/00, GC 8 July 2004, § 84). It cannot be contested that abortion consists in ending a human life; therefore, refusal to perform abortion is a case of conscientious objection as protected by international and European law. The same applies to euthanasia, which ends human life.

3.1 The right to conscientious objection in the medical area is not contested

The most recent general human rights instrument, the Charter of Fundamental Rights of the European Union, expressly recognises the right to conscientious objection, without limiting it to military service (Article 10.2).

In two cases against Poland, the European Court of Human Rights, considering that conscientious objection and the access to legal abortion respectively fall under Articles 9 and 8 of the Convention and are in conflict, judged that "*states are obliged to organise the health services system in such a way as to ensure that an effective exercise of the freedom of conscience of health professionals in the professional context does not prevent patients from obtaining access to services to which they are entitled under the applicable legislation*" (*R.R. v Poland*, 27617/08, May 26th 2011, § 206; *P. and S. v. Poland*, 57375/08, October 30th 2012, § 106). The Court refused to make one right prevail over the other and imposed the responsibility to create a mechanism reconciling the concurrent rights on the State. The Court insisted on this point, noting that the Polish law "*has acknowledged the need to ensure that doctors are not obliged to carry out services to which they object, and put in place a mechanism by which such a refusal can be expressed. This mechanism also includes elements allowing the right to conscientious objection to be reconciled with the patient's interests*" (*P. and S. v. Poland*, § 107).

The Parliamentary Assembly of the Council of Europe (PACE) has solemnly recalled in Resolution 1763 (2010): "*no person, hospital or institution shall be coerced, held liable or discriminated against in any manner because of a refusal to perform, accommodate, assist or submit to an abortion, the performance of a human miscarriage, or euthanasia or any act which could cause the death of a human foetus or embryo, for any reason.*"

This resolution is a soft law document reflecting the consensus on the state of the law and practice in Europe, which comes very close to the definition of customary international law, which is "*evidence of a general practice accepted as law*" according to Article 38 of the statute of the International Court of Justice.

The importance of conscientious objection in the medical area was recalled in Resolution 1928 (2013) of April 24th 2013 Safeguarding Human Rights In Relation To Religion And Belief, And Protecting Religious Communities From Violence. The PACE called Member States to "*ensure the right to well-defined conscientious objection in relation to morally sensitive matters, such as military service or other services related to health care and education, in line also with various recommendations already adopted by the Assembly, provided that the rights of others to be free from discrimination are respected and that the access to lawful services is guaranteed.*"

Various resolutions have also insisted on the right to freedom of conscience, which includes objection, in the workplace. Thus, in Resolution 2036 (2015) of 29 January 2015 entitled Tackling intolerance and discrimination in Europe with a special focus on Christians, the PACE called on States to "*uphold freedom of conscience in the workplace while ensuring that access to services provided by law is maintained and the right of others to be free from discrimination is protected.*"

These resolutions and recommendations are soft law instruments; though not legally binding, they reflect the consensus existing in Europe. Actually, all European countries except Sweden seem to recognise conscientious objection in the medical area, at least to some extent. The Strasbourg Court regularly relies on PACE resolutions and recommendations when deciding a case, as can be seen again in the most recent case of *Parrillo v. Italy* where it quoted two Recommendations of the Parliamentary Assembly regarding the protection of embryos, namely Rec 1046 (1986) and Rec 1100 (1989).

In the case of *International Planned Parenthood Federation – European Network (IPPF EN) v. Italy* (87/2012, 10 September 2013), the European Social Rights Committee never contested the right of conscientious objection of medical staff but simply repeated that the State was responsible for the organisation of hospitals so as to provide access to legal services: "*adequate measures must be taken to ensure the availability of non-objecting medical practitioners and other health personnel when and where they are required to provide abortion services*" (§ 163).

In the case of *Federation of Catholic Family Associations in Europe (FAFCE) v. Sweden*, (99/2013, 17 March 2015), the right to conscientious objection was not contested either: the Committee merely said it was not covered by Article 11 of the Social Charter on the right to health, which does not affect its protection under the right to freedom of conscience.

3.2 Reconciliation of concurring rights

Moreover, the Court has ruled that the possibility to change job was not sufficient effectively to protect the right to freedom of conscience: "*Given the importance in a democratic society of freedom of religion, the Court considers that, where an individual complains of a restriction on freedom of religion in the workplace, rather than holding that the possibility of changing job would negate any interference with the right, the better approach would be to weigh that possibility in the overall balance when considering whether or not the restriction was proportionate*" (*Eweida and others v. the United Kingdom*, 48420/10, 15 January 2013, § 83). A very serious reason, such as a grave breach of the rights of others, must exist to justify depriving somebody of their job.

However, the balancing required by the ECHR is not applicable where a right protected by the Convention conflicts with rights not so protected: "*It is a different matter where restrictions are imposed on a right or freedom guaranteed by the Convention in order to protect 'rights and freedoms' not, as such, enunciated therein. In such a case only indisputable imperatives can justify interference with enjoyment of a Convention right*" (ECHR *Chassagnou and others v. France*, 25088/94, 2833/95, and 2844/95, GC 29 April 1999, § 113). Now, while freedom of conscience is one of the most fundamental human rights, abortion cannot be claimed as a human right at the international or European levels. No treaty admits abortion as a right; the 1994 Cairo Conference on Population and Development not only affirmed: "*In no case should abortion be promoted as a method of family planning*" (§ 8.25) but also repeatedly called on States to prevent abortion (*e.g* §§ 7.6 and 8.25) and help women avoid abortion (§ 7.24). The ECHR has also repeated that "Article 8 cannot be interpreted as conferring a right to abortion."[2]

Even the European Social Rights Committee, in the aforementioned case of *IPPF EN v. Italy*, accepted to examine the issue of access to abortion services with regard to the right to health only because "*national legislation has classified* (abortion services) *as a form of medical treatment that relates to the protection of health and individual well-being, and* ***which therefore*** *can be considered to come within the scope of Article 11 of the Charter*" (§ 161), not because the Social Charter encompasses an alleged right to abortion.

It is thus quite clear that an alleged right to abortion, with no existence in international law, cannot prevail over one of the most fundamental human rights, namely freedom of conscience. Neither can Sweden hide behind the margin of appreciation: this margin does not concern the *existence* of the right to conscientious objection, but at most its *conditions of implementation*, provided they do not impair the substance of the right.

The balance can hardly be done with the right to health either, as abortion has no therapeutic effect. Pregnancy is not a disease, which would be cured by abortion. Only in the very rare cases where pregnancy directly threatens the life of the mother is this balance relevant, but then there is no right to objection: all possible measures to save the woman's life must be taken, even if the consequence may be the loss of the baby.

The Court has accepted that abortion may fall within the scope of the right to private life, in which case concurring rights must be reconciled, keeping in mind the outstanding position of freedom of conscience and religion in a democratic society. In the case of *Tysiac v. Poland* case (5410/03, 20 March 2007), the European Court clearly refused to limit the right to conscientious objection,

---

2 *A. B. C., v. Ireland*, 25579/05, GC 16 December 2010, § 214; *P. and S. v. Poland*, 57375/08, 30 October 2012, § 96.

when the applicant (as well as a third party) complained that *"a gynaecologist could refuse to perform an abortion on grounds of conscience"*, and further complained that *"a patient could not bring a doctor to justice for refusing to perform an abortion"* (§ 100). The Court clearly refused to undermine, at any moment in its decision, the freedom of conscience of medical practitioners. It is the State's responsibility to organise hospitals so as to permit the exercise of concurring rights.

3.3 Discrimination

The protection of freedom of conscience can also be ensured through the prohibition of discrimination, banned both by EU law and Council of Europe standards. If exercising one's right to freedom of conscience causes severe adverse consequences, the freedom is not effectively protected. Losing one's job and being obliged to change occupation is a very grave adverse consequence, with severe effects on private life. It can only be justified by very compelling reasons.

European Union's Council Directive 2000/78/EC of 27 November 2000 Establishing A General Framework For Equal Treatment In Employment And Occupation prohibits direct and indirect discrimination, based upon, inter alia, religion or belief. It applies to:

(a) conditions for access to employment, to self-employment or to occupation, including selection criteria and recruitment conditions, whatever the branch of activity and at all levels of the professional hierarchy, including promotion;
(b) access to all types and to all levels of vocational guidance, vocational training, advanced vocational training and retraining, including practical work experience;
(c) employment and working conditions, including dismissals and pay.

Article 14 of the European Convention on Human Rights prohibits discrimination based on religion or belief in the exercise of the rights guaranteed in the Convention. The Court **has** always recognised that people in a different situation must be treated differently, otherwise they would be victims of discrimination: *"the right not to be discriminated against in the enjoyment of the rights guaranteed under the Convention is also violated when States without an objective and reasonable justification fail to treat differently persons whose situations are significantly different"* (*Thlimmenos v. Greece*, 34369/97, GC 6 April 2000, § 44).

An objector and a non-objector are in radically different situations with regard to abortion or euthanasia; while the latter does not mind doing it, the former cannot because it would contradict the dictates of his conscience, his strongest and most intimate convictions based possibly on faith but mainly on rational thinking and scientific evidence that life is a continuum from fertilisation to death and abortion and euthanasia consists in ending a human life. Therefore, the situation of the objector is different and he must be treated differently, which can easily be done, by organising services accordingly.

Otherwise, the effect of the refusal to respect the freedom of conscience results in barring people who respect the life of unborn children from professions linked with pregnancy, which is both paradoxical and discriminatory. People with all the scientific skills and human qualities for these professions are deterred from them by the systematic discrimination they undergo. In the end, the patients, especially pregnant women, suffer the consequences of this obstinacy. Moreover, the lack of recognition of the right to conscientious objection not only worsens the shortage of midwives and deprives the medical staff of their right but also deprives some patients of midwives and doctors sharing their beliefs and the risk for these women to be pressured into abortion becomes very high. Therefore, claiming that the right to conscientious objection would jeopardise access to health services is false. On the contrary, it would guarantee a diversified access, corresponding to the diversity of patients.

A very simple solution permits to eliminate all problems and meet the requirements of a democratic society: recognise the right of medical staff, and organise hospitals accordingly. This would answer the ECHR findings in *Bayatyan* and conform with the consensus reflected in various PACE resolutions, such as Resolution 1846 (2011) Combating All Forms Of Discrimination Based On Religion 25 November 2011 *"when enacting legislation and implementing appropriate policies, strive to accommodate the needs of different religions and beliefs in a pluralist society, provided that any such measures do not infringe the rights of others."*

Similarly, a recent PACE resolution insists on the necessity to accommodate beliefs to ensure effective freedom of conscience, which is a foundation of a democratic and pluralist society and is necessary for peace and harmony in a pluralist society. Resolution 2036 (2015) Tackling Intolerance And Discrimination In Europe With A Special Focus On Christians underlines that acts of hostility against Christians are often overlooked by the national authorities and that *"Expression of faith is sometimes unduly limited by national legislation and policies which do not allow the accommodation of religious beliefs and practices."* This resolution insists: *"The reasonable accommodation of religious beliefs and practices constitutes a pragmatic means of ensuring the effective and full enjoyment of freedom of religion. When it is applied in a spirit of tolerance, this concept allows all religious groups to live in harmony in the respect and acceptance of their diversity."* Intolerance against objectors – who often are Christians, even if the objection is based on conscience, not necessarily religion – is a manifestation of this hostility, overlooked by some States but matter of concern for the European institutions.

Once again, *"The role of the authorities in a situation of conflict between or within religious groups is not to remove the cause of tension by eliminating pluralism, but to ensure that the competing groups tolerate each other"* (ECHR, *Holy Synod of the Bulgarian Orthodox Church*, 412/03 35677/04, 22 January 2009 § 120).

Organising health services so as to accommodate the needs of conscientious objectors would remedy the present violation of freedom of conscience and eliminate discrimination based on religion or belief.

4 Abortion and freedom of conscience in ethical professional guidelines

Members of the medical professions have a general duty to act in conscience, for the benefit of patients. This is the basis of medical ethics, already reflected in the Hippocratic Oath (5th century BC). This oath required doctors to heal patients according to their judgement, that is to say their conscience. It prohibited giving poison or abortive drugs. Though modern versions have usually erased the mention of abortion, they still oblige doctors to protect and promote health, follow their judgement or conscience and abstain from inflicting death deliberately.

For example, the World Medical Association (WMA), which was created in 1947 to ensure the independence of physicians and to work for the highest possible standards of ethical behaviour and care by physicians, states in the Declaration of Geneva,[3] its modernised version of the oath: *"I will practise my profession with conscience and dignity; the health of my patient will be my first consideration;[…] I will maintain the utmost respect for human life."*

3 Adopted by the 2nd General Assembly of the World Medical Association, Geneva, Switzerland, September 1948 and amended by the 22nd World Medical Assembly, Sydney, Australia, August 1968 and the 35th World Medical Assembly, Venice, Italy, October 1983 and the 46th WMA General Assembly, Stockholm, Sweden, September 1994 and editorially revised by the 170th WMA Council Session, Divonne-les-Bains, France, May 2005 and the 173rd WMA Council Session, Divonne-les-Bains, France, May 2006.

The WMA International Code of medical ethics[4] adds: *"A physician shall always exercise his/her independent professional judgment and maintain the highest standards of professional conduct"* and *"always bear in mind the obligation to respect human life."*

Even if the explicit prohibition of abortion has disappeared, it is all what documents insist that physicians must always act according to their conscience and respect life. The WMA Medical Ethics Manual[5] lists a number of controversial issues, the most crucial being abortion and euthanasia. Regarding the former, it states: *"Participation in abortion was forbidden in medical codes of ethics until recently but now is tolerated under certain conditions by the medical profession in many countries"* (p. 22). The manual acknowledges this diversity of opinion and belief and concludes: *"This is a matter of individual conviction and conscience that must be respected"* (p. 57). It is thus very clear that abortion is only tolerated and that no physician may be compelled to participate in abortion.

Regarding euthanasia, the manual notes: *"there is a significant difference of opinion among national medical associations. Some associations condemn it but others are neutral and at least one, the Royal Dutch Medical Association, accepts it under certain conditions"* (p. 23). The WMA concludes: *"Physicians are understandably reluctant to implement requests for euthanasia or assistance in suicide because these acts are illegal in most countries and are prohibited in most medical codes of ethics. This prohibition was part of the Hippocratic Oath and has been emphatically restated by the WMA in its 2005 Statement on Physician-Assisted Suicide and its 2005 Declaration on Euthanasia. The latter document states:"*

> *"Euthanasia, that is the act of deliberately ending the life of a patient, even at the patient's own request or at the request of close relatives, is unethical. This does not prevent the physician from respecting the desire of a patient to allow the natural process of death to follow its course in the terminal phase of sickness."* (p. 59)

The WMA thus very strongly asserts that there can be no obligation for physicians to participate in abortion or euthanasia.

Similarly, the International Federation of Gynaecologists and Obstetricians (FIGO) regularly recalls the right to conscientious objection of medical practitioners. The FIGO Committee for the Study of Ethical Aspects of Human

---

4 Adopted by the 3rd General Assembly of the World Medical Association, London, England, October 1949 and amended by the 22nd World Medical Assembly, Sydney, Australia, August 1968 and the 35th World Medical Assembly, Venice, Italy, October 1983 and the 57th WMA General Assembly, Pilanesberg, South Africa, October 2006.

5 <https://www.wma.net/what-we-do/education/medical-ethics-manual/>

Reproduction and Women's Health has gathered a number of fundamental texts in a document titled *Ethical Issues in Obstetrics and Gynaecology*, October 2012, with one concerning "Ethical Guidelines on Conscientious Objection" (pp. 25–27). This document asserts that *"Practitioners have the rights both to undertake and to object to undertake medical procedures according to their personal conscience"* (p. 26) and repeats: *"Practitioners have a right to respect for their conscientious convictions in respect both of undertaking and not undertaking the delivery of lawful procedures, and not to suffer discrimination on the basis of their conviction"* (p. 27). Many other FIGO resolutions and documents refer to conscientious objection. The only obligation of physicians is *"to disclose their objection"*[6] and *"make every effort to achieve appropriate referral."*[7] The World Health Organisation also recognises that *"Individual health-care providers have a right to conscientious objection to providing abortion."*[8]

According to the International Confederation of Midwives (ICM) *International Code of Ethics for Midwives*,[9] the aim of the profession is to *"improve the standard of care provided to women, babies and families."* Abortion is not mentioned and it is obvious that young women who want to become midwives long to help women bring babies into the world, not to abort them. The Scope of Practice in the Definition of the Profession reads as follows:

> *"The midwife is recognised as a responsible and accountable professional who works in partnership with women to give the necessary support, care and advice during pregnancy, labour and the postpartum period, to conduct births on the midwife's own responsibility and to provide care for the newborn and the infant. This care includes preventative measures, the promotion of normal birth, the detection of complications in mother and child, the accessing of medical care or other appropriate assistance and the carrying out of emergency measures.*

6 FIGO Guidelines Regarding Informed Consent, p 15 <https://www.figo.org/sites/default/files/uploads/wg-publications/ethics/English%20Ethical%20Issues%20in%20Obstetrics%20and%20Gynecology.pdf>

7 Ethical Framework for Gynaecologic and Obstetric Care, p. 13 <https://www.figo.org/sites/default/files/uploads/wg-publications/ethics/English%20Ethical%20Issues%20in%20Obstetrics%20and%20Gynecology.pdf>

8 "Safe Abortion: technical and policy guidance for health systems" (2012), p. 69 <http://apps.who.int/iris/bitstream/10665/70914/1/9789241548434_eng.pdf?ua=1>

9 Adopted at Glasgow International Council meeting, 2008, Reviewed and adopted at Prague Council meeting, 2014 <https://internationalmidwives.org/assets/uploads/documents/CoreDocuments/CD2008_001 %20V2014 %20ENG%20International%20Code%20of%20Ethics%20for%20Midwives.pdf>

> *The midwife has an important task in health counselling and education, not only for the woman, but also within the family and the community. This work should involve antenatal education and preparation for parenthood and may extend to women's health, sexual or reproductive health and child care."*[10]

This profession resolutely aims at promoting life. Abortion is not mentioned. Even if "sexual or reproductive health care" was considered a euphemism for abortion, the text only says that education and counselling *may extend* to this area, not that midwife should perform abortions or participate in them.

Abortion has very little place in the various documents of the ICM. For example, the text on the Essential Competencies[11] of midwives does not mention it in the Key Midwifery Concepts nor in the Scope of Midwifery Practice. Abortion is only mentioned at the very end of the document as a subsidiary topic under the item Facilitation of Abortion-Related Care, which clearly does not mean that a midwife is obliged to perform abortion herself. Abortion is definitely not a constituent part of the work of midwives.

Section III of the *International Code of Ethics for Midwives* specifies:

> c. *Midwives may decide not to participate in activities for which they hold deep moral opposition; however, the emphasis on individual conscience should not deprive women of essential health services*
> d. *Midwives with conscientious objection to a given service request will refer the woman to another provider where such a service can be provided.*

5 Freedom of conscience in the medical area, comparative law

Freedom of conscience of medical staff is guaranteed in the vast majority of European countries. It seems that only five states do not recognise it: Bulgaria, the Czech Republic, and three northern countries (Iceland, Finland and Sweden). In Finland, the majority of cases are resolved by local agreements.

5.1 General duty of conscience and independence

Physicians enjoy general autonomy in the exercise of their profession to allow them to exercise their judgement as required by their oath. Therefore, a physician

10 <https://internationalmidwives.org/assets/uploads/documents/CoreDocuments/CD2008_001 %20V2014 %20ENG%20International%20Code%20of%20Ethics%20for%20Midwives.pdf>

11 <http://internationalmidwives.org/assets/uploads/documents/CoreDocuments/ICM%20Essential%20Competencies%20for%20Basic%20Midwifery%20Practice%202010,%20revised%202013.pdf >

is free of his medical decisions. French law specifies that a physician can freely order what medication he deems most suitable in the case[12] and can refuse to treat a patient for professional or personal reasons.[13] A physician makes his decision according to what is good for his patient. For example, even if a patient insists on getting antibiotics, the physician can refuse if he thinks it is useless or harmful. He can also refuse to treat somebody, for example, if he thinks he is not competent or for any other reason, except in emergency cases.

Pharmacists have a similar duty to exercise their profession with conscience, as mentioned in the various codes of ethics and in some professional oaths. For example, the French oath of Galien states: *"Je jure[...] d'exercer, dans l'intérêt de la santé publique, ma profession avec conscience"*. The first Article of the French code of deontology of pharmacists asserts that they must preserve the liberty of their judgement and their independence.[14]

The fundamental principle guiding the conscience of members of all medical professions is respect for life. The French code of ethics of medical practitioners recalls that a physician must attend dying persons and cannot cause death deliberately,[15] while the code of ethics of midwives states that they must respect human life[16] and adds that they must rescue new-born infants.[17]

Similarly, the first Article of the French code of deontology of pharmacists asserts that pharmacists respect life and the human person.[18]

---

12 „Dans les limites fixées par la loi et compte tenu des données acquises de la science, le médecin est libre de ses prescriptions qui seront celles qu'il estime les plus appropriées en la circonstance." Article R4127-8 code de la santé publique (CSP).

13 „Hors le cas d'urgence et celui où il manquerait à ses devoirs d'humanité, un médecin a le droit de refuser ses soins pour des raisons professionnelles ou personnelles." Article R4127-47 (CSP).

14 „Le pharmacien doit veiller à préserver la liberté de son jugement professionnel dans l'exercice de ses fonctions. Il ne peut aliéner son indépendance sous quelque forme que ce soit" Article R4235-3

15 „Le médecin doit accompagner le mourant jusqu'à ses derniers moments, assurer par des soins et mesures appropriés la qualité d'une vie qui prend fin, sauvegarder la dignité du malade et réconforter son entourage.
Il n'a pas le droit de provoquer délibérément la mort." Article R4127-38 (CSP).

16 „La sage-femme exerce sa mission dans le respect de la vie et de la personne humaine." Article R4127-302 (CSP).

17 „Une sage-femme qui se trouve en présence d'une femme ou d'un nouveau-né en danger immédiat ou qui est informée d'un tel danger doit lui porter assistance ou s'assurer que les soins nécessaires sont donnés." Article R4127-315 (CSP).

18 „Le pharmacien exerce sa mission dans le respect de la vie et de la personne humaine." Article R4235-2 (CSP).

Equivalent provisions regarding conscience and respect for life can be found in other codes of ethics, for example, in Articles 2 and 3 of the code of deontology of the Swiss Medical Association.[19]

5.2 Abortion and euthanasia: Exception to the prohibition of killing

As already mentioned, abortion and euthanasia have long been (and still are in many countries) outside of medical action because they are not therapeutic acts. They directly contradict the oath of physicians not to inflict death.

In European countries where abortion has become legal, it is clearly an exception. The United Kingdom was the first to admit abortion, in 1967. It is only conditional: provided two medical practitioners certify that a number of conditions are fulfilled, abortion is no longer an offence. In any other circumstances, it remains an offence.[20]

Similarly, in France, where abortion became legal in 1975, the code of public health first recalls the principle of respect of human life from its beginning, then admits abortion as an exception only under the circumstances and conditions mentioned in the law.[21] The medical code of ethics insists on this exceptional character (Article R4127-18 CSP).

---

19 < https://www.fmh.ch/files/pdf18/Standesordnung_August_2016_De.pdf >

20 "Subject to the provisions of this section, a person shall not be guilty of an offence under the law relating to abortion when a pregnancy is terminated by a registered medical practitioner if two registered medical practitioners are of the opinion, formed in good faith—
(a) that the pregnancy has not exceeded its twenty-fourth week and that the continuance of the pregnancy would involve risk, greater than if the pregnancy were terminated, of injury to the physical or mental health of the pregnant woman or any existing children of her family; or
(b) that the termination is necessary to prevent grave permanent injury to the physical or mental health of the pregnant woman; or
(c) that the continuance of the pregnancy would involve risk to the life of the pregnant woman, greater than if the pregnancy were terminated; or
(d) that there is a substantial risk that if the child were born it would suffer from such physical or mental abnormalities as to be seriously handicapped." 1967 Abortion Act, section 1.

21 „Comme il est dit à l'article 16 du code civil ci-après reproduit:
„La loi assure la primauté de la personne, interdit toute atteinte à la dignité de celle-ci et garantit le respect de l'être humain dès le commencement de sa vie." Article L2211-1 (CSP).„Il ne saurait être porté atteinte au principe mentionné à l'article L. 2211-1 qu'en cas de nécessité et selon les conditions définies par le présent titre." Article L2211-2 (CSP).

In the same way, the Belgian criminal code in Article 350 prohibits abortion, except under conditions restrictively listed.[22]

The situation is identical in the very rare countries where euthanasia or assisted suicide are admitted. Ending somebody's life is a crime, except under restrictive conditions.

---

22 Article 350. „Celui qui, par aliments, breuvages, médicaments ou par tout autre moyen aura fait avorter une femme qui y a consenti, sera condamné à un emprisonnement de trois mois à un an et à une amende de cent [euros] à cinq cents [euros].
Toutefois, il n'y aura pas d'infraction lorsque la femme enceinte, que son état place en situation de détresse, a demandé à un médecin d'interrompre sa grossesse et que cette interruption est pratiquée dans les conditions suivantes:
1° a) l'interruption doit intervenir avant la fin de la douzième semaine de la conception;
b) elle doit être pratiquée, dans de bonnes conditions médicales, par un médecin, dans un établissement de soins où existe un service d'information qui accueillera la femme enceinte et lui donnera des informations circonstanciées, notamment sur les droits, aides et avantages garantis par la loi et les décrets aux familles, aux mères célibataires ou non, et à leurs enfants, ainsi que sur les possibilités offertes par l'adoption de l'enfant à naître et qui, à la demande soit du médecin soit de la femme, accordera à celle-ci une assistance et des conseils sur les moyens auxquels elle pourra avoir recours pour résoudre les problèmes psychologiques et sociaux posés par sa situation.
2° Le médecin sollicité par une femme en vue d'interrompre sa grossesse doit:
a) informer celle-ci des risques médicaux actuels ou futurs qu'elle encourt à raison de l'interruption de grossesse; b) rappeler les diverses possibilités d'accueil de l'enfant à naître et faire appel, le cas échéant, au personnel du service visé au 1°, b), du présent article pour accorder l'assistance et donner les conseils qui y sont visés; c) s'assurer de la détermination de la femme à faire pratiquer une interruption de grossesse.
b) L'appréciation de la détermination et de l'état de détresse de la femme enceinte qui conduit le médecin à accepter d'intervenir, est souveraine lorsque les conditions prévues au présent article sont respectées. 3° Le médecin ne pourra au plus tôt, pratiquer l'interruption de grossesse que six jours après la première consultation prévue et après que l'intéressée a exprimé par écrit, le jour de l'intervention, sa détermination à y faire procéder.
Cette déclaration sera versée au dossier médical.
4° Au-delà du délai de douze semaines, sous les conditions prévues aux 1°, b), 2° et 3°, l'interruption volontaire de grossesse ne pourra être pratiquée que lorsque la poursuite de la grossesse met en péril grave la santé de la femme ou lorsqu'il est certain que l'enfant à naître sera atteint d'une affection d'une particulière gravité et reconnue comme incurable au moment du diagnostic. Dans ce cas, le médecin sollicité s'assurera le concours d'un deuxième médecin, dont l'avis sera joint au dossier.
5° Le médecin ou toute autre personne qualifiée de l'établissement de soins où l'intervention a été pratiquée, doit assurer l'information de la femme en matière de contraception.

Switzerland was the first to legalise assisted suicide, provided it is not for selfish reasons. However, euthanasia (called homicide at the victim's request) is always prohibited.[23] In other words, the final lethal act must always be accomplished by the patient. The Federal Supreme Court, underlined the exceptional character of assisted suicide: *"assisted suicide cannot be considered as part of a doctor's activities, since it is self-evident that such an action goes against the aim of medicine."*[24] Physicians must respect medical ethics formulated in the end-of-life care guidelines of the Swiss Academy of Medical Sciences.[25] These rules specify the conditions under which a patient may receive this prescription, relating especially to one's health, one's information and one's expression of will.[26] A doctor who does not comply with this framework would be subject to civil, criminal and disciplinary sanctions. The Swiss National Advisory

---

6° Aucun médecin, aucun infirmier ou infirmière, aucun auxiliaire médical n'est tenu de concourir à une interruption de grossesse.
Le médecin sollicité est tenu d'informer l'intéressée, dès la première visite, de son refus d'intervention."

23 Swiss penal code: "Article 114 – Meurtre à la demande de la victime: Celui qui, cédant à un mobile honorable, notamment à la pitié, aura donné la mort à une personne à la demande sérieuse et instante de celle-ci sera puni d'une peine privative de liberté de trois ans au plus ou d'une peine pécuniaire.
Article 115 – Incitation et assistance au suicide: Celui qui, poussé par un mobile égoïste, aura incité une personne au suicide, ou lui aura prêté assistance en vue du suicide, sera, si le suicide a été consommé ou tenté, puni d'une peine privative de liberté de cinq ans au plus ou d'une peine pécuniaire."
"Article 114 – Homicide at the victim's request: Any person who for commendable motives, and in particular out of compassion, causes the death of a person at that person's own genuine and insistent request shall be liable to a custodial sentence not exceeding three years or to a monetary penalty.
Article 115 – Inciting and assisting suicide: Any person who for selfish motives incites or assists another to commit or attempt to commit suicide is, if that other person thereafter commits or attempts to commit suicide, liable to a custodial sentence not exceeding five years or to a monetary penalty."

24 Judgement of 3 November, 2006, § 6.3.4, in Haas § 16.

25 „Problèmes de l'assistance médicale au suicide", stand by the Central Commission of Ethics (CCE) of the Swiss Academy of Medical Sciences, 20th of January 2012 <http://www.samw.ch/fr/Ethique/Fin-de-vie.html> (French only).

26 <http://www.samw.ch/fr/Ethique/Directives/actualite.html>

Commission on Biomedical Ethics insisted that assisted suicide was not part of medical activity.[27]

In the Netherlands, assisted suicide and euthanasia are punished by Article 293 and 294 of the penal code.[28] However, the law of 10 April 2001 establishes the procedure to follow to transform the crimes of euthanasia and assisted suicide into medical treatments. In Belgium, the law of 28 May 2002, completed by the law of 10 November 2005, guarantees a physician will not be guilty of an offense if he respects strict conditions.[29] In both countries, the patient must be conscious and endure unbearable suffering without prospect of improvement, the request must be written and repeated, and another physician must be consulted. Additional conditions were established for minor children, above 12 in the Netherlands, without age limit in Belgium since the law of 28 February 2014. In Luxembourg, the law of 16 March 2009 on euthanasia and assisted suicide establishes the same conditions to decriminalise euthanasia and assisted suicide.

It is thus very clear that abortion and euthanasia are exceptions to the general prohibition of killing, and that they can only be performed under strict conditions. As they are not normal part of medical activity, the laws that authorised them specified that no physician or other medical staff could be obliged to participate in them.

5.3 Opting out clauses

Section 4 of the British 1967 Abortion Act is dedicated to conscientious objection:

> *Conscientious objection to participation in treatment.*
>
> (1) *Subject to subsection (2) of this section, no person shall be under any duty, whether by contract or by any statutory or other legal requirement, to participate in any treatment authorised by this Act to which he has a conscientious objection:*

---

27 Swiss national advisory commission on biomedical ethics; Prise de position n° 9/2005 Avis unanime p. 72 <http://www.nek-cne.ch/fileadmin/nek-cne-dateien/Themen/Stellungnahmen/fr/suizidbeihilfe_fr.pdf>

28 "Background about Euthanasia in the Netherlands," Patients Rights Council <http://www.patientsrightscouncil.org/site/holland-background/> and "Holland's Euthanasia Law" <http://www.patientsrightscouncil.org/site/hollands-euthanasia-law/>

29 „Le médecin qui pratique une euthanasie ne commet pas d'infraction s'il s'est assuré que: le patient est majeur ou mineur émancipé, capable et conscient au moment de sa demande;
la demande est formulée de manière volontaire, réfléchie et répétée, et qu'elle ne résulte pas d'une pression extérieure; le patient se trouve dans une situation médicale sans

Provided that in any legal proceedings the burden of proof of conscientious objection shall rest on the person claiming to rely on it.

(2) *Nothing in subsection (1) of this section shall affect any duty to participate in treatment which is necessary to save the life or to prevent grave permanent injury to the physical or mental health of a pregnant woman.*

(3) *In any proceedings before a court in Scotland, a statement on oath by any person to the effect that he has a conscientious objection to participating in any treatment authorised by this Act shall be sufficient evidence for the purpose of discharging the burden of proof imposed upon him by subsection (1) of this section.*

In France, the law on abortion provides that no physician or midwife, nurse or other medical auxiliary can be obliged to perform an abortion or participate in it.[30] This applies to termination of pregnancy for a medical reason as well (Article L.2213-2 CSP). This absence of obligation to participate in abortion is repeated in the codes of ethics of physicians[31] and midwives.[32]

Similarly, Article 350-6 of the Belgian criminal code[33] and Article 13 of the Luxembourg law of 17 December 2014 on voluntary termination of pregnancy[34] state that no medical staff or auxiliary can be obliged to participate in an abortion.

---

issue et fait état d'une souffrance physique ou psychique constante et insupportable qui ne peut être apaisée et qui résulte d'une affection accidentelle ou pathologique grave et incurable; et qu'il respecte les conditions et procédures prescrites par la présente loi. " (Law of 28 May 2002, completed by Law of 10 November 2005, Article 3, § 1).

30 „Un médecin ou une sage-femme n'est jamais tenu de pratiquer une interruption volontaire de grossesse mais il doit informer, sans délai, l'intéressée de son refus et lui communiquer immédiatement le nom de praticiens ou de sages-femmes susceptibles de réaliser cette intervention selon les modalités prévues à l'article L. 2212-2. Aucune sage-femme, aucun infirmier ou infirmière, aucun auxiliaire médical, quel qu'il soit, n'est tenu de concourir à une interruption de grossesse." Article L2212-8 (CSP).

31 „Un médecin ne peut pratiquer une interruption volontaire de grossesse que dans les cas et les conditions prévus par la loi; il est toujours libre de s'y refuser et doit en informer l'intéressée dans les conditions et délais prévus par la loi." Article R4127-18 (CSP).

32 „Conformément aux dispositions des articles L. 2212-8 et L. 2213-2, aucune sage-femme n'est tenue de concourir à une interruption volontaire de grossesse." Article R4127-324 (CSP).

33 „Aucun médecin, aucun infirmier ou infirmière, aucun auxiliaire médical n'est tenu de concourir à une interruption de grossesse." Article 350-6 penal code.

34 „Aucun médecin ne sera tenu de pratiquer une interruption volontaire de grossesse. De même aucun professionnel de santé ne sera tenu de concourir à une telle intervention." Luxembourg law of 17 December 2014 on voluntary termination of pregnancy, Article 13.

When abortion became legal, only the surgical method existed, so pharmacists were not always included in the protection. Now that medical abortion is frequent (around one half of all abortions, varying according to the country), they can have real conscience problems. As they must exercise their profession with conscience and respect life, protection from participation in an abortion should extend to them. In Belgium, the code of ethics rules that they do not have to sell abortive products.[35] In France, however, they do not enjoy such protection, as they are not considered a medical profession nor an auxiliary, but a *sui generis* category not protected by the conscience clause.

The vast majority of European States provide protection of freedom of conscience of health professionals, either by law or in their constitution, like Portugal where Article 41 guarantees the right to be a conscientious objector (without mentioning in what area). Laws that protect medical staff against compulsory participation in abortion usually require them to inform the patient timely, and sometimes organise referral to a volunteer colleague. In some countries, like Norway, referral is compulsory.

In Switzerland, Article 15 of the Constitution protects freedom of conscience and religion in general, and cantonal law goes into details. For example, the law of Geneva guarantees that nobody in the health profession can be obliged to give treatment contrary to their ethical or religious beliefs.[36] This protects all professionals of health, including pharmacists, against participating in abortion or euthanasia.

---

35 „Sans préjudice aux droits du patient, à la continuité des soins et à l'exécution de la prescription, le pharmacien a le droit de refuser la délivrance en raison de ses objections de conscience. Dans ce cas, il doit renvoyer le patient auprès d'une pharmacie où le produit en question peut bien être délivré. Si ce n'est pas le cas, le pharmacien doit exécuter la prescription. Durant le service de garde, la clause de conscience doit toujours s'effacer devant le droit du patient à la continuité des soins." Code de déontologie pharmaceutique, article 32.

36 Geneva law on health, Article 82 (RSGE K 1 03; LS):
„1 Le professionnel de la santé ne peut être tenu de fournir, directement ou indirectement, des soins incompatibles avec ses convictions éthiques ou religieuses.
2 L'objecteur doit dans tous les cas donner au patient les informations nécessaires afin que ce dernier puisse obtenir, par d'autres professionnels de la santé, les soins qu'il n'est pas disposé à lui fournir.
3 En cas de danger grave et imminent pour la santé du patient, le professionnel de la santé doit prendre toutes les mesures nécessaires pour écarter le danger, même si elles sont contraires à ses convictions éthiques ou religieuses."

The Belgian law of 28 May 2002 on euthanasia guarantees that nobody can be obliged to participate in euthanasia.[37] This protection is not limited to health professionals. Express protection of pharmacists was not added because it was already included in this general provision. A physician who refuses to perform euthanasia must inform the patient and give the medical record to the physician chosen by the patient. He has no obligation to refer the patient, but only hand over the record.

The same rule is found in the Luxembourg law of 16 March 2009, with an addition: the physician has 24 hours to inform the patient of his refusal, and give his reasons.[38]

When recognising that abortion or euthanasia are contrary to the mission of the health professions or that some other acts are not normally part of medical activity, the law provides protection of conscience, refusal to participate in these acts is not conscientious objection strictly speaking, but use of an option afforded by law.

5.4 Conscientious objection, strictly speaking

However, it may – and does – happen that some laws order health professionals to perform acts that are contrary to the aim of medicine. It must be noted that the first documented case of conscientious objection in history concerns midwives, when Pharaoh ordered Hebrew midwives to kill male newborns, and they did not obey (Ex 1, 15–21). The names of the midwives have reached us through the centuries: Shiphrah and Puah. This happened in the 14th or 13th century

---

37 „Aucun médecin n'est tenu de pratiquer une euthanasie. Aucune autre personne n'est tenue de participer à une euthanasie. Si le médecin consulté refuse de pratiquer une euthanasie, il est tenu d'en informer en temps utile le patient ou la personne de confiance éventuelle, en en précisant les raisons. Dans le cas où son refus est justifié par une raison médicale, celle-ci est consignée dans le dossier médical du patient.
Le médecin qui refuse de donner suite à une requête d'euthanasie est tenu, à la demande du patient ou de la personne de confiance, de communiquer le dossier médical du patient au médecin désigné par ce dernier ou par la personne de confiance." Article 14 Law of 14 May 2002.

38 „Aucun médecin n'est tenu de pratiquer une euthanasie ou une assistance au suicide. Aucune autre personne ne peut être tenue de participer à une euthanasie ou une assistance au suicide.Si le médecin consulté refuse de pratiquer une euthanasie ou une assistance au suicide, il est tenu d'en informer le patient et/ou la personne de confiance, s'il en existe une, dans les 24 heures en précisant les raisons de son refus.

BC, before the birth of Moses, in other words before the 10 Commandments. It clearly shows that respect for life is part of the moral law printed in human conscience.

If abortion and euthanasia are considered rights and not exceptions, then there is no opting out clause and medical staff is obliged to perform them. It is the case in Sweden regarding abortion. Doctors, midwives and other medical or auxiliary staff are obliged to perform abortion or participate in it. Students who refuse cannot get their diploma or had to choose another speciality. Gynaecologists who refuse to perform abortions cannot work in hospital and are barred from university research and teaching. Physicians and midwives can lose their jobs or be denied employment for refusing to participate in abortion. In some cases local arrangements are reached, but most of the time those who refuse suffer severe discrimination and sanctions. Recently, a midwife's contract was not renewed, then she could not find any job because of her refusal to participate in abortion. She went to court and lost her case. The only possibilities for her were to renounce her profession and become a nurse, or to go abroad, which she did. She is now a midwife in Norway. In spite of the shortage of midwives, Sweden refuses to respect and accommodate freedom of conscience. When the Parliamentary Assembly of the Council of Europe adopted Resolution 1763(2010) on the right to conscientious objection in lawful medical care, Sweden officially took a stand against it.

In the five countries which do not respect freedom of conscience of health professionals, few cases go to court or are reported abroad. In some cases, local agreements allow the objector not to participate. Most of the time, either they resign themselves to act against their will and conscience, or they choose another profession. As a consequence, people with all the personal qualities and scientific skills for these occupations are deterred from choosing the profession they want because of the discrimination they undergo.

Officially, only Sweden, Finland (where there is a debate on this issue[39]), Iceland, the Czech Republic and Bulgaria do not guarantee freedom of conscience

---

Le médecin qui refuse de donner suite à une demande d'euthanasie ou d'assistance au suicide est tenu, à la demande du patient ou de la personne de confiance, de communiquer le dossier médical du patient au médecin désigné par ce dernier ou par la personne de confiance." Article 15, Law of 16 March 2009.

39 "Citizens' initiative calls for right to conscientious objection in health care," Helsinki Times, 28 August 2014 <http://www.helsinkitimes.fi/finland/finland-news/domestic/11797-citizens-initiative-calls-for-right-to-conscientious-objection-in-health-care.html>

of medical staff. However, a worrying trend can be noted in other countries. Unavowed constraint on medical staff and creeping discrimination are developing. For example, in France, refusal to participate in abortion is theoretically protected, but public hospitals with gynaecology or surgery beds are obliged to perform abortions. Since doctors and midwives willing to perform abortions are scarce, all of them have to do it in turn. In the UK, NHS job offers specify that applicants should be "prepared to carry out the full range of duties which they might be required to perform if appointed", implicitly including duties related to termination of pregnancy. Some alleged cases of discrimination were reported, like one in Scotland in 2000.[40] Even if abortion cannot be considered a matter of medical emergency (the only possible urgency regards the legal time limit) and has no therapeutic effect, doctors are often required to perform it when adequate services for termination of pregnancy "would not otherwise be available", which is a manifest violation of professional deontology and freedom of conscience.

Until recently, this dangerous trend concerned only abortion. However, a recent case in Belgium suggests that the same could follow about euthanasia. A nursing-home in Diest refused to let a physician coming to euthanize a patient enter its premises. Finally, the patient went back to her home and was killed there. Her children are now suing the nursing-home for having refused the euthanasia to take place there, saying it increased the physical and moral suffering of their mother.[41]

The issue of assisted suicide in hospital was also discussed in Switzerland, in particular in the University Hospitals of Geneva.[42] No consensus could be reached so decision was taken on a majority vote: assisted suicide can take place in hospital under strict conditions, only for patients who cannot be sent back home, and provided no hospital staff participates. This reflexion shows the exceptional character of assisted suicide and the fact that it is not part of a doctor's mission. It is therefore very worrying to see it treated trivially or as an individual right.

---

40 "Abortion views cost job," BBC, 7 October 2000 <http://news.bbc.co.uk/2/hi/health/961169.stm>

41 "Une maison de retraite a refusé l'accès à un médecin pratiquant l'euthanasie", La Libre, 2 January 2016 <http://www.lalibre.be/actu/belgique/une-maison-de-retraite-a-refuse-l-acces-a-un-medecin-pratiquant-l-euthanasie-5687780c3570b38a57ed03d9>

42 "Autorisation/interdiction de l'assistance au suicide au sein des HUG," Hôpitaux universitaires de Genève, Conseil d'éthique Clinique <http://www.hug-ge.ch/sites/interhug/files/documents/soigner/ethique/assistanceausuicideaux.pdf>

6 Conclusion

Termination of life is a fact. Therefore, the right to conscientious objection is not part of a more general right to have "an opinion" or a religious belief; it is a right not to take part in the voluntary termination of a human life when such termination is permitted by law, whether you have a religious belief or not. Thus, the purpose of the "conscience clause" is less to permit anyone to object than to make sure that no one is forced to participate against their will. The source of the problem is not individual conscience; it is the act at stake, which contradicts the mission of medicine, and the law authorising such an act.

Roger Kiska & Robert Clarke

Conscientious Objection for Medical Practitioners in European Human Rights Law

Abstract: The chapter outlines the consistent protections found in international law for rights of conscience. In particular, it demonstrates the trend of recognising a right for medical practitioners to refuse participation in abortion on conscience grounds which reflects its status as a fundamental right. Particular regard will be to have the jurisprudence of the European Court of Human Rights ("ECtHR") as well as other international hard and soft law provisions. Turning to the national level, it will be demonstrated that all but one European Union ("EU") member state has either a general conscience provision or specific laws protecting medical staff. Each of these factors would be part of the ECtHR's consideration when it is seized of a matter raising this issue in the future. This chapter demonstrates that in affording medical practitioners legal protection, the Court would be in keeping with its own jurisprudence, in line with international law, and reflective of the fundamental nature of conscience rights as demonstrated by the clear consensus at a national level.

Keywords: conscientious objection, international law, prohibition against discrimination, margin of appreciation, rights of conscience

1 Protection of rights of conscience in international law

Protection for rights of conscience is explicitly recognised and secured in international law and is among the commitments most states have accepted through the treaty ratification process in respect of a number of documents. In each case, the State has consented to be bound by these commitments.

1.1 Jurisprudence of the European Court of Human Rights

The Grand Chamber of the ECtHR has unambiguously affirmed rights of conscience for sincerely held religious and moral beliefs as falling within the ambit of Article 9 of the European Convention of Human Rights ("the Convention"). Article 9 states:

> "1. Everyone has the right to freedom of thought, conscience and religion; this right includes freedom to change his religion or belief and freedom, either alone or in community with others and in public or private, to manifest his religion or belief, in worship, teaching, practice and observance.

2. Freedom to manifest one's religion or beliefs shall be subject only to such limitations as are prescribed by law and are necessary in a democratic society in the interests of public safety, for the protection of public order, health or morals, or for the protection of the rights and freedoms of others."

In the landmark case of *Bayatyan v. Armenia*,[1] the Grand Chamber for the first time expressly upheld the right to conscientious objection in the context of compulsory military service. The Grand Chamber held that:

"Opposition to military service, where it is motivated by a serious and insurmountable conflict between the obligation to serve in the army and a person's conscience or his deeply and genuinely held religious or other beliefs, constitutes a conviction or belief of sufficient cogency, seriousness, cohesion and importance to attract the guarantees of Article 9."[2]

While in this instance, the Court held that the guaranteed right of conscience could be expressed through exemption from military service, the judgement by no means limited the expression of conscientious objection to military service. The following reasoning of the Grand Chamber clearly indicates that the right to conscientiously object should equally apply in other contexts, including being required to take part in an abortion procedure:

"124. The Court cannot overlook the fact that, in the present case, the applicant, as a member of Jehovah's Witnesses, sought to be exempted from military service not for reasons of personal benefit or convenience but on the ground of his genuinely held religious convictions. [...] Thus, the system existing at the material time imposed on citizens an obligation which had potentially serious implications for conscientious objectors while failing to allow any conscience-based exceptions and penalising those who, like the applicant, refused to perform military service. In the Court's opinion, such a system failed to strike a fair balance between the interests of society as a whole and those of the applicant. It therefore considers that the imposition of a penalty on the applicant, in circumstances where no allowances were made for the exigencies of his conscience and beliefs, could not be considered a measure necessary in a democratic society. Still less can it be seen as necessary taking into account that there existed viable and effective alternatives capable of accommodating the competing interests, as demonstrated by the experience of the overwhelming majority of the European states [...]

126. The Court further reiterates that pluralism, tolerance and broadmindedness are hallmarks of a "democratic society." Although individual interests must on occasion be subordinated to those of a group, democracy does not simply mean that the views of a majority must always prevail: a balance must be achieved which

---

1 *Bayatan v. Armenia* [GC], no. 23459/03, 27 October 2009.

2 *Bayatan v. Armenia* [GC], no. 23459/03, at § 110.

> ensures the fair and proper treatment of people from minorities and avoids any abuse of a dominant position [...] Thus, respect on the part of the State towards the beliefs of a minority religious group like the applicant's by providing them with the opportunity to serve society as dictated by their conscience might, far from creating unjust inequalities or discrimination as claimed by the Government, rather ensure cohesive and stable pluralism and promote religious harmony and tolerance in society."[3]

The language used by the Court obliging States to uphold and maintain a healthy "democratic society" has a broader context than military service. The Court has clearly delineated a wider principle regarding the importance of States accommodating citizens' deeply held religious convictions and refraining from imposing penalties on them where there are viable alternatives available.

Bayatyan is of critical value and importance in the recognition of the right to conscientiously object because it explicitly overruled previous decisions of the Court, and of the institution it replaced, the European Commission of Human Rights ("the Commission"). In the case of *X v. Austria*,[4] the Commission had stated that in interpreting Article 9 of the Convention, it had also to consider the terms of Article 4 § 3 (b), which provide that forced or compulsory labour should not include "any service of a military character or, in cases of conscientious objectors, in countries where they are recognised, service exacted instead of compulsory military service." The Commission made a significant textual argument that, by including the words "in countries where they are recognised" in Article 4 § 3 (b), a choice was left to the High Contracting Parties whether or not to recognise conscientious objectors in the military arena and, if they were so recognised, to provide some substitute service.

Notwithstanding the textual basis of Article 4 § 3 (b), the Court in *Bayatyan* came to the conclusion, as cited above, that not providing for conscientious objection in the military field "imposed on citizens an obligation which had serious implications for conscientious objectors while failing to allow any conscience-based exceptions and penalising those who, like the applicant, refused to perform military service,"[5] and in so doing, the Armenian authorities failed to strike a fair balance between the interests of society and the interests of the applicant. The Court also noted the developments in international law on the right to conscientious objection at length in the run up to 2009.[6]

---

3 *Bayatan v. Armenia* [GC], no. 23459/03, at §§ 124§ 124 - 126.
4 Commission decision of 2 April 1973, no. 5591/72.
5 *Bayatan v. Armenia* [GC], no. 23459/03, at § 124.
6 *Bayatan v. Armenia* [GC], no. 23459/03, at §§ 50 – 70.

It should follow *a fortiori* that, in the context of medical staff and the performance of abortions, without a clear textual reference to the contrary, a failure of a State actor to recognise conscientious objection runs contrary to the obligation to strike a fair balance between the interests of the society and those of the medical staff given their objection is grounded upon the same respect for the dignity of all human life as military objectors. This is made even more compelling given a reasonable accommodation is readily available both in the case of military service and in the context of abortion. Various schemes of accommodation are practiced by almost all European States. This simple reality undermines the argument that safeguarding rights of conscience for medical staff is not possible because to so do would leave patients unable to access abortion. That argument is not persuasive in Europe which faces a shortage of qualified professionals. Moreover, given the shortage of qualified professionals in this field, by excluding otherwise competent practitioners, it is the State which is jeopardising the proper provision of healthcare services other than abortion.

Following the decision of the Grand Chamber in *Bayatyan*, the same reasoning was then applied in the similar case of *Bukharatyan v. Armenia*,[7] again in the context of compulsory military service – cementing the right of conscientious objection under Convention law and leaving no doubt about this jurisprudential line.

The ECtHR has developed the principles espoused in both *Bayatyan* and *Bukharatyan* in a number of decisions, recently upholding the right to act according to one's deeply held convictions in a number of settings using the concept of reasonable accommodation to guarantee protection of rights enshrined under Article 9 of the Convention. An example of this is the case of *Vartic v. Romania (No. 2)*,[8] where the Court found a violation of a Moldovan prisoner's rights under Article 9 for refusing to serve him a vegetarian diet in accordance with his convictions.

More recently, in the case of *Eweida and Others v. the United* Kingdom,[9]the Court held that there was no requirement for an applicant to establish "that he or she acted in fulfillment of a duty mandated by the religion in question" in order for Article 9 to have been engaged.[10] The United Kingdom courts had found, on the basis of previous decisions of the ECtHR, that a religious manifestation

7 *Bukharatyan v. Armenia*, no. 37819/03, 10 January 2012.

8 *Vartic v. Romania (No. 2)*, no. 14150/08, 17 December 2013.

9 *Eweida and Others v. the United Kingdom*, nos. 48420/10, 59842/10, 51671/10, 36516/10, 15 January 2013.

10 *Eweida and Others v. the United Kingdom* § 82.

had to be a requirement of a religion to be protected, but significantly the Court overruled this reasoning.[11] Further, the Court in *Eweida* overruled decades of pre-existing Commission case law which had indicated that the ability to resign from a job led to a conclusion that there was no interference with Article 9. The Court reasoned that:

> "Given the importance in a democratic society of freedom of religion, the Court considers that, where an individual complains of a restriction on freedom of religion in the workplace, rather than holding that the possibility of changing job would negate any interference with the right, the better approach would be to weigh that possibility in the overall balance when considering whether or not the restriction was proportionate."[12]

Turning specifically to rights of conscience for medical professionals, while the Court has not yet been called upon to rule specifically upon this, it clearly anticipates their existence. In *R.R. v. Poland*,[13] the Court reasoned that where abortion is legalised, it must be available under the following terms:

> "States are obliged to organize the health services system in such a way as to ensure that *an effective exercise of the freedom of conscience of health professionals in the professional context* does not prevent patients from obtaining access to services [...]"[14]

The recognition that health professions can and do exercise "freedom of conscience in the professional context" is qualified only by the access argument, exposed above, in this insightful paragraph which takes for granted a system securing the "effective exercise of the freedom of conscience of health professionals."

1.2 Relationship between rights of conscience and the prohibition against discrimination

Article 14 of the Convention provides as follows:

> "The enjoyment of the rights and freedoms set forth in this European Convention on Human Rights shall be secured without discrimination on any ground such as sex, race, colour, language, religion, political or other opinion, national or social origin, association with a national minority, property, birth or other status."

The Jurisprudence of the Court has considered that the freedom from discrimination encompassed by Article 14 is a freedom not to be discriminated against

11 *Eweida and Others v. the United Kingdom*
12 *Eweida and Others v. the United Kingdom*, § 83.
13 *RR v. Poland*, no. 27617/04, ECHR 2011.
14 *RR v. Poland*, § 83§ 83.

in the enjoyment of the rights guaranteed under the Convention. The Court has found Article 14 to be violated when States treat differently persons in analogous situations without providing an objective and reasonable justification.

In *Thlimmenos v. Greece*,[15] the Court held that a difference of treatment is discriminatory for the purposes of Article 14 if it "has no objective and reasonable justification," that is if it does not pursue a "legitimate aim" or if there is no "reasonable relationship of proportionality between the means employed and the aim sought to be realised":

> "The Court has so far considered that the right under Article 14 not to be discriminated against in the enjoyment of the rights guaranteed under the Convention is violated when States treat differently persons in analogous situations without providing an objective and reasonable justification (see the Inze judgment cited above, p. 18, § 41). However, the Court considers that this is not the only facet of the prohibition of discrimination in Article 14. The right not to be discriminated against in the enjoyment of the rights guaranteed under the Convention is also violated when States without an objective and reasonable justification fail to treat differently persons whose situations are significantly different."[16]

This issue arose in *Thlimmenos* in connection with a refusal by the Greek authorities to allow the applicant to gain qualification as an accountant on the ground of his having a former conviction for having refused to wear military uniform during a national mobilisation in 1983 because of his religious convictions. What was at issue was not the distinction made by domestic law between convicted persons and others for access to a profession but the lack of distinction between convicted persons whatever their offences, and the fact that no account was taken of the applicant's offence being of a special nature because of its moral motivation. The Court therefore considered that Article 14 had been violated in conjunction with Article 9.

In this regard, the Court reaffirmed the complimentary aspect of an Article 14 discrimination claim. The applicant complained that no distinction was made by the national authorities as between persons grounding their exemption from military service in an exercise of their freedom of religion, conscience and belief, or other persons convicted when subsequently being disbarred from seeking to apply for a professional role. The Court noted that the applicant's own conviction resulted from the very exercise of his Article 9 freedoms. The Court gave weight

15 *Thlimmenos v. Greece* [GC], no. 34369/97, ECHR 2000-IV.
16 *Thlimmenos v. Greece* [GC], § 44.

to the fact that no account was taken of the applicant's offence being of a special nature because of the moral motivation. The Court stated:

> "Seen in this perspective, the Court accepts that the "set of facts" complained of by the applicant – his being treated as a person convicted of a serious crime for the purposes of an appointment to a chartered accountant's post despite the fact that the offence for which he had been convicted was prompted by his religious beliefs – "falls within the ambit of a Convention provision," namely Article 9."[17]

Again, the ECtHR can be seen recognising the special nature of a conscience-based objection and the protection it should be afforded. In *Thlimmenos*, the Court took the unusual step of indicating that it was the legislation itself, which provided for no exceptions for applicants in the position in question, which directly violated the applicant's rights under Article 14.[18]

1.3 The margin of appreciation

It should be noted that the ECtHR does afford a degree of deference to member states through the doctrine of the margin of appreciation. This is aimed at ensuring the subsidiarity of the Convention machinery given that "national authorities are in principle better placed than an international court to evaluate local needs and conditions."[19] This sensitivity to the history, culture, and law of member states is a source of the legitimacy of the Court's judgements given that the Convention is "built on diverse economic, cultural, and legal traditions [...]"[20]

The doctrine has recently been formally recognised and is soon to be entrenched into the preamble of the Convention by Protocol 15 when it comes into force.[21] It is a powerful method of ensuring a balance of uniformity in the protection of Convention rights whilst also supporting the diversity of social realities in different member states.

---

17 *Supra* n 19 at 42.

18 *Supra* n 19 at 48

19 Explanatory Report on "Protocol No. 15 amending the Convention on the Protection of Human Rights and Fundamental Freedoms," article1., <http://www.echr.coe.int/Documents/Protocol_15_explanatory_report_ENG.pdf>

20 Onder Bakircioglu "The Application of the Margin of Appreciation Doctrine in Freedom of Expression and Public Morality Cases," *German Law Journal,* Vol. 8 (2007), p. 717.

21 "Protocol No. 15 amending the Convention on the Protection of Human Rights and Fundamental Freedoms," article1.<http://www.echr.coe.int/Documents/Protocol_15_ENG.pdf>

In cases which raise complex scientific, legal, moral, and social issues, particularly in the absence of a social consensus among the member states, the Court affords greater discretion to member states, yielding a wider margin of appreciation.[22] This is an indispensable manifestation of the exercise of the Court's supervisory, rather than appellate, function.

However, the presence of an emerging or established consensus throughout the member states can be a clear indication of the fundamental nature of the right in question, and therefore leads the Court to adopt a more exacting standard of scrutiny of impugned measures or practices.

For example, in *Evans v. UK*,[23] the Court recalled the fact that "there is no clear common ground amongst the member states" on questions relating to IVF and went on to say that "the Court considers that the margin of appreciation to be afforded to the respondent State must be a wide one."[24]

Given the clear consensus that exists amongst European states in protecting the conscience of their healthcare practitioners demonstrating the fundamental nature of the right,[25] it is inevitable that alleged violations in this subject area will attract heightened scrutiny from the ECtHR.

2 Wider international recognition of the right of conscientious objection

a) The Court of Justice of the European Union

The ECtHR is not isolated in recognizing the importance of conscientious objection and developing the law in this area. In recent cases before the Court of Justice of the European Union ("CJEU"), *Federal Republic of Germany v. Y*[26] and *Federal Republic of Germany v. Z*,[27] the Advocate General gave his opinion on the correct understanding of Article 9 of the Convention. The Advocate General stated that if the so-called "core area" of religious belief comprised only of "private conscience," it would render any protections for "the external manifestation of that freedom" effectively "meaningless."[28] In its final ruling, the CJEU held that

22 *X, Y, and Z v. UK*, Application no. 21830/93, 22 April 1997, see §§ 44, 52.
23 *Evans v. UK*, no. 6339/05, 7 March 2006.
24 *Evans v. UK*, § 81.
25 See Annex
26 Case C-71/11.
27 Case C-99/11.
28 Advocate General opinion at § 46.

the right to act upon sincerely held religious or moral beliefs must include public manifestations of those beliefs.

An understanding of Article 9 void of a right to act on one's deeply held convictions becomes the far more limited freedom of "worship,"[29] which protects only private manifestations of faith.[30] In this context, belief-motivated action would only be allowed so long as it does not touch any other boundaries of civil society. This is not what the Convention envisioned, nor what it protects. Indeed, Article 9 § 1 explicitly lists a number of forms which manifestation of one's religion or belief may take: not only worship but teaching, practice, and observance as well.[31]

b) The Parliamentary Assembly of the Council of Europe

With regard to the issue of rights of medical professionals and abortion in particular, the Parliamentary Assembly of the Council of Europe ("PACE") could not be more clear than as set out in the provisions of Resolution 1763 (2010) titled "The right to conscientious objection in lawful medical care":

> "No person, hospital or institution shall be coerced, held liable or discriminated against in any manner because of a refusal to perform, accommodate, assist or submit to an abortion, the performance of a human miscarriage, or euthanasia or any act which could cause the death of a human foetus or embryo, for any reason.
> The Parliamentary Assembly emphasises the need to affirm the right of conscientious objection together with the responsibility of the state to ensure that patients are able to access lawful medical care in a timely manner. The Assembly is concerned that the

29 The Court of Appeal decision in *Ladele v. London Borough of Islington* [2009] EWCA Civ 1357 illustrates this narrowing of freedom of religion to freedom of worship. Lord Neuberger held at § 51: "[…] the effect on Ms Ladele of implementing the policy (performing same sex civil partnerships) did not impinge on her religious beliefs: she remained free to hold those beliefs, and free to worship as she wished."

30 For example, when the Charity Tribunal found against the last remaining Catholic adoption agency in England, it stated that "religious conviction in the sphere of personal belief is protected in both domestic and European equality law, so that acts of devotion, worship, and prayer (including ceremonies) are exempt from equality obligations" but held that there is an "essential distinction" between private acts of worship and the provision of a public service. *Catholic Care v. The Charity Commission for England and Wales*, CA/2010/0007, 26 April 2011 § 60.

31 See *Hasan and Chaush v. Bulgaria* [GC], no. 30985/96, § 60, ECHR 2000-XI and *Metropolitan Church of Bessarabia and others v. Moldova*, no. 45701/99, § 114, ECHR 2001-XII.

unregulated use of conscientious objection may disproportionately affect women, notably those with low incomes or living in rural areas.
In the vast majority of Council of Europe member states, the practice of conscientious objection is adequately regulated. There is a comprehensive and clear legal and policy framework governing the practice of conscientious objection by health-care providers ensuring that the interests and rights of individuals seeking legal medical services are respected, protected and fulfilled.
In view of member states' obligation to ensure access to lawful medical care and to protect the right to health, as well as the obligation to ensure respect for the right of freedom of thought, conscience and religion of health-care providers, the Assembly invites Council of Europe member states to develop comprehensive and clear regulations that define and regulate conscientious objection with regard to health and medical services, and which:

4.1. guarantee the right to conscientious objection in relation to participation in the medical procedure in question;
4.2. ensure that patients are informed of any conscientious objection in a timely manner and referred to another health-care provider;

ensure that patients receive appropriate treatment, in particular in cases of emergency."[32]

If one completes an investigation of the voting list, there is to be found deputies voting in favor of the Resolution from Malta, Spain, Romania, the Netherlands, Italy, France, Hungary, Germany, Slovak Republic, Moldova, Austria, Luxembourg, Poland, Albania, Georgia, Latvia, Ireland, Switzerland, Lichtenstein, Ukraine, Sweden, Norway, Bulgaria, Lithuania and Portugal, comprising a total of 25 countries.

Not only did the Resolution pass by a majority of votes, but it was also passed by a majority of countries. It is clear the vote enjoyed a robust debate including 89 amendments and that the final text was voted for by a numerical majority of those present.

Furthermore, PACE Resolution 2036 (2015) titled "Tackling intolerance and discrimination in Europe with a special focus on Christians" provides that member states should "promote reasonable accommodation within the principle of indirect discrimination *so as to [...] uphold freedom of conscience in the workplace* while ensuring that access to services provided by law is maintained and the right of others to be free from discrimination is provided."[33]

The position of PACE is therefore one that robustly respects freedom of conscience in the context of employment in addition to protecting military objectors.

---

32 PACE Resolution 1763 (2010).
33 PACE Resolution 2036 (2015), § 6. Emphasis added.

c) The United Nations Human Rights Committee

The International Covenant on Civil and Political Rights ("ICCPR"), which Sweden ratified in 1971, provides that:

> "1. Everyone shall have the right to freedom of thought, conscience and religion. This right shall include freedom to have or to adopt a religion or belief of his choice, and freedom, either individually or in community with others and in public or private, to manifest his religion or belief in worship, observance, practice and teaching. [...]"[34]

The United Nations Human Rights Committee ("HRC"), the body that monitors implementation of the ICCPR, initially took the view that the ICCPR did not provide for the right to conscientious objection.[35] However, more recently, much like the ECtHR, it has recognised the importance of rights of conscience as an important component of freedom of thought, conscience and religion. The HRC noted in General Comment 22 that while "[...] the [ICCPR] does not explicitly refer to a right to conscientious objection, [...] the Committee believes that such a right can be derived from Article 18 [...]"[36]

Further to General Comment 22, the HRC has found violations of Article 18 in cases concerning compulsory military service. Firstly, it found that in *Frédéric Foin v France* the applicant "was discriminated against on the basis of his conviction of conscience."[37] In 2006, the Committee found violations of Article 18 in two cases against South Korea, stating:

> "[W]hile the right to manifest one's religion or belief does not as such imply the right to refuse all obligations imposed by law, it provides certain protection, consistent with Article 18, paragraph 3, against being forced to act against genuinely-held religious belief [...] [R]espect on the part of the State for conscientious beliefs and manifestations thereof is itself an important factor in ensuring cohesive and stable pluralism in society [...]"[38]

The HRC has gone even further in recognizing that conscientious objection is *inherent* in freedom of thought, conscience, and religion:

---

34 Article 18.

35 See *L.T.K. v. Finland*, Communication no. 185/1984, UN doc. CCPR/C/25/D/185/1984, 9 July 1985.

36 General Comment No. 22: The right to freedom of thought, conscience and religion (Article 18), 30 July 1993, § 11.

37 Communication No. 666/1995, 9 November 1999, at § 10.3.

38 *Yoon v Republic of Korea* and *Choi v Republic of Korea*, communication nos. 1321/2004 and 1322/2004, UN Doc. CCPR/C/88/D/1321-1322/2004, January 23, 2007, §§ 8.3 - 8.4.

> "The right to conscientious objection to military service inheres in the right to freedom of thought, conscience and religion. It entitles any individual to an exception from compulsory military service if this cannot be reconciled with that individual's religion or belief."[39]

Mr. Hipólito Solari-Yrigoyen suggested that the issue of the conscientious objection to military service should be examined under Article 18.1, *forum internum*, and not 18.3, as mere manifestation and reasoned:

> "[E]ven if it were wrongly supposed that the present Communication does not concern recognition of the objector's right, but merely its public manifestation, the statement that public manifestations may be subject only "to such limitations as are prescribed by law" in no way implies that the existence of the right itself is a matter for the discretion of state parties."[40]

d) The European Union

Within the military context, the European Parliament has determined that the right to conscientious objection was inherent in the concept of freedom of thought, conscience and religion, as recognised in Article 9 of the Convention, and called upon the member states of the European Union to incorporate the right to conscientious objection as a fundamental right in their legal systems.[41]

The Charter of Fundamental Rights of the European Union entered into force with the Lisbon Treaty in December 2009. It contains explicit protection for conscientious objection in Article 10(2) which provides that: "the right to conscientious objection is recognized, in accordance with the national laws governing the exercise of this right." Whilst this provision is aimed at the area in which conscience protections were first codified, military service, the principal is not so limited and the emphasis of the provision is on the place of national laws to regulate the framework which *a priori* assumes the existence of conscience protections.

---

39 *Min-Kyu Jeong et al. v Republic of Korea*, communication nos. 1642-1741/2007, UN Doc. CCPR/C/101/D/1642-1741/2007, 27 April 2011, para 7.3; *Atasoy v Turkey*, communication nos. 1853/2008 and 1854/2008, UN Doc. CCPR/C/104/D/1853-1854/2008, 19 June 2012, para 10.4.

40 *See* n 38, Dissenting Opinion of Mr Hipólito Solari-Yrigoyen, paras 8.2 and 8.3.

41 For example, see Resolution of the European Parliament of 7 February 1983 on *Conscientious Objection*, Doc.1-546/82; Resolution of the European Parliament on Conscientious Objection and Alternative Civilian Service, 13 October 1989, Doc. A3-15/89; Resolution of the European Parliament on Conscientious Objection in the Member States of the Community, 18 January 1994, Doc. O.J. (C 44) 103.

The European Court of Human Right in *Bayatyan* specifically noted that, in the context of compulsory military service, the majority of European States had found "viable and effective alternatives" to accommodate conscientious objectors. A comparative survey of the laws regarding rights of conscience in member states of the European Union clearly highlight the possibility of adopting a similar approach.

Among member states of the European Union, all but one State has explicit Constitutional or statutory protections for rights of conscience. Most countries provide *specific* protections for medical staff in connection with performing abortions. Even those member states without explicit textual reference to abortion nonetheless broadly define the enumerated right of conscience within their domestic law. A detailed listing of the protections afforded to conscience in the European Union follows which not only illustrates the practicability of legislating for conscientious objection but demonstrates the undeniable support in favour of conscience protections, reflective of the fundamental nature of this right. The ECtHR would take into account both of these things in assessing any complaint grounded on this basis.

3 Statistical summary on laws protecting conscience across EU member states

With the exception of Sweden, *every EU member state* has either a general law protecting freedom of conscience, or a specific law protecting medical practitioners' rights of conscience. The majority of states have both a general provision and a specific law.

Number of EU member states with *general clause(s) guaranteeing freedom of conscience*: 22 out of 28 (Austria, Belgium, Bulgaria, Croatia, Cyprus, Czech Republic, Estonia, Finland, France, Germany, Greece, Hungary, Ireland, Latvia, Lithuania, Malta, Poland, Portugal, Romania, Slovakia, Slovenia, Spain).

Number of EU member states *with specific laws protecting medical practitioners' rights of conscience*: 22 out of 28 (Austria, Belgium, Croatia, Cyprus, Czech Republic, Denmark, France, Germany, Greece, Hungary, Ireland, Italy, Luxembourg, Malta,[42] Netherlands, Poland, Portugal, Romania, Slovakia, Slovenia, Spain, United Kingdom).

42 Malta is included in this list as abortion is generally unavailable there, removing the need for a specific provision to protect the conscience of healthcare workers – none of whom are required to participate.

4 The interests at stake

As demonstrated in Annex 1 below, while there is a strong European consensus on the protection of individual rights of conscience in Europe, there are those who argue, explicitly or implicitly, that conscience rights will violate a fabricated "right" to abortion. No such right to abortion exists in international law. The ECtHR has explicitly stated that the Convention does not contain a right to abortion.[43] The Court further recognises that with the advancement of science and various forms of research involving the embryo, greater protections are now afforded to the pre-born child in international law.[44]

Furthermore, the issue of abortion is not a competence of the European Union. For example, in 2006, the European Council stated that: "The European Union treaties have not bestowed on the Community or the Union the competence whereby the Union could regulate on abortions."[45] Further, the European Council has stated that the term "reproductive health" does not include any reference to a right to abortion and the Council does "not accept that abortion should form part of policies on reproductive and birth control education."[46]

Finally, not a single binding international human rights document describes abortion as a right. Both the 1994 International Conference on Population and Development in Cairo and the Fourth World Conference on Women that took place in Beijing in 1995 held that governments have an obligation to eliminate and reduce abortions and to help women avoid repeat abortions.[47] The outcome documents also hold that abortion should never be promoted as a method of family planning.[48] If abortion was indeed a "right," clearly international law would not be describing it as something governments need to reduce or eliminate.

---

43 *A, B and C v. Ireland* [GC], no. 25579/05, 16 December 2010.

44 *Vo v. France*, no. 53924/00, § 84, 8 July 2004.

45 Paula Lehtomäki, President-in-Office of the Council, 13 December 2006, Reply to an Oral Question (H-0983/06) by Bastiaan Belder, MEP. Emphasis added. <http://www.europarl.europa.eu/sides/getDoc.do?type=CRE&reference=20061213&secondRef=ITEM-021&language=EN#3-429>

46 Answering questions from MEPs Bernd Posselt (H-0729/03) and Dana Scallon (H-0794/03), 4 December 2003 <http://www.europarl.europa.eu/sides/getDoc.do?type=CRE&reference=20031216&secondRef=ITEM-005&language=EN#2-178>

47 ICPD Programme of Action at § 8.25.

48 ICPD Programme of Action at § 7.24.

5 Conclusion

Given that the margin of appreciation in this area concerning a fundamental right is narrow, and the protection found in international law for those with conscience-based objections, as compared to the absence of a "competing right to abortion," any future application to the ECtHR on this basis will, or at least should be, looked on favourably.

The oft-cited argument surrounding access to abortion is outside the competence of the European Union and, in reality, is not practically at stake in any event. Weighing heavily against it are the interests of a relatively small number of medical practitioners, bound by a moral code which says they cannot take life, supported by all but one European country in at least general terms (and 22 where their rights would be protected explicitly under law) and by international law. The impact of this policy is seen in the personal cost for the medical practitioners who are forced out of a profession they love. It is also felt in the healthcare system, and the patients it seeks to treat, which struggles to fill positions and is left unrepresentative of the population it serves.

The ECtHR has held that guaranteeing freedom of thought, conscience and religion is at least part of the duty of State neutrality.[49] Where necessity and proportionality are lacking, a State must accommodate religious and moral beliefs no matter how irksome it finds them. This notion stems from the reluctance of European civilisation – born of decency, forbearance, and tolerance – to compel our fellow citizens to humiliate themselves by betraying their own consciences. *(For more details see Annex.)*

---

49 See n 30, above.

Michał Skwarzyński

Impact of the ECHR Case Law on the Use of Conscientious Objection in Poland

Abstract: The objective of this chapter is to present the influence of the jurisprudence of the European Court of Human Rights in Strasbourg upon the use of conscientious objection in Poland. The chapter describes whether the jurisprudence of the ECHR influences the jurisdiction of the Polish Court Tribunal as well as the jurisdiction of the Supreme Court and common courts.

Keywords: conscientious objection, polish courts, Strasbourg jurisprudence

1 Introduction. The essence of conscientious objection

The problem of applying the right of conscientious objection in the Polish literature is rarely researched from the perspective of the European judicial decisions or on the normative basis of the legal regulations governing international human rights. The fundamental direction of the research concerns the rights of medicine doctors and nurses,[1] if need be, the axiological problems to the extent of conscience[2] or the axiological normative[3] context are being indicated;

---

1 P. Stanisz, J. Pawlikowski, and M. Ordon, *Sprzeciw sumienia w praktyce medycznej – aspekty etyczne i prawne* (Lublin, 2014), passim; A. Zoll, "Prawo lekarza do odmowy udzielenia świadczeń zdrowotnych i jego granice," *Prawo i Medycyna*, No. 13 (2003), p. 18; L. Bosek, "Prawo osobiste do odmowy działania sprzecznego z własnym sumieniem na przykładzie lekarza," *Forum prawnicze,* No.1 (2014), p. 17; L. Bosek, "Problem zakresowej niekonstytucyjności art. 39 ustawy o zawodach lekarza i lekarza dentysty," in: *Sprzeciw sumienia w praktyce medycznej – aspekty etyczne i prawne*, eds. P. Stanisz, J. Pawlikowski, and M. Ordon (Lublin, 2014), pp. 96–100, O. Nawrot, "Klauzula sumienia w zawodach medycznych w świetle standardów Rady Europy," *Zeszyty Prawnicze BAS*, No. 3 (2012), pp. 12–16.

2 A. Szostek, "Kategoria sumienia w etyce," in: *Sprzeciw sumienia w praktyce...*, pp. 15–25.

3 A. Zoll, "Klauzula sumienia," in: *Sprzeciw sumienia w praktyce...*, pp. 77–85; M. Skwarzyński, "Sprzeciw sumienia w europejskim i krajowym systemie ochrony praw człowieka," *Przegląd Sejmowy,* No. 6 (2013), pp. 17–21; L. Bosek, "Prawo osobiste...," pp. 87–89, 92–95; L. Bosek, "Problem zakresowej...," pp. 87–90, 100–103; O. Nawrot, "Prawa człowieka, sprzeciw sumienia i państwo prawa," in: *Sprzeciw sumienia w praktyce...*, pp. 107–109.

by contrast, the conscientious objection is infrequently associated with legal professions.[4]

The conscientious objection, referred to as the conscience clause, is defined as *"the right to act according to one's own conscience, and, as a consequence, also the freedom from the coercion to act in defiance of one's own conscience."*[5] Conscientious objection is material in a situation when a specific obligation arises or is abandoned and consists in the right to refuse to fulfil such an obligation. The conscientious objection is an individual right.

The objective of this chapter is to present the influence of the jurisprudence of the European Court of Human Rights in Strasbourg upon the use of conscientious objection.

It is a current problem that is often addressed in practice, which the Polish Court Tribunal had to face in 2015. Consequently, it is necessary to examine whether the jurisprudence of the ECHR influences the jurisdiction of the Polish Court Tribunal, as well as the jurisdiction of the Supreme Court and common courts.

2 Legal regulations governing conscientious objection within the framework of the system of human rights

The fundamental legal regulation to the extent of conscientious objection in the freedom of conscience and creed. The Article 9 (1) of the European Convention on Human Rights stipulates that: *"[e]veryone has the right to freedom of thought, conscience and religion; this right includes freedom to change his religion or belief and freedom, either alone or in community with others and in public or private, to manifest his religion or belief, in worship, teaching, practice and observance."*

In the light of the foregoing, the linguist interpretation makes it possible to state that the aforementioned standard may constitute the source of conscientious objection.

4 Conf. Z. Cichoń, "Klauzula sumienia w różnych zawodach," in: *Prawnik katolicki a wartość prawa* (Kraków, 1999), pp. 44–51, where the case of a conscientious objection of a barrister or solicitor was briefly discussed on the grounds of the system of the French Law, see also M. Skwarzyński, „Sprzeciw sumienia w adwokaturze," in: *Standardy bezstronności światopoglądowej władz publicznych*, eds. A. Mezglewski and A. Tunia (Lublin, 2013), pp. 201–220.

5 Conf. P. Stanisz, "Klauzula sumienia," in: *Prawo wyznaniowe*, A. Mezglewski, H. Misztal, and P. Stanisz (Warszawa, 2011), p. 104, point 111.

This results from the essence of human freedom. The aforementioned is also reflected by the fact that the Article 9 (1) of the European Convention on Human Rights *encompasses "the right to manifest his religion or belief, either alone or in community with others and in public or private [...] in practice [...]."* In this context, the conscientious objection appears to be a measure of last resort for protecting the conscience, because there is no other legal institution protecting the conscience of an individual.

A similar standard as in the Article 9 of the European Convention on Human Rights is included in the Article 10 of the Charter of Fundamental Rights of the European Union, stipulating that: *"Everyone has the right to freedom of thought, conscience and religion. This right includes freedom to change religion or belief and freedom, either alone or in community with others and in public or in private, to manifest religion or belief, in worship, teaching, practice and observance."*

In addition, the recognition of the thesis that the conscientious objection results from the human right to freedom of conscience is supported, not only by the content of the standards determining this law, but also by the content of the limitation clauses.

The Article 9 (2) of the European Convention on Human Rights stipulates that: *"Freedom to manifest one's religion or beliefs shall be subject only to such limitations as are prescribed by law and are necessary in a democratic society in the interests of public safety, for the protection of public order, health or morals, or for the protection of the rights and freedoms of others."* The content of this provision *per se* indicates that the objective thereof does not entail the limitation to the right to freedom of conscience and belief, but merely the *"[f]reedom to manifest one's religion or beliefs."*[6]

It has to be emphasized that the scope of the limitation clause to the right to freedom of conscience and belief is decidedly narrower than the limitation clause set forth in Article 10 (2) of the European Convention on Human Rights,[7]

---

6 See also: L. Garlicki, "Komentarz do art. 9 EKPCz (Comments to Article 9 of the Charter of Fundamental Rights of the European Union)," in: *Konwencja o ochronie praw człowieka I podstawowych wolności. Komentarz do artykułów 1–18 (Convention on Protection of Human Rights and Fundamental Freedoms. Comments to Articles 1–18), eds. L. Garlicki, P. Hofmański, and A. Wróbel, Vol. I, Warszawa (2010), p. 4.*

7 The exercise of such freedoms entailing obligations and responsibility may be subject to formal regimes, conditions, encumbrances, and sanctions that may be provided for in the act of law and that may be deemed necessary in a democratic society to secure national security, territorial integrity or public safety due to protection of health and morality, protection of the good name and third parties' rights, as well as due to

which pertains to the freedom of speech, even though the freedom of speech is deemed fundamental in the human rights protection system. The comparison of the two aforementioned clauses makes it possible to draw a conclusion that the religious freedom protection is much wider than the freedom of speech, since the essence of religious freedom cannot be restricted; the limitation clause refers to manifesting this freedom, that is to one of the aspects thereof.

It is therefore appropriate to state that the beliefs of an individual, which give rise to the conscientious objection are protected by the internal protection of conscience and belief, in which, as in scope of freedom, the state cannot interfere.

However, manifesting this objection consists in execution of the right to manifest one's own religion or beliefs and within scope thereof a state may examine the validity of the conscientious objection, taking into account replicable premises to apply the clause of conscientious objection, which was indicated in the conclusion to this text.

At the same time, the nation does not have right to question the belief of an individual, nor to specify the scope or the essence thereof. The state may only assess the manifestation of the freedom of conscience and belief[8] within the context of the conditions set forth in the limitation clauses, while examining whether it is justified to use the conscientious objection.

It has to be confirmed that, in respect of applying the right to freedom of conscience and belief, the ban on interfering is a negative obligation of public authorities, unless such an interference is made within the boundaries of the Article 9 (2) of the Charter of Fundamental Rights of the European Union.[9]

Accordingly, the opinion that the "*The concept of practising and ritual activities will not, however, apply to all activities inspired by the professed beliefs, even when they are deeply rooted.*"[10] However, it is indispensable to meet requirements of the limitation clause, which has to correspond to the specificity of the conscientious objection.

The most plausible argument for the understanding of the source of conscientious objection can be found in Article 10 (2) of the Charter of fundamental rights of the European Union, which in its official translation, that is in the official Polish version, stipulates that *"the right to refuse to act in contravention of*

prevention from disclosure of confidential information or earnestness and impartiality of judicial authority.

8 See also: Nawrot, "Prawa człowieka, sprzeciw sumienia...," p. 108.

9 See Garlicki, "Komentarz do art. 9 EKPCz," in: *Konwencja...*, point 30.

10 I. C. Kamiński, "Komentarz do art. 10 KPP," in: *Karta Praw Podstawowych Unii Europejskiej. Komentarz*, ed. A. Wróbel (Warsaw, 2012), point 31.

one's own conscience shall be recognised in conformity with the national law and related regulations governing the exercise of that right."[11] An identical content is to be found in the English language version: "*the right to conscientious objection is recognised, in accordance with the national laws governing the exercise of this right,*"[12] as well as in the French language version: "*le droit à l'objection de conscience est reconnu selon les lois nationales qui en régissent l'exercice.*"[13]

The content of the Article 10 (2) of the Charter of Fundamental Rights of the European Union is connected to the obvious phenomenon of making human rights more specific, which, especially in the American literature, is referred to as "formulation of human rights."

Taking into account that an international legislative body expressed the necessity to protect the right to conscientious objection, along with the right to freedom of conscience and belief, in the process of making the aforementioned rights more specific, the same international legislative body also indicates that the aforementioned elements, which are subject to normative regulations, are interconnected. For this reason, it appears legitimate to draw the conclusion that conscientious objection results from human right to freedom of conscience and belief.

3 Dignity as the essence of normative regulation of human rights

It has to be ascertained that even though the provisions of international conventions stipulate that a given human right exists, the provisions do not constitute it in any case. The universality of human rights consists also in the fact that the legal standards contained in international conventions are of declaratory and not of constitutive nature. The nature of the convention specifying human rights indicates that the source of these rights is outside the positive law and is based on axiological system and natural law. The objective of human rights is to

---

11 Translation included in the *European Journal of Laws* of 2010, C. 83, p. 389, last access: 11 November 2015 <http://eur–lex.europa.eu/LexUriServ/LexUriServ.do?uri=OJ:C:2010:083:0389:0403:PL:PDF>

12 Translation included in the *European Journal of Laws* of 2010, C. 83, p. 389, last access: 11 November 2015 <http://eur-lex.europa.eu/LexUriServ/LexUriServ.do?uri=OJ:C:2010:083:0389:0403:EN:PDF>

13 Translation included in *the European Journal of Laws* of 2010, C. 83, p. 389, last access: 11 November 2015 <http://eur-lex.europa.eu/LexUriServ/LexUriServ.do?uri=OJ:C:2010:083:0389:0403:FR:PDF>

formulate, in a normative manner, the inherent dignity of a human being, which is the source of all the rights of an individual.

Conscientious objection effectively protects the aforementioned dimension of human dignity, related to beliefs concerning religion and outlook. The human right to freedom of conscience and belief is one of rights that is most deeply rooted in the dignity of a human being. If it were not for the conscientious objection and if the freedom of an individual were not protected, the free will of an individual would not be protected. It would concern the dignity of human personality and it would translate into lack of protection of personal dignity. The reason for referring to the conscience clause is that the legal standard makes the subject of the law to take actions against one's conscience or belief; consequently, it makes the subject to act in defiance of conscience of belief and at the same time it interferes with the essence of human right to freedom of conscience and belief. If the conscientious objection did not constitute a law, then, the protection of this area of human dignity, expressed in the form of the right to freedom, would be hypocritical.

Conscience as a normative standard, or even, morality and values as an imperative and determinant of behavior, mirror the legal order. Accepting the mere concept of the "minimum of natural law in positive law," or sociological positivism or regulatory and natural concept, which is presented by the author, one has to recognize that the conscience clause protects this moral and axiological element at the source of legal system which is connected to human dignity. If there was not such a right protecting the conscientious objection, then one would have to look for some another axiological source expressed in a normative order, exactly in the system of human rights.

Human rights constitute an attempt to include human dignity in a normative text and the execution thereof consists in the conscience clause, that is the ability to act according to one's conscience. The assumption that conscientious objection constitutes a statutory right, which is not connected to human dignity and axiological order, expressed in the system of human rights, would only be possible if one assumed that the legal system is of positive nature; this, in turn, could bear direct consequences and remind of the case of lawful genocides committed in the Third Reich for the reason of belief or racial origin.

Moreover, if the aforementioned right were purely statutory, then referring in vows or oaths to conscience as to a category by the voice of which the representatives of specific professions shall act.

Referring to conscience would be possible only in the event of a specific statutory entitlement to objection, and it is reserved exclusively for a doctor and a nurse, even though the category of conscience is also referred to in other professions. In addition, it would raise obvious doubts concerning discrimination and equality before the law.

Therefore, it seems unjustified to "separate" conscientious objection from the human right to freedom of conscience and religion, so, as a consequence, separate it from free will and personal dignity.[14] After all, forcing a person to act against their belief or conscience affects the substance of the dignity of the individual.

Is it possible to "dehumanize" a human being, then to make it act against the system of values upheld by this person? Moreover, depriving conscientious objection of lawful protection would make the right to freedom of conscience and belief an apparent right, not protected in its essence. This right, despite being formally vested, would not give anyone the competence to act in harmony with conscience, so, in fact, this normative category would not be protected.

Public authority may violate the human right to freedom of conscience and religion, for example, by forcing a person to act against her or his convictions; the protection of freedom of conscience and belief, as a human right, was developed to protect this right. However, the aforementioned protection is not total. Conscientious objection, as a rule, is the ultimate means of expressing one's beliefs and religious orders in a situation where the rule of law requires whom to do otherwise. Without the protection thereof the individual beliefs and religion would not, in fact, be protected. One must accept the results of an analysis conducted by Oktawian Nawrot which proves that restrictions towards the white collar workers "*can touch upon the essence of the recognised system of values and not only restrict its expression, but also result in limiting freedom of thought, conscience and belief as such.*"[15]

---

14 To find out more about the dignity of a human being, please, confront K. Orzeszyna, "Godność ludzka podstawą praw człowieka," in: *Człowiek - jego prawa i odpowiedzialność,* ed. R. Tabaszewski, (Lublin 2013, KUL) p. 23 [in]; J. Krukowski, "Godność człowieka podstawą konstytucyjnego katalogu praw i wolności jednostki," in: *Podstawowe prawa jednostki i ich sądowa ochrona,* ed. L. Wiśniewski (Warszawa, 1997), pp. 39–42; W. Jedlecka, J. Policiewicz, "Pojęcie godności na tle Konstytucji RP," in: *Z zagadnień teorii i filozofii prawa. Konstytucja*, ed. A. Bator (Wrocław, 1999), p. 146; J. Zajadło, "Godność jednostki w aktach międzynarodowej ochrony praw człowieka," *RPEiS*, No. 2 (1989), p. 111; K. Complak, "Uwagi o godności człowieka oraz jej ochrona w świetle nowej konstytucji," *Przegląd Sejmowy,* No. 5 (1998), p. 42 ff; *Prawa Człowieka, Zarys wykładu*, eds. Z. Hołda, D. Ostrowska, J. Hołda, and J. A. Rybczyńska (Warszawa, 2008), p. 12; M. Piechowiak, *Filozofia praw człowieka. Prawa człowieka w świetle ich międzynarodowej ochrony* (Lublin, 1999), pp. 343–347; F. J. Mazurek, *Godność osoby ludzkiej podstawą praw człowieka* (Lublin, 2001), pp. 75–80.

15 Nawrot, "Klauzula sumienia w zawodach…," p. 15.

4 The judicial decision of the ECHR with regard to conscientious objection. Typology of cases before the ECHR

The judicial decisions of the ECHR with regard to the conscience clause would certainly require a separate study,[16] so for the purposes of this work, I will present the most important issues indispensable for further analysis.

The Strasbourg Court expressed the view that conscientious objection is not protected under the Article 9 (1) of the ECHR,[17] which suggests that conscientious objection does not result from freedom of conscience and religion, nonetheless such reasoning is logically flawed,[18] and was mitigated in subsequent judgments.[19] The main case appearing in the judicial decisions of the ECHR in respect of conscientious objection is a right to refer to refusal of military service.[20]

Another group of judicial decisions includes the decisions concerning the powers of a doctor and a nurse. The Court stated that "*the state is obliged to organise the health care system in such a way as to ensure the effective exercise of freedom of conscience of healthcare workers*"[21] and this view was expressed on the

---

16 See M. Skwarzyński, "Orzecznictwo Europejskiego Trybunału Praw Człowieka w zakresie klauzuli sumienia," in: *Aktualne problemy wolności myśli, sumienia i religii*, eds. P. Stanisz, A. M. Abramowicz, M. Czelny, M. Ordon, and M. Zawiślak (Lublin 2015), pp. 286–291.

17 The Case of *Bayatyan vs. Armenia*, the Complaint No. 23459/03, the Judgement of the ECHR of 7 July 2011, point 110.

18 See Skwarzyński, "Sprzeciw sumienia w europejskim…," pp. 17–23.

19 The Case of *Eweida et al. vs. Great Britain*, Complaints No. 48420/10, 59842/10, 51671/10, 36516/10, the Judgement of the ECHR of 15 January 2013, points 105, 106 and point 109; M. Skwarzyński, "Sprzeciw sumienia w europejskim…," p. 16 and subsequent pages.

20 Examples: *Tsaturyan vs. Armenia*, the Complaint No. 37821/03, the Judgement of the ECHR of 10 January 2012; *Bukharatyan vs. Armenia*, the Complaint No. 37819/03, the Judgement of the ECHR of 10 January 2012; *Thlimmenos vs. Greece*, the Complaint No. 34369/97, the Judgement of the ECHR of 6 April 2000; *Ülke vs. Turkey*, the Complaint No. 39437/98, the Judgement of the ECHR of 24 January 2006, but also the religious convictions of Jehovah's Witnesses, to the extent of refusal of military service e.g. the cases: *Jehovah's witnesses in Moscow et al. vs. Russia*, the Complaint No. 302/02, the Judgement of the ECHR of 10 June 2010, amended on 18 August 2010; *Taganrog (LRO) et al. vs. Russia*, the Complaint No. 32401/10.

21 *R. R. vs. Poland*, the Complaint No. 27617/04, the Judgement of the ECHR of 26 May 2011, point 206.

basis of a judgment concerning abortion. The Court stipulated that the requirement that the state, despite its obligation to ensure "freedom of conscience" for medical staff, is to establish a review procedure for the patient, who is willing to undergo abortion, if such a case is allowed by law, which of course does not mean that there is an individual right to abortion.

The most extensive reference to the Court in Strasbourg in respect of conscientious objection may be found in the ECHR judgment of 15 January 2013, on *Eweida et al. v. the United Kingdom*.[22] The ECHR did not question the fact that the legal duty consisting in registration of homosexual relationships was extremely painful for the plaintiff and was falling within the scope of protection under the Article 9 and 14 of the European Convention on Human Rights; by contrast, it assessed the conduct of the authorities rated in terms of whether the failure to make exception and excluding Ms. Ladele from registering homosexual relationships was proportional and had a legitimate objective.[23] The Court's position, according to which the refusal to comply with a legal obligation because of a conflict with religious beliefs, falls within the scope of protection under the Article 9 of the ECHR, also to the extent of the matters other than military service should be considered as righteous and innovative.

However, the Court stated that within the scope of freedom of assessment of local authorities, the authorities could have given the priority to protection against discrimination in access to public services for gay couples and to the requirement that the workers should conduct activities in a non-discriminatory manner, so the purpose of the action was justified.[24]

Accordingly, despite serious consequences for the plaintiff resulting from the strength of her religious beliefs, the ECHR stated that the action of local authorities was proportionate in view of the wide margin of assessment in the protection of competing rights set out in the Convention.[25]

Further to the above, it seems reasonable to assume that conscientious objection as a specific right resulting from the right to freedom of conscience and belief

22 *Eweida et al. vs. Great Britain*, Complaints No(s). 48420/10, 59842/10, 51671/10, 36516/10, the Judgement of the ECHR of 15 January 2013.

23 *Eweida et al. vs. Great Britain*, point 104 in connection with point 83.

24 *Eweida et al. vs. Great Britain*, point 105.

25 *Eweida et al. vs. Great Britain*, point 106.

consists in execution of the right to external freedom and, in this regard, has the nature of a human right.

This means that duties are imposed on a state to protect this specific right in such a way as to allow the legal system to effectively implement it. This anchors also in the fact that conscientious objection is an individual right[26] and taking into account the fact that freedom of conscience and religion is of such a nature,[27] the resulting conscientious objection should also have such a form.

5 The concept of the margin of appreciation and its impact upon the use of conscientious objection in Polish law

First of all, one should distinguish between the ideological propaganda regarding the judicial decisions taken by the Strasbourg Court and the contents expressed in the judgments. Of paramount importance is the fact that the judgments of the ECHR are binding in a given case and do not fulfil the function of judicial precedents, even though they are often mistakenly perceived in this way.

In addition, a decision concerning one country does not necessarily mean a similar decision in another case concerning a different state. This is due to the concept of margin of appreciation[28] used by the Strasbourg Court, which is a theoretical and practical model, which *"allows for taking into account the specifics of the social and cultural context of each country. It is obvious that this specificity is particularly clear in cases concerning morality or religion, and therefore the Court uses the concept of margin of appreciation in the application of Article 9,"* in a manner slightly different from those applied with regard to other "liberty provisions."[29]

---

26 Bosek, "Problem zakresowej niekonstytucyjności…," p. 89 and subsequent pages; Skwarzyński, "Sprzeciw sumienia w europejskim…," p. 12.

27 J. Sobczak, W. Sobczak, "Komentarz do art. 10 KPP (Comments to Article 10 of the Charter of Fundamental Rights)," in: *Karta Praw… (the Charter…)*, p. 386 and subsequent pages.

28 *Bayatyan vs. Armenia*, the Complaint No. 23459/03, the Judgement of the ECHR of 7 July 2011, points 121–123; *Eweida et al. vs. Great Britain)*, Complaints No(s). 48420/10, 59842/10, 51671/10, 36516/10, the Judgement of the ECHR of 15 January 2013, pp. 106 and 109.

29 Garlicki, "Komentarz do art. 9 EKPCz (Comments to Article 9 of the European Charter of Human Rights)," in: *Konwencja… (Convention…)*, point 4; and, A. Wiśniewski, *Koncepcja marginesu oceny w orzecznictwie ETPCz* (Gdańsk, 2008), pp. 130–131, 136, 187.

This concept means that judges of the Court of Justice do not undermine the assessment of axiological hierarchy of human rights in specific national systems recognizing that the national court is in a better position to decide such issues. This is due to the fact that national judges have a better understanding of the given legal order and social structure, determined by culture and history.

6 Judicial decisions of the Polish Constitutional Tribunal

Taking into account the analysis conducted so far, it is clear that the position of the Polish Constitutional Court is of pivotal importance for the assessment of the impact of the judicial decisions of the Strasbourg Court. The shape of case law on the issue of conscience clause has formed from the early nineties. At that time, the Court stated that the conscience clause was grounded in the constitutional freedom of conscience and belief.[30] It is, therefore, justified to accept the position of the Constitutional Court in this respect as binding.

Similar position was taken by the Constitutional Court in case No. K 12/14, where examining the constitutionality of the law regulating the profession of doctor and dentist[31] the Court, in its judgment of 7 October 2015, in point 2, stated that: "*Article 39 of the Law referred to in the Section 1 in so far as it imposes on the doctor restraining from performing health services inconsistent with his conscience is obliged to indicate different feasible possibilities of obtaining such services from another doctor or in other therapeutic entity, it is inconsistent with Article 53(1) in connection with Article 31(3) of the Constitution.*" The operative part of the judgement shows clearly that the Constitutional Court associates the protection for conscientious objection directly with the human right to freedom of conscience and belief. This confirms the oral justification for interpreting the decision.[32]

---

30 The Decision of the Constitutional Tribunal of 15 January 1991, File No. U 8/90, OTK ZU 1991, No. 1, item 8, p. 134; Decision of the Constitutional Tribunal of 7 October 1992, File No U 1/92, OTK ZU 1986–1995, Vol. 3/1992, particle 2, p. 38. The decisions referred to the legal position from the time before the adoption of the Constitution of the Republic of Poland of 1997, but they are still binding, in particular in respect of the Decision of the Constitutional Tribunal of 7 October 2015.

31 Acts of Law of 5 December 1996 on professions of the doctor and dentist, Journal of Laws from 2015, item 464.

32 Until now the grounds for the decision have not been published in writing yet.

Thus, in the light of the concept of margin of appreciation, and the well-established position of the Polish Constitutional Court, it should be noted that Article 53[33] of the Polish Constitution of 2 April 1997[34] protects the right to conscientious objection held by an individual. This is important, because of the wide scope of power, to adopt a national human rights protection system under the concept of a wide margin of appreciation in cases connected to confession, where such a margin is wider than usual.[35]

Moreover, it strengthens the interpretation of rules governing the human right to freedom of conscience and belief, where the interpretation results allow the conclusion that conscientious objection is subject to the protection of this fundamental right of an individual. The scope of this standard also allows to deduce the normative basis for the conscience clause. It seems, therefore, that the right to freedom of conscience and religion is a normative source for the conscience clause[36] and the correctly interpreted judicial decisions of the Court in Strasbourg confirm this conclusion.

---

33 Article 53. 1. Freedom of conscience and religion shall be ensured to everyone. 2. Freedom of religion shall include the freedom to profess or to accept a religion by personal choice as well as to manifest such religion, either individually or collectively, publicly or privately, by worshipping, praying, participating in ceremonies, performing of rites or teaching. Freedom of religion shall also include possession of sanctuaries and other places of worship for the satisfaction of the needs of believers as well as the right of individuals, wherever they may be, to benefit from religious services. 3. Parents shall have the right to ensure their children a moral and religious upbringing and teaching in accordance with their convictions. The provisions of Article 48, para. 1 shall apply as appropriate. 4. The religion of a church or other legally recognised religious organisation may be taught in schools, but other peoples' freedom of religion and conscience shall not be infringed thereby. 5. The freedom to publicly express religion may be limited only by means of statute and only where this is necessary for the defence of State security, public order, health, morals or the freedoms and rights of others. 6. No one shall be compelled to participate or not participate in religious practices. 7. No one may be compelled by organs of public authority to disclose his philosophy of life, religious convictions or belief.

34 Journal of Laws from 1997, No. 78, item 483, with subsequent amendments, hereinafter referred to as the Constitution of the Republic of Poland.

35 See L. Garlicki, "Komentarz do art. 9 EKPCz (Comments to Article 9 of the European Charter of Human Rights)," in: *Konwencja… (Convention…)*, p. 4; A. Wiśniewski, *Koncepcja marginesu oceny…*, pp 27, 187, 272.

36 See also Bosek, "Problem zakresowej…," p. 90 and subsequent pages.

In addition, as Piotr Tuleja once put it: the Constitution of the Republic of Poland aims at identifying the limits of the protection of individual human rights[37] and, in this respect, is of a binding nature.[38]

7 Conditions for applicability of conscientious objection in the light of human rights standards

It is a truism to state that there is no unlimited rights. The individual's right to conscientious objection cannot be unlimited, because it would archaize the law, and consequently, the social order. However, this does not excludes the necessity to protect the aforementioned right and the need to set without limits thereto.

In determining standard cases in which the use of conscientious objection may be justified, it is helpful to refer to limitation clauses concerning human rights. Article 9(2) of the ECHR stipulates that *"the freedom to manifest one's religion or beliefs may be subject only to such limitations as prescribed by law and necessary in a democratic society with regard to the interests of public safety, public order, health or morals or the protection of the rights and freedoms of others."*

The very wording of this provision shows that it is not intended to limit the core of the right to freedom of thought, conscience and belief, but merely the *"freedom to manifest one's religion or belief."*[39] A similar meaning and scope is included in Article 53(5) of the Constitution of the Republic of Poland, which stipulates that *"freedom to manifest one's religion may be limited only by means of law and only where this is necessary for the protection of national security, public order, health, morals or the rights and freedoms of others."*[40]

The considerations should be commenced with imposing the limitation clause concerning freedom of conscience and religion upon the conditions for applicability of conscientious objection, that is the requirement of being a statutory law, the necessity in a democratic society, which is justified in respect of the interest of public safety, law enforcement, health and morals, or the rights and freedoms of other specific conditions, to be met by conscientious objection.

---

37 P. Tuleja, "Prawo naturalne i prawo pozytywne jako podstawa konstytucyjnych praw człowieka," *ETHOS*, No(s). 1–2 (1999), pp 200, 201, 211 and subsequent pages.

38 Tuleja, "Prawo naturalne i prawo pozytywne…," pp. 204 – 209, 211 ff.

39 See also Garlicki, "Komentarz do art. 9 EKPCz (Comments to Article 9 of the European Charter of Human Rights)," in: *Konwencja… (Convention…)*, point 4.

40 See also P. Sarnecki, "Komentarz do art. 53 Konstytucji RP," in: *Konstytucja Rzeczypospolitej Polskiej. Komentarz, Rozdział I. Rzeczpospolita*, ed. L. Garlicki (Warsaw, 2003), p. 9.

Thus, after examining whether such conditions to use the limitation clause are the case, which are recognized as legality, necessity and desirability,[41] these are to be referred to conscientious objection.

The subject of determining the validity of the application of the conscience clause should consist exclusively in examining, firstly, whether such an objection was a subsidiary right, that is the one that may be executed as the ultimate manner to protect the human right to freedom of conscience and belief, and whether the conflict could possibly have been resolved otherwise.

Secondly, the right to conscientious objection must, in a particular case, be justified and it seems useful to apply the criterion of natural law, which is intended to protect the interests protected in a system of positive law and man-made law. The Court in Strasbourg described the reference to the criterion of views, which have an appropriate level of persuasion, seriousness, cohesion, and importance in the society.[42]

Thirdly, the good that the person referring to conscientious objection is willing to protect should also be proportionate – in proportion to the obligations imposed by the law, which, due to a conflict of conscience, is obliged not to perform.[43] The role of the state is to create a legal system where each and every individual, including the one that appeals to the conscience clause, has the right to enjoy all of his or her human rights.

Such a structure of the legal system is possible and can be found, even in the form of institution of excluding a judge or a doctor in a particular case. Thus, the state shoulders the burden of developing a procedure that ensures the execution of the rights of an individual in situations where a person required to perform a specific actions refuses to do it because of the conflict with their conscience. A given state must anticipate that the situation of justified reference to conscientious objection can occur and must be prepared for that.

---

41 See Nawrot, "Prawa człowieka, sprzeciw sumienia…," p. 108.

42 *Bayatyan vs. Armenia*, the Complaint No. 23459/03, the Judgement of the ECHR of 7 July 2011, p. 110, *Eweida and others vs. the United Kingdom*, Complaints No. 48420/10, 59842/10, 51671/10, 36516/10, the Judgement of the ECHR of 15 January 2013, p. 82, *Jakóbski vs. Poland*, the Complaint No. 18429/06, the Judgement of the ECHR of 7 December 2010, p. 44, *Leela Förderkreis e.V. et al. vs. Germany*, the Complaint No. 58911/00, the Judgement of the ECHR of 6 November 2008, p. 80.

43 See M. Skwarzyński, "Sprzeciw sumienia w europejskim…," pp. 23–26.

Part III: National Perspectives

William L. Saunders

Threats to Conscience Protection in the United States During the Years of the Obama Administration[1]

Abstract: The chapter presents issues of protecting freedom of religion and conscience in the United States as of 2015. The conclusion is that American society is one in which the rights of medical professionals, and indeed of all citizens, to freedom of conscience is on shaky ground. The reasons for such a situation are three. First is that constitutional safeguards for constitutional freedoms depend currently more upon the philosophy of Supreme Court judges than on the written text of the constitutional provisions. The second reason is that many judges – and other American cultural and political leaders – often regard religion as superstition that must yield to enlightened opinions. Finally, the crucial element for assessment of the right to conscientious protection is the status of abortion, which is considered by many powerful American elites not as a threat to constitutional rights but as basic healthcare service.

Keywords: abortion, conscience, constitution, freedom, rule of judges

---

1 The election of Donald Trump has brought some significant changes. Within a few months in office, Trump took action to extend protection for religious freedom and conscience, including the issuance of an executive order requiring religious liberty to be given as much protection as any other civil right. He also created a division within the legal office at the Department of Health & Human Services to focus upon the protection of conscience rights of health care professionals. The Trump administration also ended the litigation over the "HHS contraception mandate" by making the exemption from the mandate as broad as possible for religious entities and persons. President Trump also nominated, and the Senate confirmed, two justices for the Supreme Court, Neil Goresuch and Brett Kavanaugh, both of whom are "originalist" jurists. While these and other actions show what can be done through the political process to protect rights of conscience, some of these protections may last only through the administration of Donald Trump, and might be swept aside by a new president with a different view of the rights of conscience and new nominees to the Supreme Court. Further, despite what happens at the national level, much happens at the level of the individual states. There are deep forces and cultural attitudes at work that must be changed if conscience is to be truly protected, as the reader will discover in my article.

1 The principle

The First Amendment to the Constitution of the United States[2] protects religious liberty – "[government] shall make no law respecting an establishment of religion, or prohibiting the free exercise thereof." While "freedom of conscience" is not directly mentioned in the First Amendment, it was generally understood – by both the founders of the American republic[3] and the Supreme Court[4] – to be within the protection afforded by the First Amendment.[5]

Furthermore, freedom of religion/conscience may be protected *expressly* in specific federal laws, such as what are called the "Church amendments" (named after a member of the United States Senate, not because of any reference to churches or religion) of 1973.[6] The Church amendments were passed shortly after the Supreme Court legalized abortion in *Roe v. Wade*[7] in order to protect healthcare providers who refuse to participate in abortion (or any other lawful health service) for religious or moral reasons.

---

2 The Constitution is the fundamental law or legal document of the United States. It prescribes both the system of "federalism" between the national and state governments (under which many powers reside in the various states) and the separation of powers between the various branches (judicial, executive, and legislative) at the national level.

3 For instance, as America's first President, George Washington, stated: "The conscientious scruples of all men should be treated with great delicacy and tenderness; and it is my wish and desire that the laws may always be extensively accommodated to them, as a due regard for the protection and essential interests of the nation may justify and permit." Letter to Religious Society Called Quakers (1789).

4 For example, the Court said: "If there is any fixed star in our constitutional constellation, it is that no official, high or petty, can prescribe what shall be orthodox in politics, nationalism, religion, or other matters of opinion or force citizens to confess by word or act their faith herein [...] [L]ocal authorities [may not] transcend [...] constitutional limitations on their power and invade[...] the sphere of intellect and spirit which it is the purpose of the First Amendment of our Constitution to reserve from all official control." *West Virginia State Board of Education v. Barnette*, 319 U.S. 624, 642 (1943).

5 A parallel situation is that of those who conscientiously object to serving in the military. In Welsh v. U.S., 398 U.S. 333 (1970), despite the fact that the statute protected only those who objected on religious grounds and the fact the objector in the case was not objecting on religious grounds, the Court broadly read the statute to apply to "all those whose consciences, spurred by deeply held moral, ethical or religious beliefs, would give them no rest or peace [...]" The decision illustrates the strong tendency in the U.S. to understand "religious" protections broadly, beyond the strictly "religious" to include the moral and ethical.

6 44 U.S. Code, section 300–7.

7 410 U.S. 113.

As good as this no doubt appears, the Church amendments and other national laws, nevertheless, do not, for various reasons, provide comprehensive protection.[8] Thus, under America's federal system of government, the laws of individual states (such as California or New York) must be heavily relied upon to provide protection for conscience rights. Usually such laws *do* offer some form of conscience protection for medical professionals (47 out of 50 states do so).[9]

2 Its practical operation

However, despite this initial positive picture – that is, the existence of constitutional, national, and state laws protecting conscience – the actual picture is much darker and more troubling. Several points in this regard should be noted. First, the existing national laws are a patchwork, not a coherent, comprehensive protection with effective remedies;[10] they offer some protection but large gaps remain.[11] Second, most of the state laws offer limited protection (for instance, usually not covering pharmacists[12]) and apply only to abortion

8 For example, the Church amendments are tied to the flow of federal (national) funds to an entity. If federal funds are not involved, then the Church amendments do not prohibit anti-conscience discrimination.

9 Only the states of Alabama, New Hampshire, and Vermont provide no protection.

10 Some of the other federal (national) laws regarding conscience protection for healthcare providers are: (1) 42 U.S. Code section 238 n (regarding residency and training programs for physicians) and (2) the "Hyde/Weldon Amendment," Sec. 507 (d) of Title V of the Consolidated and Further Continuing Appropriations Act, 2015, Public Law No. 113–235. The former, in addition to being limited in scope, is also tied to receipt of federal funds; the latter is a "rider" to restricting the appropriation of funds and requires annual renewal. Neither provides for a private right of action to sue in court. Both apply only to abortion.

11 The Constitution itself, as quoted, while good as a general precept, lacks specificity. Thus, whenever possible, advocates of religious/moral freedom/conscience choose to rely upon specific statutory language. It should be noted that the Supreme Court historically has created a variety of tests to put into practice the guarantees of the First Amendment, including most recently, the test of *Employment Division v. Smith*, 494 U.S. 892. That case, in 1990, held that, so long as a law did not target religious behavior specifically and applied to the populace at large, it was not prohibited by the Constitution despite its "incidental" effect on religious believers. Note, that in response to *Smith*, the Congress enacted the Religious Freedom Restoration Act ("RFRA"), which will be discussed subsequently herein.

12 A case concerning the freedom of conscience of pharmacists is pending for review before the Supreme Court, which has not yet decided whether to grant review. That

(and even if broad protection is provided, such laws may still be ineffective if they fail, as most do, to provide for the right of the affected party to sue in a court of law to enforce the right). Third, and most significant, is the fact that serious efforts are underway to undermine freedom of conscience where it is protected.

On the state level, Illinois illustrates this third point. That state has the most comprehensive protection for conscience of any state in the United States (matched by only one other state – Mississippi). Its protection extends to *all* healthcare providers, institutions and payers who object to participating in *any* healthcare service based on a religious, moral or ethical objection. Illinois's existing law states: "It is the public policy of the State of Illinois to respect and

---

case is *Stormans v. Wiseman*, no. 12-35221, Ninth Circuit, July 23, 2015, available at <http://cdn.ca9.uscourts.gov/datastore/opinions/2015/07/23/12-35221.pdf>.The case concerns the law in the state of Washington, which until 2005 protected the conscience rights of pharmacists. However, in 2005, a new regulation was adopted requiring pharmacists to provide abortifacient drugs. While the pharmacists who objected were allowed to provide a list of other pharmacies in the area, those pharmacists were specifically prohibited from doing so *if their refusal was based on reasons of conscience.* In other words, only those who had conscientious objections were prohibited from exercising them! (The new regulations expressly permitted the pharmacy to refuse to provide any and all drugs if that refusal was based on *business reasons*, such as fraudulent prescriptions or a customer's inability to pay.) Pharmacies were required to have at least one person on staff who was present in the pharmacy and who was willing to provide the abortifacients. The Stormans family, who work for and operate pharmacies, filed suit in federal court under the First Amendment (RFRA, discussed elsewhere herein, was not involved because it applies only to actions of the *national* government). The pharmacists won in the district court, which held that the regulations violated the religious freedom of the pharmacists because it intentionally discriminated against religious/conscience beliefs. However, on appeal to the Ninth Circuit, the lower court's decision was reversed. The Ninth Circuit, on July 23, 2015, ruled that the law was "neutral". It is difficult to imagine that the Supreme Court, following its decision in *Hobby Lobby* (discussed subsequently), will uphold the Ninth Circuit, if it grants review, because the regulation seems clearly targeted against – and is, hence, not "neutral" toward - those pharmacies that, as small family-owned businesses, refuse, for reasons of conscience, to provide abortifacients (or even to have available in the store). (Of course, if the Supreme Court does not grant review, the decision in the Ninth Circuit will remain the law for the states in its jurisdiction – California, Oregon, Washington, Arizona, Nevada, Idaho, Alaska, Hawaii, and Montana. Even so, it seems certain the issue of pharmacists' rights of conscience will arise in future cases and that, eventually, the Supreme Court will have to rule on the issue.)

protect the right of conscience of all persons" regarding "medical services" whose morality is disputed.[13] Yet, legislation was recently introduced in the state legislature in Illinois (Senate Bill, or SB, 1564) to amend existing law to, among other things, add new language regarding "access to care and information protocols." This section would require "health care facilities, physicians, and health care personnel" who are opposed for reasons of conscience to performing an abortion to, nevertheless, "refer, transfer, or give information […] about other health care providers who they reasonably believe may offer […] the […] service," which includes abortion. So the objector has to make one of three choices – refer, transfer, or provide a list.

Obviously, requiring the objector to refer (or to transfer) the person to a different medical provider who *will* perform the abortion is radical – and unacceptable – because it implicates the objector in the obtaining of the disputed "medical service." It makes her or him *a participant*, that is, one who facilitates the procedure by assisting in its being obtained. This conclusion holds whether the referral is direct or indirect.

It might be thought that the third possible choice – to "give information" – is not so problematic regarding freedom of conscience. But, in fact, it is. It is not innocent or neutral – as requiring provision of an ordinary phonebook (i.e., an unfiltered list of local phone numbers) would be. In requiring the objector to provide a list of those whom he or she "reasonably believes" may offer the "service," SB 1564 requires that the objector facilitate the very procedure to which he or she objects – because the list *necessarily* is comprised solely of those of whom it is "reasonable" to believe they would perform the abortion. (If one has *no reason* to believe a facility performs abortions, it would not be "reasonable" to put it on the list. Similarly, if one knows a facility does *not* perform abortions, it would not be reasonable to put it on the list. Hence, the list will be comprised of those who *will* – if asked and paid – provide an abortion. Without such a list, the abortion-seeker would have to find an abortionist by their own efforts.)

Thus, it is clear the proposed amendment would dramatically undermine (if it does not, in fact, vitiate entirely) the conscience protection for medical professionals in one of the states where conscience is currently best protected. If the amendment is not passed during the current session of the Illinois legislature,

13 745 Illinois Compiled Statutes 70, the Health Care Right of Conscience Act (public law 90-246, effective Jan. 1, 1998)

political forces supporting it are likely to re-introduce the amendment in subsequent sessions.

The effort in Illinois to undermine conscience protection is not aberrational. In other states, by one count, during the 2015 legislative sessions in the states, more states considered measures coercing conscience than protecting it (9 to 7). By contrast, in 2013, more states sought to protect conscience than coerce it (12 to 3).[14] The difference might at first seem small, but for reasons discussed below, it appears, upon close examination, to illustrate a disturbing trend in the wrong direction.

3 Coercion that has been afforded

On the national level, consider the controversy in the United States over what has been called the "HHS contraceptive mandate," but which may be more accurately called the "HHS 'preventive services' mandate."

To summarize: when Congress passed the Affordable Care Act in 2010, it included a provision that insurance plans *must* include coverage of "preventive services" for women. The law did not define "preventive services" but left it to a federal agency, the Department of Health & Human Services (HHS) to do so. HHS adopted a regulation that defined "preventive services" to include all "contraceptive services" approved by the Food & Drug Administration (FDA), another federal agency. (In fact, FDA has misleadingly labeled as "contraceptive" certain devices and drugs that have an abortifacient effect by, for example, preventing the implantation of an embryo in the womb).

Many Americans objected to this requirement for contraception and/or abortion coverage in insurance, for a variety of religious and moral reasons. In response, HHS amended its regulation to exempt churches (and other houses of worship) from having to provide such insurance. In response to protests about the narrowness of that exemption, HHS amended its regulations still further to provide what it called an "accommodation." Under the accommodation, the objector was not required to provide the contraceptives, *but* the government would require the objector's insurance company to do so. But the accommodation was available only to some, not to all, of those with conscientious objections. For example, the accommodation only applied to *religious non-profit institutions*, not to private employers, and it only applied to religious institutions that satisfied

14 See "2015 Final State Legislative Session Report," Americans United for Life, 14 July 2015 <www.aul.org>

a certain set of criteria. The regulation went through a number of additional iterations, as objections continued to be made and HHS continued to revise its criteria.[15]

4 Defending freedom of conscience in courtroom

During this time, there were many complaints filed in courts challenging the regulations. Some of these lawsuits were filed by religious institutions, and some by private businesses who objected to conducting their businesses in a manner that violated their consciences (by providing insurance that covers abortion and/or contraception). The lawsuits by the private employers argued that they had a right to religious freedom that was being violated by the fact they were not given any accommodation at all. Those by the religious institutions argued that the accommodation they had been given was too restrictive – it infringed their religious liberty by requiring them to be complicit in the immoral acts (abortion, contraception) to which they objected.

On June 30, 2014, in the *Hobby Lobby* case,[16] the Supreme Court ruled on the objections of the private individuals/businesses. The Court held that these small, private (essentially, family-owned) businesses did have a right, under the Religious Freedom Restoration Act (hereafter, "RFRA"),[17] to religious liberty that HHS could not violate by requiring them to provide coverage of services to which they had religious objections.[18] In doing so, it referred favorably to the

15 The long and convoluted development of the HHS mandate regulation is beyond the scope of this chapter, but I have reviewed those developments in several "Washington Insider" columns I have written for the National Catholic Bioethics Quarterly, available at <www.ncbcenter.org>.

16 570 U.S.(2014) <http://www.supremecourt.gov/opinions/13pdf/13-354_olp1.pdf>

17 All of the cases – both by religious non-profit institutions and by for-profit businesses – have proceeded under RFRA, 42 U.S. Code Chapter 21B <http://prop1.org/legal/rfra.htm> RFRA states that a law that produces a "substantial" infringement of a person's religious freedom is only valid if it is of general applicability (i.e., is not targeting those with religious objections) and if the government has a "compelling interest" in enforcing the law and does so with the "least restrictive" means.

18 In the *Hobby Lobby* decision, after holding that "person" includes small, family-owned businesses, the Court assumed (but did not decide) that the governmental interest (providing the "contraceptives") was "compelling," but nonetheless held that the government had not used the "least restrictive" means of doing so. The Court noted (see pages 40–45 of its opinion) that two obvious examples of how the government could make the contraceptives available without requiring the objector to do so would be if

"accommodation" HHS had made for religious institutions, suggesting it should be extended to small for-profit businesses.[19]

Turning now to the cases involving religious institutions rather than for-profit businesses, it is to be observed that the Supreme Court subsequently granted "interlocutory" requests (i.e., requests for injunctive relief pending final resolution of the case) in several cases in which religious institutions lost in lower courts, saying that the court below should reconsider in light of the Court's holding in *Hobby Lobby*. Eventually, many of these lower (or inferior) courts did reconsider, but most still held *against* the religious institution.[20]

Thus, the current state of things is this: the Supreme Court is being asked to review decisions holding, contrary to the claims of religious institutions, that the "accommodation" does not violate their religious freedom under RFRA[21] by forcing them to participate in the provision of services (such as contraceptives) to which they object on religious/moral grounds. It is expected the Court will

---

the government itself subsidized the provision of them to the employees of an objector, or if HHS extended the "accommodation" so it protected the small family-owned businesses. Technically, the Court did not hold that the accommodation survived RFRA-scrutiny, but its favorable language towards the accommodation has led many to speculate that the Court would, in a later case, uphold the mandate. Precisely that issue is raised in the cases currently pending before the Court.

19 In addition to the comments from the majority opinion that were noted in the prior footnote, the concurring opinion of Justice Anthony Kennedy says that the means for "reconciling" religious liberty with the demands of the common good regarding the HHS mandate has been found by the government in its "accommodation."

20 It is too complicated – and beyond the scope of my presentation – to recite all of the details of all the cases in this chapter. To summarize, of the intermediate (or Circuit) courts that considered the issue, all but one ruled against the non-profit religious institution (i.e., the courts held that RFRA did not protect the institution and that it must provide the contraceptives or pay large fines to the government). See, for instance, the July 14, 2015 decision by the Tenth Circuit in *Little Sisters of the Poor v. Burwell*, 794 F.3d 1154, available at: <http://scholar.google.com/scholar_case?case=13480747407526409338&q=little+sisters+of+the+poor+v.+burwell&hl=en&as_sdt=20006&as_vis=1> One of the legal organizations that has represented the non-profit religious institutions in many of these cases has a helpful web site that provides information about these cases, at: <http://www.becketfund.org/hhsinformationcentral/>

21 If the Court holds that the enforcement of the HHS mandate against the institutions does not violate RFRA, it might well do so on the ground that the burden is "insubstantial," as most of the circuit courts have said. If, as noted in my discussion of RFRA above, the burden is insubstantial, the government is not put to the task of justifying its action as the "least restrictive means" to accomplish a "compelling state interest."

grant review and decide the matter during its term that begins in October 2015 and ends in June 2016.[22]

There is a substantial possibility the Court will uphold the lower courts and rule against the religious institutions (and, by implication, the small family-owned businesses).[23] If so, many of these institutions will close – they will refuse to comply. That will, in turn, severely damage the provision of educational, medical and other charitable services to the general public. The question to consider is this: why were they put to the choice to comply or close? Why would HHS, and the administration of President Barrack Obama, insist the institutions comply with the mandate even if it means diminished service to the general public? After all, the government could provide contraceptives itself or provide vouchers or tax credits for anyone who wants them so that they can purchase them privately. It does not need the assistance of morally opposed institutions. Why attempt to force objecting institutions (and businesses) to supply them?

5 Reasons for coercion

This question in the context of the HHS mandate points more generally toward the reasons, I believe, for the increased pressure that is being placed on conscience protection in the United States, both at the national and at the state levels. The reasons are, I believe, threefold: (1) the conviction that abortion should be treated as ordinary health care,[24] (2) growing hostility to religion (which is seen as

22 The Supreme Court has consolidated most of these pending law suits, and heard oral arguments on them in February 2016.

23 The death of Justice Antonin Scalia means that the Court now has eight, rather than nine, members. However, nothing in the Constitution requires that there be nine justices or that all vacant seats be filled prior to the Supreme Court deciding a case. Thus, it could be the Court will split four votes to four votes between what are often considered to be "liberal" and "conservative" groupings of justices. In that eventuality, the lower courts' decisions would be affirmed, meaning that across most of the United States religious institutions would be required to comply with the HHS mandate. (But not everywhere – as noted one circuit, the Eighth, ruled in favor of the institutions. The Eighth Circuit is comprised of federal courts in seven states – Minnesota, Missouri, North Dakota, South Dakota, Arkansas, Iowa, and Nebraska.) The need for *uniformity* of interpretation of national law throughout *all* the states is one important reason that the Supreme Court often grants review in order to resolve a split among the different circuit (or, intermediate appellate) courts.

24 The state of California has gone so far as to require that all insurance plans cover abortion, regardless of conscientious objection, as part of "basic health care." See,

irrational) and to any claims associated with it,[25] and (3) the rise of "living constitution" jurisprudence.

This third – the rise of "living constitution" jurisprudence – operates by untethering the judiciary from any restraint (including what we might call the "common sense of the common man" that is reflected in written laws) and enables the judiciary to "read" elite policy preferences *into* legal guarantees.[26] Indeed, *that is precisely what the Supreme Court did in Roe v. Wade*, the case that created "abortion rights" in the United States.[27] The Court held that, despite scant historical evidence and no textual support, the constitutional requirement that no one shall be "deprived of life, liberty or property without due process of law" [28] included the right to have an abortion. When combined with the companion case issued the same day, *Doe v. Bolton*,[29] which held that no more than "one doctor" need be consulted[30] and that abortions could be granted for any

---

e.g., <http://www.christianpost.com/news/churches-abortion-healthcare-mandate-california-planned-parenthood-148335/>

25 An example is Barrack Obama's dismissive comment about those who "cling to guns and religion." See, e.g., <http://www.theguardian.com/world/2008/apr/14/barackobama.uselections2008>

26 An extensive and enlightening analysis of this problem in the United States is by Christopher Wolfe, *The Rise of Modern Judicial Review: from constitutional interpretation to judge-made law*, rev. ed. (Rowan & Littlefield, 1994).

27 410 U.S. 113 (1973).

28 The doctrine of "substantive" due process, deriving from this language from the Fourteenth Amendment to the Constitution, has been used since *Roe* and *Doe* to find/create "new" rights from this general guarantee of "liberty". Though the Court, under the leadership of then-Chief Justice William Rehnquist cut back this doctrine substantially, requiring that the newly discovered rights could only be so if they were rooted in the history and traditions of the nation and, therefore, rejecting such a "right" to assisted suicide, see *Washington v. Glucksberg*, 521 U.S. 702 (1997), the Court has overthrown those restraints – and relegated *Glucksberg* to its facts – in *Obergefell v. Hodges*, 576 U.S. (2015), which found a right to same-sex marriage. The Court was unrestrained in its assertion – and celebration - of its right to find "new meanings" of the "liberty" interest in the Fourteenth Amendment. The seriousness of this embrace of judicial activism was emphasized by Justice Samuel Alito in dissent: "If a bare majority of Justices can invent a new right and impose that right on the rest of the country, the only real limit on what future majorities will be able to do is their own sense of what those with political power and cultural influence. Are willing to tolerate [...] Today's decision shows that decades of attempts to restrain this Court's abuse of its authority have failed."

29 410 U.S. 179.

30 410 U.S. at 199. The "attending physician" will certainly be an abortionist, who has a financial incentive for the woman to decide to have an abortion. Hence, the state of

reason,[31] the Supreme Court created an essentially unlimited "abortion right" for the entire nine months of pregnancy.[32] As Justices Byron White and William Rehnquist said in dissent, the combined rulings were simply "an act of raw judicial power."[33]

An example of the first and second reasons – that is, that abortion is considered ordinary health care and that religions are viewed as irrational enemies of progress – may be found, for instance, in a statement made by Hillary Clinton a few months ago that "deep-seated [...] religious beliefs [...] have to be changed for the sake of giving access to women to reproductive health care."[34] Ever since the Cairo Conference on Population and Development in 1994, abortion advocates have claimed that "reproductive health care" includes abortion. Clinton's speech was so understood by the left-leaning crowd at the event. She may be the next president of the United States, and she seems to believe that religious beliefs are unenlightened and hinder access to the "basic right" of abortion.

6 Will the Western culture survive?

The prospects for protection of conscience for medical professionals in a world in which these three views are rising, if not regnant, are not encouraging. Many years ago, the American-born, English poet and critic, T. S. Eliot, reflected upon how cultures can forget, and eventually become hostile to, their religious culture-forming roots: "I do not believe that the culture of Europe could survive the complete disappearance of the Christian Faith. And I am convinced of that, not

---

Georgia, in its statute, had required the opinion of a second physician that an abortion was necessary. But the Court seems to have missed this obvious point.

31 The Court asserted "that the medical judgment may be exercised in light of all factors – physical, emotional, psychological, familial, and the women's age – relevant to the well-being of the patient. All these factors may relate to health." U.S. 410 at 192. It is difficult to imagine a broader definition of "health." The test from *Roe* was that a state could regulate abortion *unless* it risked a woman's life *or health*.

32 If the abortionist is the one deciding whether an abortion will be performed, and if that decision may be based on any factor he decides is relevant to the woman's "health," then it is unlimited. (See my discussion in the two prior footnotes.)

33 "As an exercise of raw judicial power, the Court perhaps has authority to do what it does today, but, in my view, its judgment is an improvident and extravagant exercise of the power of judicial review that the Constitution extends to this Court." 410 U.S., page 422.

34 See, e.g., <http://cnsnews.com/news/article/susan-jones/clinton-deep-seated-cultural-codes-religious-beliefshave-be-changed>

merely because I am a Christian myself, but as a student of social biology. If Christianity goes, the whole of our culture goes. Then you must start painfully again, and you cannot put on a new culture ready-made. You must wait for the grass to grow to feed the sheep to give the wool out of which your new coat will be made. You must first pass through many centuries of barbarism."[35]

Eliot's point, of course, is that our culture cannot survive the disappearance of the Christian faith that created it. Do his words describe our current Western situation? Has Christianity and the values it creates and incarnates in the culture run its course? Are we so far gone that we must begin all over again? Or is such a judgment too pessimistic? Is there still hope in the here-and-now? There may well be, for there are hopeful signs, including efforts to enhance conscience protection for healthcare professionals on the national and state levels.

But a society in which judges, not written constitutions, rule, in which religion is regarded as superstition that must yield to enlightened opinions, and in which abortion is regarded as basic health care, is one in which the rights of medical professionals, and indeed of all citizens, to freedom of conscience is on very shaky ground.

35 Thomas S. Eliot, *Notes Toward the Definition of Culture* (1948), p. 122.

Danuta Brańska

Conscience Clause of Pharmacists and Other Pharmacy Staff

Abstract: The chapter presents problems with conscience clause of pharmacist in Poland. Conscience clause in pharmacist's employment can be defined as a regulation, which allows a pharmacist or technician pharmacist to refuse particular professional duty imposed by law due to demands of his or her conscience with both ethical and religious foundations. It is explained how professional knowledge about real operation of some of the medical products allowed for distribution provokes conflict of conscience. It is argued that imposing statutory obligation on pharmacists to act in a way threatening fundamental right to protect human life and health is contrary to constitutional protection of their dignity. It seems that state allowing distribution of medical products of controversial operation should ensure equal freedom to all citizens. If a patient cannot be forced by someone else to use controversial medical products, no one should be expected (including the pharmacist) to participate in their production or distribution.

Keywords: conscience clause, professional knowledge, ethical dilemmas, pharmacist, legal duties

1 Introduction

Conscience clause in pharmacist's employment can be defined as a regulation which allows a pharmacist or technician pharmacist to refuse particular professional duty imposed by law due to demands of his or her conscience with both ethical or religious foundations.

2 Legal-professional situation

In the current legal system in Poland, a pharmacist, like any other citizen, can benefit from the freedom of conscience if he or she applies the rights guaranteed by the Constitution of the Republic of Poland. However, by vague provisions of Pharmaceutical Law and by social pressure from groups imposing unlimited access to contraceptives, we are being suggested that this possibility is legally restricted.

The main law regulating profession of pharmacist is Pharmaceutical Law. It states in paragraph 95 that: "With regard to the pharmacy, there is an obligation to have medicinal products and medical devices in quantity and range necessary to meet the health needs of local population" [Article 95 paragraph 1] and also "[…] if the public pharmacy lacks a medicinal product, including prescription medicine, pharmacy manager should provide his acquisition at the time agreed with the patient" [Article 95 paragraph 3].[1]

Pharmacies' owners fearing the loss of concessions or breaching of contract by National Health Found refer to the above articles and require from employees to sell preparations that are objectionable for conscience even though the same Pharmaceutical Law contains an article which reads: "The pharmacist and pharmacy technician may refuse to hand over medicinal product if it can endanger the life or health of the patient" [Article 96 paragraph 4].[2] The pharmacies' owners feel entitled to do so because of different interpretations of existing legislations.

Bioethics Committee of the National Academy of Science explicitly do not recognize the right of pharmacists to invoke the conscience clause.[3] On the other hand, according to legal opinion of the Office of Parliamentary Analysis depriving pharmacists of the right to act according to conscience restricts the basic (constitutional) rights and freedoms.[4] In practice, many pharmacists pay high price to work according to their conscience – some are losing their jobs or drop out of the profession of pharmacy.

For this reason, it seems almost necessary to regulate the issue of invoking conscious clause objection by pharmacists at the level of statutory law, especially because it does not apply to marginal group of people as it is usually said. Research made in three universities (University of Warsaw, Medical University in Lublin and University of Warmia and Mazury) shows that approximately 25 % of Polish pharmacists expresses readiness to use clause of conscious (or sees purposefulness to introduce such regulation). Eight percent of the respondents currently use the conscience clause (in most cases it is the refusal of "morning-after pill" containing levonorgestrel).[5] In another research,

---

1 Prawo Farmaceutyczne, Dz.U. 2001 Nr 126 poz. 1381, article 95.

2 Prawo Farmaceutyczne, Dz.U. 2001 Nr 126 poz. 1381, article 96.

3 *Stanowisko Komitetu Bioetyki przy Prezydium PAN nr 4/2013 z dnia 12 listopada 2013 roku w sprawie tzw. Klauzuli sumienia.*

4 *Opinia prawna dotycząca możliwości wprowadzenia do polskiego prawa klauzuli sumienia dla farmaceutów i techników farmacji*, Biuro Analiz Sejmowych, BAS-WAL-910/12, 10 May 2012.

5 S. Bąk and J. Pawlikowski, "Aspekty etyczne klauzuli sumienia dla farmaceutów w opinii pracowników aptek," Farmacja Polska, Vol. 69, No. 10 (2012), pp. 561–566.
M. Gryka, et al., Stosunek polskich farmaceutów do tzw. klauzuli sumienia, XXII Naukowy Zjazd Polskiego Towarzystwa Farmaceutycznego, streszczenia,

every third pharmacy student expressed his/her acceptance for the clause of conscience.[6]

This is not just a Polish phenomenon - pharmacists from other countries also report this need. In the USA about 15 % (n = 2,725) of surveyed pharmacy employees want to be able to use conscientious objection clause (Nevada 13 %, Florida 11 %, Texas 14–27 %, Mexico 30 % Arkansas 40 %), in Australia 6 %.[7] In some US states,[8] in the UK and Ireland[9] the right to use conscientious objection clause by pharmacists is respected by the society.

In Poland, the conflict of conscience in the case of pharmacists concerns mainly hormonal contraceptives (especially the so-called "after" pills) and intra-uterine devices due to their possible abortifacient action.

(2013).Małgorzata Prusak, Sprzeciw sumienia farmaceutów. Aspekty etyczne, teologiczne i prawne, Kraków, pp. 93–101. (Wydawnictwo św.Stanisława BM 2015)

6 M. Prusak, *Opinie studentów farmacji na temat wątpliwości moralnych wobec sprzedaży środków antykoncepcyjnych oraz możliwości wprowadzenia klauzuli sumienia*, XXII Naukowy Zjazd Polskiego Towarzystwa Farmaceutycznego, streszczenia, (2013).

7 L.A. Davidson, et al., "Religion and conscientious objection: A survey of pharmacists' willingness to dispense medications," *Social Science & Medicine,* Vol. 71 (2010), p. 163.
G. Sutkin, et al., "Opinions of West Texas pharmacists about emergency contraception," *Pharmacy Practice*, Vol. 4 (2006), p. 154.
S. K. Griggs and C. M. Brown, "Texas community pharmacists' willingness to participate in pharmacist-initiated emergency contraception," *Journal of American Pharmacists Association*, Vol. 47 (2007), p. 52.
D. Hopkins and D. West, "Arkansas pharmacists' perceptions toward emergency contraception and nonprescription Plan B," *Pharmacy Practice*, Vol. 6 (2008), pp. 100–101.
S. Landau et al., "Pharmacist interest in and attitudes toward direct pharmacy access to hormonal contraception in the United States," *Journal of the American Pharmacists Association*, Vol. 49 (2009), p. 47.
S. G. Downing et al., "Emergency contraception over-the-counter: Practices and attitudes of pharmacists and pharmacy assistants in far North Queensland," *Australian and New Zealand Journal of Obstetrics and Gynaecology*, Vol. 51 (2011), p. 530.
M. E. Borrego et al., "New Mexico pharmacists' knowledge, attitudes, and beliefs toward prescribing oral emergency contraception," *Journal of the American Pharmacists Association*, Vol. 46 (2006), p. 42.

8 Guttmacher Institute, "Refusing to Provide Health Services", *State Policies in Brief*, 1 July 2013.

9 *Standards of conduct, ethics and performance,* General Pharmaceutical Council (UK, 2012).
Guidance on the provision of pharmacy servicies affected by religious and moral beliefs, General Pharmaceutical Council, UK, 2010).*Code of Conduct for Pharmacists*, The Pharmaceutical Society of Ireland (2009).*Supply by pharmacist of non-prescription*

After application of the hormone contraceptives (either oral, transdermal, or intrauterine as gestagen insert devices), four basic processes are observed in the female body:

1. inhibition of ovulation,
2. changes in the lining of the uterus preventing the implantation of the embryo,
3. decrease in motility of the fallopian tubes,
4. thickening the cervical mucus.

It is widely believed that the contraceptive efficacy advertised at just over 99 % corresponds to the inhibition of ovulation. However, studies did not confirm that. In the case of simple gestagenic tablet ovulation occurs in 18–84 %, in the case of a binary hormonal tablet ovulation there are some reports that ovulation can occur in 10–25 %, in case of hormonal implant ovulation may occur in 15–75 %.[10] It shows that the efficacy of hormonal contraceptives consists largely of other mechanisms of action, of which two in three means death for the newly conceived life.

In case of the emergency postcoital contraception ("morning-after pill") the delay or inhibition of ovulation is only possible when the pill is taken before the moment ovulation took place. Once the ovulation has already occurred, pill action becomes purely abortive (second mechanism of action).[11] Because such preparations are applied between 1st and 5th day after the intercourse then if conception occurred, the pill can work as abortifacient.

Intrauterine devices containing copper have no inhibitory ovulation effect. Their effectiveness results from toxic effects of copper on the sperm and the effect of presence of a foreign body in the uterine, meaning local inflammation changing the membrane of the uterus to the stage that implantation is not possible.

---

medicinal products containing levonorgestrel (Norlevo 1.5 mg tablets) as emergency hormonal contraception, The Pharmaceutical Society of Ireland (2011).

10 A. R. Baewald, R. A. Walker and R. A. Pierson, "Growth rates ovarian follicles during natural menstrual cycles, oral contraception cycles, and ovarian stimulation cycles," Fertility and Sterility, Vol. 91 (2009), pp. 443–444.
R. A. Pierson, D. F. Archer, M. Moreau et al., "Ortho Evra/Evra versus oral contraceptives: follicular development and ovulation in normal cycles and after an intentional dosing error," Fertility and Sterility, Vol. 80, No. 1 (2003), p. 38.
K. A. Petrie, A. H. Torgal, and C. L. Westhoff, "Matched-pairs analysis of ovarian suppression during oral
vs. vaginal hormonal contraceptive use," Contraception, Vol. 84 (2011).

11 P. Ventura-Juncá, "Objection of Conscience, Witness in Medical Health Practice: the Case of Emergency Contraception," in: *Christian Conscience in Support of the Right to Life*, eds. E. Sgreccia and J. Laffitte (Vatican, 2008), p. 184.

Other conscience objectionable products are vaccines produced from cell lines derived from aborted human fetuses, products used in an *in vitro* procedure, homeopathic remedies due to a lack of clinical evidence for their therapeutic effects and spiritual damage signaled by exorcists, and addictive substances sold to addicts. Beyond Poland, the conflict of conscience is raised also by the obligation to sell means to perform euthanasia, assisted suicide, and medical abortion (by mifepristone – RU486).

Pharmacists who are aware of mechanisms of action and effects resulting from use of these preparations and are aware of their professional and moral responsibility for any substance they give to the patient, rightly demand respect of their conscience and wait for clear laws to protect the inviolable character of human life from conception to natural death.

3 Difficulties arising from discussions about objection of conscience[12]

According to some, granting pharmacists the right to use conscience clause could violate the dignity and privacy of people who legitimately expect to be provided with access to "legal" products. They express concern that ultimately the patient will not be able to exercise his right to fill the prescription or at least it will be made significantly more difficult. Often it is proposed that an apparent conflict between the right to act according to conscience and the right of access to legal means of health care should be solved for the benefit of the patient. It is required from health workers and, thus, also from the pharmacists to "sacrifice" their deepest values in favor of obligations arising from their role. But it is difficult to agree on such specific moral relativism based on the fact that the pharmacist will use other moral standards at work and other in his/her private life.

Others propose a compromise solution that a patient has access to contested specifics through compulsory sending away to another pharmacist or pharmacy. Such a solution also is not accepted by those who wish to act ethically. Indication of "another specialist" is forcing pharmacists to indirectly participate in unacceptable actions in the same way as directly issuing the preparation.

Both the patient and the pharmacist have the right to act in according with their conscience and to self-determine in accordance with their recognized moral principles, that is to conduct it autonomously. It seems that the proposed solution based on the principle or the right of the patient or pharmacist's right

12 See M. Prusak, Sprzeciw sumienia w praktyce aptecznej (KUL, 2013), pp. 223–224.

causes damage to one of the parties. It should rather go in the direction of a "mature relationship" based on responsibilities and obligations and not just on vested rights. The pharmacist should be able to clearly and openly express their objections and the patient has the right to look for a pharmacist (pharmacy) sharing his/her views. Conversation on this subject should take place in conditions that ensure the patient's privacy. Currently, in Polish pharmacies privacy and intimacy of conversation are guaranteed in a limited way. In many pharmacies, there are windows hindering contact or where the patient has at his back already another patient, who, whether he wants it or not, hears the conversation with the pharmacist. Regardless of the particular situation discussed, the very fact of being sick is a sufficient reason to ensure that any advice coming from the pharmacist was not for open public. Every pharmacy should ensure a place to hold a conversation with a patient without exposing him to the public.

Another issue is the use of contraceptives in other than registered indications in treatment of certain women's diseases. Here, opinions of practitioners vary, for example, doctors who use NaProTechnology, in general, do not apply these preparations in their practice. Until the moment of resolving this issue by physicians, authorities might introduce labeling of prescriptions in order to indicate for which purpose contraceptives are prescribed, what is partially implemented in Great Britain or introducing labels on pharmacies, for example, in the expeditionary hall that they do not sell such products and make it easier for the patient to select an appropriate pharmacy.

4 Conclusion

In the light of data presented, it seems that in a pluralistic society the conscientious objection pharmacists should be recognized and strengthened by statutory regulations. In practice, so far existing constitutional warranties does not seem to provide sufficient protection of the pharmacists' freedom of conscience. Obliging pharmacists to participate in actions threatening fundamental right to protect human life and health is contrary to their dignity. It seems that state introducing on the market preparations if their actions or usage are morally questionable (especially those that may affect the beginning or end of human life and their use may violate fundamental right to life) should ensure equal freedom to all citizens. Just like the patient cannot be forced by someone else to use these medical products, no one should be expected (including the pharmacist) to participate in their production or distribution.[13] Pharmacists in their professional engagement

13 See M. Prusak, Sprzeciw sumienia w praktyce aptecznej (KUL, 2013), p. 225.

deal with many other problems provoking ethical dilemmas (product bundling promotions, preferring particular companies, unexamined dietary supplements, etc.). These situations however are not imposed as statutory duties. Therefore, even though they often provoke serious moral issues and require strong opposition, they do not belong to the category of cases subject to the conscience clause.

Part IV: Courtroom Perspective

Konstanty Radziwiłł

Medical Doctor's Right to Act According to His/Her Conscience

Since antiquity medical ethics (so-called Hippocratic Oath – 5th/4th century BC) has imposed on each physician the obvious duty to help every sick person. It forbids to discriminate patients in any way, also on grounds of their views or expectations. The basic dictate, included as well in the Polish Medical Oath and in the Medical Code of Ethics (MCE),[1] is the ancient principle "Salus aegroti suprema lex esto" (The health of the ancient is to be the supreme law). As there are various, often difficult circumstances, under which physicians work, MCE phrases this duty unequivocally: "Market mechanisms, social pressure or administrative requirements do not exempt physicians from the obligation to follow this principle." At the same time MCE orders physicians to fulfill their duties, on one hand "with respect for human beings regardless of their age, sex, race, genetics, nationality, religion, social background, material situation, political views or any other circumstances," but on the other hand it forbids "to influence a patient with a purpose different from the medical one."

Over the millennia this duty of physicians was convergent with patients' expectations towards them. The public opinion in Europe, based on Christian values, agreed even more on physician's tasks. Along with an increasingly diverse 20th century (also as regards the attitude towards fundamental values concerning life) and with the creation of public healthcare systems (Bismarck-type insurance based and Beveridge-type security based), the "third party" appeared in the patient-physician relationship, that is the State or any other public administrator or a public or a private payer. Physicians have been increasingly faced with patients' expectations that are inconsistent with the traditional system of values (often followed by physicians) however "guaranteed" by the third party.

At the same time it is clear in fact that patients expect medical doctors to enjoy an extensive professional freedom in order to carry out their tasks not only in accordance with actual medical knowledge, but also with their conscience. There is a strongly held belief in this respect that professional autonomy understood in

1 <http://www.nil.org.pl/__data/assets/pdf_file/0003/4764/Kodeks-Etyki-Lekarskiej.pdf>

this way is, in fact, a precondition for good quality of general healthcare and for patient's safety.

Thus, questions arise on how to enforce patients' "rights" (in-vitro fertilization, especially embryo manipulation, termination of pregnancies, euthanasia) being often directly in conflict with traditional values concerning, above all, the beginning and the end of life, and at the same time to guarantee the physicians' natural right to act in accordance with their conscience. Some think that this right is guaranteed by the Polish Constitution, and by numerous international regulations, so it does not require any additional provisions that might lead to its restrictive interpretation.

It seems, however, appropriate to describe how the "conscience clause" is being practiced by physicians, at least for practical and "educational" reasons. It is widely recognized that a medical doctor who refuses to fulfill a patient's expectation that is inconsistent with his/her system of values, has to inform the patient, with full respect for his/her dignity, about the reasons behind this refusal (the doctor cannot say, falsely, that the refusal is based on medical grounds). This information should not contain any condemnation of the patient's attitude, but should come down to explaining the physician's position in a tactful and simple way. In such circumstances, a physician cannot be forced to help in order to fulfill the patient's expectations. Especially, he/she cannot be obliged to help the patient finding a different physician willing to do so.

It is widely recognized that invoking conscientious objection cannot take place in an emergency that requires the procedure objected to, to be carried out. Therefore, if a doctor foresees a situation where the conflict of conscience might arise, he/she should consider changing the place of work.

It seems that the conscience clause cannot apply to ordinary evidence-based medicine (EBM) activities, and the conflict of conscience cannot justify actions inconsistent with EBM (e.g., refuse to vaccinate a child, recommend unscientific methods of treatment, etc.).

Medical specialties, where the conflict of conscience can arise quite often (family medicine, gynecology and obstetrics, clinical genetics), cannot be "forbidden" to physicians following the traditional system of values. Those who plan to begin such a specialty and those who begin to work in one of them, cannot be classified in any way or committed to make a prior declaration concerning their outlook or beliefs. This would simply mean that they are discriminated against.

Therefore, the physician's right to refuse to act against his/her conscience should be treated, not only as a citizen's right, but, as the patient's right to be treated by a professional with integrated personality, who not only has an extensive knowledge and know-how, but is also ready to carry out a wise ethical reflection, is sensitive to what is good and wrong, acts in accordance with his/her conscience and eventually does not act under extreme pressure of a payer, administration, authorities etc., but follows the patient's well-being. Moreover, to a certain extent, even if this right is not respected, physicians should be expected not to accept actions raising their conscientious objection, even if this can mean ramifications for them. Patients should be able to expect such heroism from their doctors.

In 2014, the Polish Chamber of Physicians and Dentists recognized that there was a serious doubt concerning conformity of the Physicians and Dentists Act as of 5 December 1996 with the Polish Constitution as regards the possibility for a physician to abstain from providing treatment inconsistent with his/her conscience. Thus the Chamber asked the Constitutional Court to analyse the respective provisions of this Act in this respect.[2] At the same time the Chamber recalled that:

a) every physician has the duty to help every patient regardless of their age, sex, race, genetics, nationality, religion, social background, material situation, political views or any other circumstances;
b) every physician has the right to act in accordance with his/her conscience as guaranteed by general provisions concerning all citizens (including the Polish Constitution and international regulations ratified by Poland);
c) every physician has the right to refuse treatment being at odds with his/her conscience or current medical knowledge;
d) every physician has the right to enjoy the freedom to exercise their profession in agreement with their conscience and contemporary medical knowledge, with respect for the patient's dignity and bearing in mind the patient's good in accordance with the principle "Salus aegroti suprema lex esto."[3]

The Chamber also recalled that physicians had the right to enforce their right to refuse any action that is against their conscience and cannot be put under pressure, subject to discrimination or be victimized because of this.

The court issued a judgment in this case. A selection of the justification of the court judgment is reprinted below.

2 <http://www.nil.org.pl/__data/assets/pdf_file/0004/93685/ru003-14-VI.pdf>
3 <http://www.nil.org.pl/__data/assets/pdf_file/0003/98121/rs019-14-VII.pdf>

Constitutional Tribunal of the Republic of Poland

Judgement K12/14 of 7th October 2015

File No. K 12/14*

On behalf of the Republic of Poland

The Constitutional Tribunal (...) after examination, with the participation of the applicant and of the Marshal of the Sejm and the Public Prosecutor General, at the hearing held on 7 October 2015, the application by the Supreme Medical Council (pl. Naczelna Rada Lekarska - NRL) (...) decides:

1. Article 39, first sentence, in connection with Article 30 of the Act of 5 December 1996 on Professions of Doctor and Dentist (Journal of Laws of 2015 item 464) in so far as it imposes on the doctor the obligation to perform incompatibly with his conscience medical services "in other urgent cases", is inconsistent with the principle of correct legislation based on Article 2 of the Constitution of the Republic of Poland and Article 53 para. 1 in connection with Article 31 para. 3 of the Constitution.
2. Article 39, first sentence, of the Act referred to in the Point 1., in so far as it imposes on the doctor, who refrains from the performance of a medical service incompatible with his conscience, the obligation to indicate a real possibility of obtaining that service from another doctor or entity, is incompatible with Article 53 para. 1 in connection with Article 31 para. 3 of the Constitution.
3. Article 39, second sentence, of the Act referred to in the Point 1., in so far as it obliges the doctor practicing on the basis of the employment or service relationship, who exercises his right to refuse providing a medical service incompatible with his conscience, to the prior notice in writing to his supervisor:
   a) is in compliance with Article 53 para. 1 in connection with Article 31 para. 3 of the Constitution,
   b) is not incompatible with Article 53 para. 7 of the Constitution.
4. Article 39, first sentence, of the Act referred to in the Point 1., in so far as it obliges the doctor exercising his right to refuse providing a medical service incompatible with his conscience, to substantiate it and record that fact in medical documentation,

---

* The Judgement was announced on 16 October 2015 in the OJ. item 1633.

a) is in compliance with Article 53 para. 1 in connection with Article 31 para. 3 of the Constitution,
b) is not incompatible with Article 53 para. 7 of the Constitution.

Relevant legislation:

THE CONSTITUTION OF THE REPUBLIC OF POLAND:

Article 31 (…)

3. Any limitation upon the exercise of constitutional freedoms and rights may be imposed only by statute, and only when necessary in a democratic state for the protection of its security or public order, or to protect the natural environment, health or public morals, or the freedoms and rights of other persons. Such limitations shall not violate the essence of freedoms and rights.

Article 53. [Freedom of conscience and religion]

1. Freedom of conscience and religion shall be ensured to everyone. […]

7. No one may be compelled by organs of public authority to disclose his philosophy of life, religious convictions or belief.

ACT OF 5 DECEMBER 1996 ON PROFESSIONS OF DOCTOR AND DENTIST:

Article 30 [Obligation to provide assistance] The doctor is obliged to provide medical aid in any case, when the delay in its delivery would result in the danger of loss of life, severe personal injury or serious health disorder, and in other urgent cases.

Article 39 [Development] The doctor may refrain from the performance of medical services that are incompatible with his conscience, with the reservation for the Article 30, provided that he has the duty to indicate a real possibility of obtaining that service from another doctor or medical entity, and justify and state that fact in the medical documentation.[6] A doctor practicing on the basis of the employment or service relationship is also obliged to submit to his supervisor a prior notification in writing.

REASONING OF THE TRIBUNAL:

(…)

1.2. The applicant indicated that, the joint reading of art 39 and Article 30 of the Act on Professions of Doctor and Dentist engenders a rule of law, according to which the physician is unconditionally obliged to perform a medical service incompatible with his conscience in every case of extreme urgency, and thus beyond the must of providing assistance in an emergency or a danger of bodily harm or serious health disorder. In the case of refusing the patient medical assistance in such a situation, the doctor may incur disciplinary, civil or employee's, and even criminal liability, for an offence committed unintentionally. The Act does not explicitly provide for any circumstance that would exclude fulfilling that obligation.

The Supreme Medical Council emphasised that "other urgent cases" referred to in the contested act should not have "priority" over the doctor's right to exercise his freedom of conscience. The specially supporting it fact might be, that the term applies to both medicinal and non-medicinal. In case of the latter services, as they are not preserving, saving, restoring and improving the patient's health, the doctor should absolutely retain the right to refuse to perform them in such situations, where it poses no risk to the patient's life, neither causes serious bodily injury nor serious health disorder. The applicant appealed also to Article 4 of the Code of Medical Ethics, adopted at the Second Extraordinary National Convention of Medical Chambers II in 1991(revised twice: in 1993, and in 2003; hereinafter Code of Medical Ethics or CME), according to which the doctor, for the fulfilment of his tasks, must have the freedom to act according to his or her conscience and the liberty to perform professional activities in line with the present standards of medical knowledge.

1.3. The applicant also pointed out that obligating a doctor, who uses the clause of conscience, to indicate a real possibility of obtaining that service from another doctor or entity, is in fact a legal obligation to help in the performance of a service deemed evil by the doctor. That provision in fact obliges the doctor to provide active, specific and real aid to obtain a service incompatible with his conscience. In the light of the literal wording of that provision, the doctor may not be exempt from that obligation by directing the patient to the National Health Fund (hereinafter also: NHF). The Supreme Medical Council also stated that obligating the doctor to indicate the real possibility of performance of the service by another doctor or another entity is impossible to perform in practice, because the doctor refusing to provide a medical service incompatible with his conscience does not know beliefs of other doctors, to whom he would direct the patient. For that reason the provision in question infringes also the principle of correct legislation derived from Article 2 of the Constitution.

1.4. The applicant also pointed out the unconstitutionality of obligating a doctor to inform his supervisor about his intention to take advantage of the clause of conscience, because that is in conflict with the absolute prohibiting public authorities to impose on the citizen the obligation to disclose his beliefs (Article 53 para. 7 of the Constitution). Besides, the existence of the contested regulation may cause in practice that the superior, informed by the doctor about his intention to exercise the clause of conscience, will persecute him. Thus the consequence of the contested regulation in practice may be the effect of deterring, which will discourage doctors to use their right to the freedom of conscience. According to the applicant, the doctor's legal obligation of written "self-incrimination" arouses also concerns from the point of view of the applicability of the prohibition of discrimination on religious or faith-based grounds in labour relations.

1.5. Similar allegations were reported by the applicant as regards the obligation to document and justify in the medical documentation the fact that the doctor refrained from performing a service contrary to his conscience. Also that obligation remains in conflict with the absolute prohibition of imposing on citizens by public authorities any obligation to disclose their worldviews, and may cause the above indicated "deterring effect " or discrimination of the doctor by his superior. In addition, the imposition on the doctor of the obligation to state the reasons his the use of the freedom of conscience means ordering the person to disclose facts or experiences belonging to the sphere of his or her freedom of conscience, which is unacceptable under the rule of law in a democratic state.

(…)

2.2. The introduction in the Act on Professions of Doctor and Dentist of conditions limiting the use of the conscience clause by doctors is justified by such constitutional values as the necessity to respect the individuals' right to healthcare (Article 68, para. 1, of the Constitution) and their right to privacy (Article 47 of the Constitution). Such a restriction may be deemed necessary from the point of view of Article 31 para. 3 of the Constitution.

The Marshal of the Sejm emphasised also that, although the wording "urgent cases" included in Article 30 of the Act on Professions of Doctor and Dentist can be qualified as "an imprecise concept", that fact alone cannot lead to the recognition of its unconstitutionality. In that case the legislator has chosen to apply such a concept to enable the doctor *a casu ad casum* to assess himself whether in the given situation there occurred substantive reasons for invoking the clause of conscience in the light of current medical knowledge and professional experience. The legislator could not use an expression characterised by a higher level of conclusiveness because of the "diversity of actual conditions subject to the doctor's professional evaluation". The contested law does not either affect the principle of the freedom to practice a profession, expressed in Article 65 para. 1. 1 of the Constitution, because it is a part of the gist of the doctor's profession to be each time obliged to assist the ill in all cases of urgency.

2.3. According to the Marshal of the Sejm, Article 39 of the Act on Professions of Doctor and Dentist does not make the doctor "a guarantor" of the performance of a medical service incompatible with his conscience, and the very obligation to inform the patient about the real possibility of obtaining the service from another doctor or entity "neither charges the doctor's conscience nor breaks it". (…)

In the view brought to the Tribunal it was also assumed that the doctor – in order to comply with the obligation specified in Article 39 of the Act on Professions of Doctor and Dentist – should check where the patient can get the service, that he refused. In the view of the Marshal of the Sejm, such checking does not consists in getting to know other doctors' worldviews, but it is "a matter of a technical nature" that can be "resolved at an organisational level". The party also expressed the view that each doctor should be able to "get prepared for situations in which his moral integrity will be threatened" which means for example, a search for medical entities, in which are provided services unacceptable for the doctor. Getting such information was deemed by the Marshal of the Sejm to be equal with the doctor's ability to "acquire and upgrade the data concerning the list of reimbursable drugs". (…)

2.4. In the view of the Marshal of the Sejm, a doctor is required to annotate in the medical documentation only that he refrains from the performance, and justify the reason for his decision. Despite the literal wording, the Marshal ascertained that the law contained in Article 39 of the Act on Professions of Doctor and Dentist does not oblige the doctor to justify his belief, because it "is individual and autonomous". (…)

2.5. The party of the proceeding emphasised that the doctor's obligation of prior notification of his superior in writing is purely informational. It should allow the superior to assess, why the doctor did not perform the specific service and confirm that it was not for any other reason (such as lack of the doctor's knowledge or lack of medical devices necessary for the performance of the service). (…)

3.1. Referring to the principal control pattern indicated by the Supreme Medical Council, i.e. Article 53 para. 1. of the Constitution, the Public Prosecutor General pointed out that: "freedom of conscience and religion" is a concept binding, existing and accepted in international terminology, though differently understood. Undoubtedly it is the freedom inherently associated with the human person, and inalienable. The freedom of thought, conscience and religion is a personal right of each individual, and therefore the State has the obligation to ensure every citizen protection in that regard. The Public Prosecutor General called international acts, from which it follows that the freedom is fundamental, and the judgments of the European Tribunal of Human Rights (ETHR) confirming its importance in a democratic society. He distinguished two realms of freedom, which are protected: *forum internum* – the absolute right to create and have one's own opinions and views and *forum externum* – the right to express them, which is subject to certain restrictions. (…)

3.2. Referring to the first allegation of the Supreme Medical Council, the Public Prosecutor General (…) reckoned that in a democratic State the restriction of the doctor's freedom of conscience is necessary for the protection of privacy. As a consequence, the Public Prosecutor General stated that "the conscience clause is (…) a compromise solution, so that both doctors and patients may proceed in accordance with their consciences, and the price of that compromise is enduring certain difficulties or inconveniences by both parties"which gives no grounds to state a violation of the Constitution.

3.3. The applicant's second allegation, regarding the imposition on the doctor using the clause of conscience the duty of notification (the first sentence of Article 39 of the Act on Professions of Doctor and Dentist), according to the Public Prosecutor General, neither deserves consideration. (…)

3.4. Considering the third allegation of the Supreme Medical Council, concerning the unconstitutionality of the obligation of the doctor (working within the framework of an employment or service relationship) to inform his supervisor in writing about using the right to refuse a medical service (the second sentence of Article 39 of the Act on Professions of Doctor and Dentist), the Public Prosecutor General acknowledged that the required notification is prospective ("acts for the future") and generic. Such notification constitutes for the employer the basis to determine the range of health services, which may be included the contract with the National Health Fund and allows him to plan properly the work of employed doctors. According to the Public Prosecutor General, introducing the obligation to notify is therefore applied for the exercise of patients' rights and the formation of rational employment policy. Thus it is not tantamount to allowing the employer to collect data about doctors' beliefs, which makes the applicant's appeal groundless. (…)

3.5. The requirement to annotate the fact of refusal to provide a medical service and its justification by the doctor in the medical documentation (the first sentence of Article 39 of the Act on Professions of Doctor and Dentist), which is the subject of the applicant's fourth allegation, in the judgment of the Public Prosecutor General, is not only natural but also necessary, because it ensures that the conscientious objection will not be misused. The party of the proceeding emphasised that medical documentation constitute a guarantee of the patients' rights and interests in terms of the quality of treatment, and also grants the basis for the control of the process of providing medical services. The obligation to make an appropriate statement in the medical documentation does not mean that the doctor is obliged by the public authorities to disclose his worldview. That is why the introduction of that obligation cannot be considered as the violation the Article 53 para. 1. 7 of the Constitution.

4. The Minister of Health, in the letter of August 20, 2014, written at the request by the President of the Constitutional Tribunal, took the position that none of the applicant's allegations is justified, since the contested provision is compatible with the Constitution. The Minister of Health assumed that the "so-called conscience clause referred to in Article 39 of the Act, is not the same as the freedom of conscience and religion expressed in Article 53 para. 1. of the Constitution of the Republic of Poland", and consequently it is not a constitutionally protected right or freedom, but is an extension of the guarantee expressed in the Constitution.

(…)

III

The Constitutional Tribunal weighted the following:

(…)

2. Subject matter of the application and benchmarks of constitutional control.

In the application initiating the procedure in the adjudicated case, the SMC formulated four allegations, although the first of these was presented alternatively. Generally speaking, all allegations addressed one provision of the Act on Medical Profession, Article 39, which states: "The doctor may refrain from performing healthcare services contrary to his conscience, with reservation of Article 30, however, he is obliged to indicate real possibilities of obtaining this service from a different doctor or in a healthcare entity, as well as to substantiate and annotate this fact in the medical documentation. The doctor practicing his profession on the basis of employment relationship or within the framework of his service is obliged, furthermore, to inform his superior thereof in advance in writing". From the quoted provision, complemented, in accordance with its literal wording, with the content of Article 30 of the UMP, pursuant to which: "The doctor is obliged to provide medical assistance in every case, wherein delay in their provision could result in a danger for the patient's life, serious injury to his body or grave health disorder, as well as in other urgent cases", the SMC derives four legal norms contested in the application:

1) norm according to which the doctor is obliged to perform, against his conscience, a healthcare service, even though delay in its provision would not result in a danger for the patient's life, serious injury to his body or grave health disorder; this norm is accused by the SMC of violation of Article 2, Article 53 para. 1 and Article 65 para. 1 with relation to Article 30 and Article 31 para. 3 of the Constitution, as well as infringement of Article 18 para. 1 and 2 International Covenant on Civil and Political Rights, open for signature in New York on 19 December 1966 (Dz. U. z 1977 Nr 38, item 167; hereinafter: ICCPR),

2) norm, from which the obligation is derived for the doctor invoking the conscience clause to provide real possibilities to obtain the service in question from another doctor or healthcare entity; this norm is accused by the SMC of violation of Article 2, Article 53 para. 1, Article 65 para. 1 with relation to Article 30 and Article 31 para. 3 of the Constitution,

3) norm according to which the doctor practicing his profession on the basis of employment relationship or within the framework of his service is obliged to inform his superior of his refusal to provide healthcare services contrary to his conscience in advance in writing; this norm is accused by the SMC of violation of Article 53 para. 7 and Article 2, Article 53 para. 1 with relation to Article 31 para. 3 of the Constitution,

4) norm, from which the obligation is derived for the doctor invoking the conscience clause to annotate this fact in the medical documentation; this norm is accused by the SMC of violation of Article 53 para. 7 and Article 2, Article 53 para. 1 with relation to Article 31 para. 3 of the Constitution.

As follows from the above specification, allegations formulated by the SMC, although diverse to a certain extent, have their common, fundamental benchmark of constitutional control, which is Article 53 para. 1 of the Constitution, establishing freedom of conscience and religion. Due to the significance of this benchmark, the Tribunal assumed as purposeful to analyse, in a broader comparative legal perspective, the origin and contemporary normative content of the principle freedom of conscience.

3. Origin and contents of the principle of freedom of conscience and religion.

3.1. Freedom of conscience in the historical perspective.

Freedom of conscience and religion is in the modern world, and particularly in Europe, a fundamental principle, and, at the same time, a determining factor of a democratic state and society. Freedom to autonomously define one's attitude towards faith and religion, encompassing adoption and profession of philosophical and ideological beliefs of antireligious or non-religious nature, to reveal these thoughts and convictions and to act in accordance with their imperatives has established itself in the European civilisation as one of the main manifestations of individual freedom (see P. Winczorek, *Komentarz do Konstytucji Rzeczypospolitej Polskiej z dnia 2 kwietnia 1997 r.*, Warszawa 2000, s. 73).

In its first days, the idea of freedom of conscience was closely related with requests for religious tolerance and freedom of religion, it is, therefore, not surprising that it took shape against the background of ecclesiastical and political disputes of the Reformation. Its origin lies, however, deeper. The term "freedom of conscience" (*libertas conscientiae*) may be found in a work created much earlier "*De consolatione philosophiae*", written around 524 AD by a Roman lawyer and theologian Boethius (see J. Grzybowski, *Boecjusz, czyli posłannictwo filozofii. Analiza przemiany i duchowej drogi ku Dobru na podstawie De consolatione philosophiae*, "Warszawskie Studia Teologiczne" nr XX/2/2007, s. 95 and the following). The framework of this freedom was narrow and corresponded with what nowadays would be referred to as *forum internum* – internal freedom of thought, a domain, wherein, in accordance with the principle *de interis non iudicat praetor*, the judge does not decide.

In Middle Ages, freedom of conscience was transmitted into the domain of politics and feudal relations between the rulers. John of Salisbury already in the 12th century claimed that all of them, including the king, may request from their vassals submissiveness and obedience, with the exception of infringing a person's conscience and dignity (*salva indemnitate conscientiae et honestate* – see E. Schockenhoff, *Jaką pewność daje nam sumienie?*, Opole 2006, s. 13). Nonetheless, these opinions enjoyed only limited resonance and the medieval socio-political order failed to acknowledge neither political nor religious freedom of conscience. It was not, in any case, distinguished from respecting religious orders. To act against the latter was identified as acting against conscience. Only once in a while contrary opinions were voiced, an example thereof being the speech by Paweł Włodkowic, rector of the Cracow Academy, at the Council of Constance in 1415. Claiming that the choice of religion should be made in a conscious, rational manner for the entire life, he condemned the use of coercion against religious dissenters, gaining believers by military methods and war as a means of conversion and Christianisation.

Creation of the modern of feudal social structures as a consequence of religious wars waged in Europe in the 16th and 17th century. Freedom of conscience began to be perceived not in the categories of freedom to independently live one's life according to one's own conviction, but as a specific instrument for protection of religious minorities. The long way to the individualised freedom of conscience was marked with i.a. the peace of Augsburg (1555), in which, against the principle *cuius regio, eius religio*, private religious practices in the privacy of the household were accepted, the union of Utrecht (1579) or the peace of Westphalia (1648).

In Poland, a momentous breakthrough for the establishment of freedom of conscience and religious confession was the adoption of the Act of the Warsaw Confederation on 28 January 1573. It guaranteed "under the obligation of an oath, loss of faith, respect and conscience" religious tolerance in the Commonwealth and unconditional and eternal peace among the religions (*pax inter dissidentes in religione*). The Confederation became a laudable example of how the "jewel of freedom of conscience" may be protected in Europe, which was at that time overwhelmed with religious conflicts. Its provisions were further confirmed in the Henrician Articles and introduced in the parliamentary constitutions as a part of the binding law (see J. Bardach, B. Leśnodorski, M. Pietrzak, *Historia ustroju i prawa polskiego*, Warszawa 2005, s. 209–210).

During the Age of Enlightment, demands for ethical, political and legal autonomy of man enabled further enhancement of the scope of the discussed freedom, as well as its clear differentiation from religious freedom. Declaration of the Rights of Man and of the Citizen of 26 August 1789, taking inspiration from the ideals of the era and the doctrine of natural law, included in the list of "natural rights of man, inalienable and sacred", the right to religious freedom, stating that no-one may be disturbed for their opinions, including religious ones, if their manifestation fails to disturb the public order established by law (Article 10 of the Declaration). The Prussian Landrecht, as well as German constitutions preceding the Spring of Nations also asserted "freedom of religion and conscience" (see E. Schockenhoff, *Jaką pewność daje nam sumienie…*, s. 15).

Full "emancipation" of the freedom of conscience took place thanks to the liberal ideology that developed in the 19th century. It postulated to vest freedom of conscience and belief with the status of a public right, whose scope, in a religiously and ideologically neutral state could only be limited exceptionally and for important reasons. The liberal doctrine pointed to the necessity to juridise the right to freedom of conscience and belief. It demanded its acceptance as a constitutional right and guarantee of specific individual rights in positive law (see. M. Pietrzak, *Prawo wyznaniowe*, Warszawa 2005, s. 29–30).

3.2. The international standard.

3.2.1. The juridisation of freedom of conscience took place only after the 2nd World War together with the renaissance of the doctrine of natural law and fulfilment of the postulate related with the doctrine to create a catalogue of fundamental individual rights and freedoms. Freedom of conscience, together with freedom to profess a religion, related with the former, constitutes nowadays the universal standard and one of fundamental rights and freedoms of man and is expressed in numerous acts of international law (see for many: W. Sobczak, *Wolność myśli, sumienia i religii – poszukiwanie standardu europejskiego*, Toruń 2013, s. 183 and the following and M. Piechowiak, *Wolność religijna i dyskryminacja religijna – uwagi w kontekście rezolucji Parlamentu Europejskiego z 20 stycznia 2011 r.*, [w:] *Urzeczywistnianie wolności przekonań religijnych i praw z niej wynikających*, red. S. Stadniczeńko, S. Rabiej, Opole 2012, s. 107 i nast.).

3.2.2. According to Article 18 of the Universal Declaration of Human Rights of 10 December 1948 adopted by the United Nations, everyone enjoys the right to freedom of thought, conscience and religion; this right includes freedom to change one's religion or opinions, as well as freedom to manifest one's religion or one's opinions individually or in community with others, in public or private, by teaching, religious practices, professing the cult and rituals.

The ICCPR included, among the rights derived from the inherent dignity of the human person, the right to freedom of thought, conscience and religion. According to Article 18 para. 1 of the ICCPR, which constitutes one of control benchmarks in the present case, this right includes freedom to have or adopt a religion or belief of one's own choice and to manifest one's religion or belief either individually or in community with others and in public or private, in worship, observance, practice and teaching. At the same time, the ICCPR stipulated that no one shall be subject to coercion which would impair his freedom to have or to adopt a religion or belief of one's own choice (Article 18 para. 2). Freedom to manifest one's religion or belief may be subject only to such limitations as are prescribed by law and are necessary to protect public safety, order, health or morals or fundamental rights and freedoms of others (Article 18 para. 3 of the ICCPR).

3.2.3. Freedom of thought, conscience and religion is stated also by the Convention for the Protection of Human Rights and Fundamental Freedoms, signed in Rome on 4 November 1950 (Dz. U. z 1993 Nr 61, item 284, as amended; hereinafter: the Convention). According to Article 9 para. 1 of the Convention everyone has the right to freedom of thought, conscience and religion; this right includes freedom to change one's religion or belief and freedom to manifest one's religion or belief individually or in community with others, in public or private by worship, teaching, practice and rituals. Freedom to manifest one's religion or belief may be subject to only such limitations as are prescribed by law and necessary in a democratic society to protect public safety, order, health or morals or protection of rights and freedoms of others (Article 9 para. 2 of the Convention).

The significance and scope of freedom of thought, conscience and religion, according to of the Convention cannot be determined without taking into account the jurisprudence of the European Tribunal of Human Rights (hereinafter: the ETHR), whose decisions also lead to standardisation of its normative contents in each of the States Parties to the Convention. According to the established case law by the ETHR, freedom of conscience and religion, as understood in the Convention, forms "one of the foundations of a pluralistic democratic society". It is, in its religious dimension, one of the crucial elements forming the believers' identity and their idea of life, yet, it is also "a value for atheists, agnostics, sceptics and persons indifferent to faith" (see the judgement of 13 December 2001, Église métropolitaine de Bessarabie and others against Moldova, complaint no. 45701/99; all the rulings by ETHR are available in the HUDOC system at www.hudoc.echr.coe.int).

What is protected above all, is the sphere of individual personal and religious beliefs (the so-called internal forum), which are characterised by certain strength of conviction, seriousness, integrity and significance (see M.A. Nowicki, *Wokół Konwencji Europejskiej. Komentarz do Europejskiej Konwencji Praw Człowieka*, Warszawa 2013, s. 740 and the following.; ruling of 25 May 1993, Kokkinakis against Greece, complaint no. 14307/88 and the ruling of 6 November 2008, Förderkreis e.V. and others against Germany, complaint no. 58911/00). Independence in the spiritual domain, guaranteed by Article 9 para. 1 of the Convention, is subject to no limitations. In other words, everyone enjoys autonomy of thought, conscience and religion, which in practice translates as freedom to choose one's own system of values. It is different, however, with reference to manifestation (expression) of one's religion or beliefs. From Article 9 para. 2 of the Convention it follows that in a democratic society certain limitations may result necessary to reconcile the interests of different groups and ensure the respect for each individual's beliefs. Exercising its regulatory powers in this sphere, as well as in relations with different religions, cults and faiths, the state must remain neutral and impartial. It results from the obligation to preserve pluralism and to ensure proper functioning of democracy (see. M.A. Nowicki, *Wokół Konwencji Europejskiej. Komentarz…*, s. 740 and the following). This is the perspective, wherein the actions undertaken by the state which limit the discussed freedom are assessed for their lawfulness, necessity and advisability (see O. Nawrot, *Klauzula sumienia w zawodach medycznych w świetle standardów Rady Europy*, "Zeszyty Prawnicze Biura Analiz Sejmowych" nr 3/2012, s. 11 ant the following).

The individual right of "conscientious objection" was initially considered by the European Commission of Human Rights against the background of cases related with the refusal to perform military service, maintaining for a long time that this right is neither guaranteed by the Convention, nor by any of its protocols (see, e.g., decision of 6 December 1991, Tomi Autio against Finland, complaint no. 17086/90). This stance was changed with the judgement of 7 July 2011, Bayatyan against Armenia (complaint no. 23459/03), wherein the ETHR adopted, under the influence of transformation in European states and in the international scale that objection to military service, if motivated by a serious and insurmountable conflict between obligatory conscription and the conscience of a given person or one's deep and authentic religious or other beliefs, has sufficient persuasive power, seriousness, integrity and significance to be covered by the guarantees stipulated in Article 9 of the Convention.

In the opinion by the Great Chamber of the ETHR, imposition of a penalty on the plaintiff with relation to lack of statutory guarantees concerning conscientious objection, could not be accepted as proper in a democratic society, since the regulations failed to ensure appropriate balance between the interest of the society and the interest of the individual, whose objection was not motivated by his own comfort, but resulted from religious beliefs, professed and truly practiced by the plaintiff (member of the Jehovah's Witnesses community). Moreover, this penalty could not be considered as the only necessary means of solving conflicts as indicated by the experience from the majority of European states. This view has been upheld by the judgement issued on 10 January 2012 in case Bukharatyan against Armenia (complaint no. 37819/03).

3.2.4. Discussing international standards concerning protection of freedom of conscience in the context of the contested measure, one may not ignore resolution no. 1763 by the Parliamentary Assembly of the Council of Europe of 7 October 2010 regarding the right to conscientious objection within the framework of lawful medical care (hereinafter: CoE resolution of 7 October 2010). According to this resolution, no person, hospital or institution may be lawfully coerced, held liable or discriminated against for refusal to perform or to assist in a performance of termination of pregnancy, induction of miscarriage, euthanasia or any other act, which could result in a death of a human foetus or embryo for any reason. According to the CoE resolution of 7 October 2010, the responsibility to guarantee the respect for the freedom of thought, conscience and religion of healthcare professionals, and, at the same time, to provide the patients with access to legitimate healthcare services without unnecessary delay, is borne by the state. Because of the obligation of Member States to provide access to legitimate healthcare services and to ensure the right to medical care, as well as taking into account the obligation to respect the right to freedom of thought, conscience and religion of healthcare professionals, the Parliamentary Assembly encouraged the Member States of the Council of Europe to elaborate comprehensive and transparent solutions defining and regulating the right to conscientious objection with regard to health and healthcare services, which would: first, guarantee the right to conscientious objection against participation in the contested service; secondly, ensure that patients are informed of the refusal without unnecessary delay and referred to another healthcare provider; thirdly, ensure that patients receive appropriate treatment, especially in urgent cases (see J. Pawlikowski, *Prawo do sprzeciwu sumienia w ramach legalnej opieki medycznej. Rezolucja nr 1763 Zgromadzenia Parlamentarnego Rady Europy z dnia 7 października 2010 r.*, "Studia z Prawa Wyznaniowego"t. 14/2011, s. 313 i nast.).

Although the CoE resolution of 7 October 2010 has no binding power, it could not remain without significance for the considerations of the present case, as it establishes a universal standard of protection for medical care professionals (see O. Nawrot, *Klauzula sumienia w zawodach medycznych…*, s. 20–22). In the light thereof, the right to conscientious objection is determined in a particularly broad manner both objectively and subjectively, for it encompasses also other subjects providing medical services rather than only natural persons.

One must also note that the CoE resolution of 7 October 2010 is a natural consequence of the position by the Parliamentary Assembly of the Council of Europe, adopted already in the 60ties of the 20th century, which in the resolution no. 337 of 1967 with regard to the right to conscientious objection, as well as in the recommendation no. 478 of 1967 with regard to the right to conscientious objection stated that the possibility to refer to a conscience clause constitutes one of human rights.

3.3. Other legislations.

3.3.1. Guarantees for the freedom of conscience and religion, as fundamental individual freedoms, are included in most post-war European constitutions (see for many to be discussed M. Safjan, *Wolność religijna w konstytucjach państw europejskich*, [w:] *Kultura i prawo, tom 3. Religia i wolność religijna w Unii Europejskiej. Materiały III Międzynarodowej konferencji na temat "Religia i wolność religijna w Unii Europejskiej", Warszawa 2–4 września 2002 r.*, red. J. Krukowski, O. Theisen, Lublin 2003, p. 44 ff; J. Waszczuk-Napiórkowska, *Opinia prawna dotycząca wolności sumienia w konstytucjach krajów Unii Europejskiej*, "Zeszyty Prawnicze Biura Analiz Sejmowych" nr 3/2012, p. 231 ff). In all states, freedom of conscience does not mean only the right to have a given worldview, but above all the right to act in accordance with one's conscience and freedom from coercion to act against it. In most states, the issue of conscientious objection has been regulated by the law (particularly with reference to members of medical professions, soldiers and journalists).

Protection of freedom of conscience and belief may be considered a classical and relatively uniformly established element of contemporary constitutional systems. The particular standing of the freedom of conscience is influenced by the well-grounded conviction that it forms an indispensable component of values constituting the idea of dignity of the human person. This circumstance additionally favours harmonisation of fundamental principles and constitutional values of most European states rooted in the Christian culture they share (see M. Safjan, *Wolność religijna w konstytucjach*..., s. 44 i nast.).

Universally accepted is the principle that everyone has the inalienable right to independently determine his own religious, antireligious or indifferent approach. Freedom encompassing one's image of what is divine and transcendent, may not be disturbed or infringed by the state, therefore, coercion by the state regarding persuasion to profess a determined worldview or to dissuade from it is out of question (see W. Johann, B. Lewaszkiewicz-Petrykowska, *Wolność sumienia i wyznania w orzecznictwie konstytucyjnym – status jednostki*, [w:] *Wolność sumienia i wyznania w orzecznictwie konstytucyjnym*, XI Conference of European Constitutional Courts, Bulletin of the Constitutional Tribunal, special edition, Warszawa 1999, s. 15 and the following).

In European constitutional systems, in a similar manner the premises for limitation of the scope of freedom of conscience and religion are determined. These are public safety and order, health, public morals, as well as rights and freedoms of others. Possible limitations must, however, result from the Constitution itself, constituting a specific remedy against collision with other constitutional rights (see W. Johann, B. Lewaszkiewicz-Petrykowska, *Wolność sumienia i wyznania w orzecznictwie konstytucyjnym*..., s. 17).

The intimate sphere of individual conscience is treated as a reflection of the universal idea of dignity of the human person. As stated by the Italian Constitutional

Court: "it is, therefore, impossible to provide complete and effective protection of inviolable human rights without having guaranteed the mutually related constitutional protection of one's intimate and privileged relation with oneself" (ruling by the Constitutional Court of the Republic of Italy of 16 December 1991, C. Cost. 467/1991, after: J. Waszczuk-Napiórkowska, *Opinia prawna na temat klauzuli sumienia lekarzy, farmaceutów oraz pielęgniarek w prawie włoskim*, "Zeszyty Prawnicze Biura Analiz Sejmowych" nr 3/2012, s. 259). From this point of view, the conscience clause "may be considered a constitutionally guaranteed human right, which results from the directly applicable provision of the Constitution, forming the foundation od freedom of conscience, understood as freedom to live and act according to one's own beliefs, as long as these are not contrary to constitutional principles" (ruling by the Constitutional Court of the Republic of Italy of 2 October 1979, N. 117, C. Cost. 117/1979, after: J. Waszczuk-Napiórkowska, *Opinia prawna na temat klauzuli sumienia lekarzy*..., s. 259).

The French Constitutional Council also relied on a strong constitutional foundation of freedom of conscience (and, in consequence, also of the conscience clause), referring, in this respect, to Article 10 of the Declaration of the Rights of Man and of the Citizen and the Article 5 of the preamble to the Constitution from 1946, pursuant to which no one may be disadvantaged in his work for reasons of origin, opinions or beliefs (see decision by the Constitutional Council of 27 June 2001, no. 2001-446).

Conscience clause, approached as a right of fundamental nature, whose limitation may only take place exceptionally, was supported by the Spanish Constitutional Court, which declared unconstitutional the bill on abortion failing to acknowledge the possibility to refer to conscience clause by doctors and health care professionals (see W. Johann, B. Lewaszkiewicz-Petrykowska, *Wolność sumienia i wyznania w orzecznictwie konstytucyjnym*..., s. 21). Although freedom of conscience has not been *expressis verbis* stated in the Spanish constitution from 1978, this freedom is related with dignity of the human person and the "ideological" freedom specified in Article 16 of the Spanish Basic Law. Furthermore, what should be noted, is explicit constitutionalisation of conscience clause as one of possible reasons to refuse military service (see J. Waszczuk-Napiórkowska, *Opinia prawna dotycząca wolności sumienia w konstytucjach*..., s. 244). An analogous stance was taken by the German legislator, stating in Article 4 of the Basic Law the integrity of freedom of religion, conscience, religious and philosophical beliefs, as well as prohibition to coerce anyone, against his conscience, to perform armed military service. A similar solution may be found also in Article 15 para. 3 of the Charter of Fundamental Rights and Freedoms of the Czech Republic and in Article 41 para. 6 of the Portuguese constitution.

Reference to conscience clause may occur in various situations. Although initially it was used to solve the conflict of conscience related with the performance of the citizen's obligatory military service, nowadays its practical significance has expanded to include the performance or certain medical interventions, particularly termination of pregnancy, but also artificial insemination, sterilisation or assisted suicide.

3.3.2. Most European legal systems provide for the possibility of refusal to perform a medical treatment. The differences among these regulations regard both the objective and subjective scope of this law.

First, one may indicate legislative systems, where this right is enjoyed only by doctors (i.a. Latvia and Swiss cantons of Zurich and Solothurn) or encompasses a broader circle of professionals i.e. nurses, midwives, members of auxiliary medical staff (i.a. Austria, Belgium, France, Spain, the Netherlands, Luxembourg, Slovakia, Great Britain, Italy and Swiss cantons of Aargau, Appenzell, Bern, Freiburg and Luzern). The possibly broadest subjective scope was adopted in German act of 27 July 1992 on avoiding and overcoming conflicts related with pregnancy, which states that no one is obliged to collaborate with the pregnancy termination procedure, as well as in Belgian act of 28 May 2002 on euthanasia, which in Article 14 reserves that no one is obliged to participate in euthanasia.

Secondly, from the objective point of view, in some states conscience clauses are of a general nature, that is, they are related to all kinds of medical procedures m (as i.a. in France, Spain, Italy and Luxembourg). Other states introduced regulations related with specific kinds of medical procedures, such as abortion (i.a. Austria, Germany, Belgium, France, Spain, the Netherlands, Luxembourg, Latvia, Great Britain, Italy), operations performed on human embryos (i.a. Austria, Germany, France), artificial insemination procedures (Great Britain, Italy), euthanasia (Belgium), assisted suicide (the Netherlands, Luxembourg) or sterilisation for contraceptive reasons (France). In practice, however, these "type-based" conscience clauses may become subject to a broadening interpretation. For instance, in Germany, the right of refusal is also enjoyed by a doctor responsible for issuing an opinion, whether the premises for permissibility of abortion stipulated in § 218a para. 2 and 3 of the German penal code are met, even if he would not perform the procedure himself (see *Zur Ausübung des Rechts, die Mitwirkung an einem Schwangerschaftsabbruch zu verweigern* – Guideline of the German Association of Gynaecology and Obstetrics and the Association of Medical Law of 2010). Also in Italy refusal of abortion is not limited to the procedure itself, but includes actions directly aiming at the termination of pregnancy.

As concerns reasons for refusal to perform a medical procedure, certain legal systems confer the right of refusal regardless of the reason (Belgium, Latvia,

Austria, Germany; specific clauses exist also in France and Luxembourg), or speak of personal or medical reasons (general clauses in France and Luxembourg), technical and scientific convictions (Italy), medical opinions (i.a. Swiss cantons of Aargau, Appenzell, Bern, Freiburg, Luzern) or indicate that these reasons must be of an important nature (i.a. Austria, Germany, Swiss cantons of Zurich and Solothurn). In certain legislations, the premise of the conflict of conscience is expressed in a direct manner (Spain, the Netherlands, Slovakia, Great Britain, Italy, Swiss cantons of Aargau, Bern, Freiburg) or ethical reasons are invoked (i.a. Swiss cantons of Appenzell and Luzern).

In a number of European legal systems, there have been introduced certain conditions that must be met in case of refusal to provide healthcare services. This might be the obligation to inform of the refusal within a given period of time (e.g., "without delay", "in due time", "within 24 hours", "during the first visit"), the obligation to annotate the fact in the medical documentation (e.g., with reference to refusal to perform the procedure of euthanasia for medical reasons in Belgium), the obligation to transfer the documentation to another doctor in order to provide the continuity of medical care or the obligation to submit a written statement thereof.

Some of the European legislative systems, with respect to the principle *salus aegroti suprema lex*, treat the danger to human life or health as a premise for the limitation of the right to conscientious objection. Such solution was adopted e.g. by the French Public Health Code, wherein the right of refusal to provide medical care for professional or personal reasons may not be invoked in cases which are urgent or when the doctor's activity constitutes his "human obligation". An analogous solution is envisaged in Article 67 of the Luxembourgish Code of Medical Ethics.

According to the German Act on Avoiding and Overcoming Conflicts Related With Pregnancy, the possibility of refusal to perform an abortion is only excluded in case of a sudden and impossible to delay in any other manner (from the medical perspective) danger to life or serious threat to the woman's health. The right of refusal to perform an abortion is, however, not excluded, if, despite a "crisis situation", the procedure may be performed by a different person, without the participation of the doctor, who raised his objection. The German Federal Constitutional Tribunal created its own definition of a "decision of conscience" as: "any serious decision based on the categories of good and evil, taken by an individual in a particular situation, which the individual considers indispensable and binding, so that any action contrary to this decision would result in a serious psychological discomfort" (E. Tuora-Schwierskott, *Pojęcie sumienia w doktrynie konstytucjonalistów niemieckich w świetle ochrony prawnej wolności sumienia i religii*, "Państwo i Prawo" z. 8/2014, s. 96). Also the representatives of the German doctrine of constitutional law assume that the state shall create for the man a possibility to choose in order to prevent him from being exposed to conflicts of conscience. Its duty is only to establish the necessary ethical minimum, and not to establish the contents of freedom of conscience; "legal order shall be shaped in such a manner so that the individual may act in accordance with the criteria of conduct of his own choice" (E. Tuora-Schwierskott, *Pojęcie* ..., s. 95).

A regulation of a similar nature to the German one is included in § 97 para. 2 of the Austrian Penal Code, pursuant to which no doctor is obliged to perform a procedure of termination of pregnancy or to collaborate in such procedure, unless the procedure is necessary to save the life of the pregnant woman, without the possibility of delay, from the direct danger to her life, which is impossible to be averted otherwise.

Pursuant to the Italian Act no. 194 of 22 May 1978 on protection of maternity and termination of pregnancy, the statement including/of refusal to perform actions related with termination of pregnancy for religious or moral reasons may not be invoked by a healthcare professional or a member of auxiliary medical staff, as long as special circumstances occur, which render their intervention indispensable to save the life of a woman facing direct danger.

4. Freedom of conscience and religion in the Constitution of the Republic of Poland.

4.1. The position of freedom of conscience in Polish constitutional system.

4.1.1. Freedom of conscience and religion enjoys in the Republic of Poland a strong basis, not only in the acts of international law discussed above, but also in the provisions of the Constitution. Already the preamble to the Constitution contains a reference to conscience, speaking of "[each citizen's] feeling of responsibility before God or before one's own conscience". In Article 25 para. 2 of the Constitution, located in its first chapter, the legislator decided that "Public authorities of the Republic of Poland maintain impartiality with respect to religious, ideological and philosophical beliefs, guaranteeing their freedom of manifestation in the public life". The legal significance of conscience is also emphasised, apart from the regulations which are control benchmarks in the present case, in Article 85 para. 3 of the Constitution (which introduces the right to refuse the performance of military service as a result of religious beliefs or moral principles one professes), Article 48 para. 1 of the Constitution (regarding the right of the parents to upbringing their children in accordance with their own beliefs), as well as in Article 233 para. 1 of the Constitution (which prohibits the limitation of this freedom under martial law or state of emergency).

Doubtless, however, of essential importance to determine the form of the freedom occupying the central place in the investigated question is Article 53 of the Constitution. Freedom of conscience, traditionally quoted together with the freedom of religion, and in Article 53 para. 1 of the Constitution together with the freedom of religion enjoys a special standing among the rights and freedoms of man. For certain authors, the position of freedom of conscience and religion results above all from its chronological antecedence and substantial significance. They assume that "from the human rights perspective, freedom of conscience and religion is chronologically the first, indeed a rudimentary freedom, crucial for the entire system of rights and freedoms" (see J. Szymanek, *Wolność sumienia i wyznania w* of the Constitution *RP*, "Przegląd Sejmowy" nr 2/2006, s. 39). It is a freedom immanent for the very nature of man, therefore, it is described as inherent, and, thus, inalienable. Freedom of conscience, itself being a fundamental human right, is at the same time the source of numerous other rights and freedoms, a unique "right of rights". The aforementioned results from the personalistic notion of rights and freedoms in the Constitution, as evidenced by its numerous provisions (see J. Szymanek, *Wolność sumienia i wyznania…*, s. 41, 42). Other authors, who do not vest freedom of conscience and religion with such an importance, link it, nonetheless, directly with the notion of human dignity specified in Article 30 of the Constitution, being the source of freedoms and rights. Dignity of man expresses itself i.a. in his inborn (immanent) search and experience of certain transcendent values, to which a clear reference is made in the preamble to the Constitution, establishing thereby a basis for the acknowledgement of freedoms listed in Article 53 of the Constitution (see. P. Sarnecki, commentary to Article 53 of the Constitution, [w:] *Konstytucja Rzeczypospolitej Polskiej. Komentarz, t. 3,* red. L. Garlicki, Warszawa 2003, pt. 4, s. 2). As concerns freedom of religion, the Tribunal declared that it is "not only an individual freedom of personal nature, but also a founding principle of the political system, which correspondingly increases the significance of this freedom" (see judgement of 10 December 2014, sygn. K 52/13, OTK ZU nr 11/A/2014, item 118, part III, pt. 5.2 of the substantiation).

4.1.2. The Polish legislator decidedly abandoned the idea of granting protection, guarantees or tolerance for freedom conscience and belief. Such approach would assume the existence of a certain authority entitled to determine the scope of protection or tolerance, whereas the discussed freedom is considered extra-positive, axiologically related with the very nature of man, a fundamental element of his dignity. As a consequence, a legal system which would fail to guarantee this freedom, "would be *ab initio* incomplete, ineffective and inefficient, and thereby also undemocratic, as it would diverge from the model of state respecting the necessary *minimum minimorum* within the scope of human rights protection" (J. Szymanek, *Wolność sumienia i wyznania…*, s. 39). The necessity to respect it is closely related with respect and protection of human dignity, which constitutes an obligation for public authorities.

The Tribunal in its case law assumes that human dignity is "an axiological foundation and premise for the entire constitutional system", it is a value "of vital importance for the establishment of axiology for the present constitutional regulations" (see M. Granat, *Godność człowieka z Article 30* of the Constitution *RP jako wartość i jako norma prawna*, "Państwo i Prawo" z. 8/2014, s. 3 and the following, as well as quoted by the author rulings by the CT of: 9 July 2009, sygn. SK 48/05, OTK ZU nr 7/A/2009, item 108 and of 30 September 2008, sygn. K 44/07, OTK ZU nr 7/A/2008, item 126). At the same time, the Tribunal acknowledges the connection between human dignity and specific rights or freedoms and generally assumes that their infringement "has its impact on human dignity" (M. Granat, *Godność …*, s. 9). Article 30 of the Constitution is almost never referred to on its own as a control benchmark, but is usually linked with the provision stating a particular freedom or right. Although the subjects initiating constitutional control usually use the same arguments to justify the infringement of a particular freedom or right and dignity, the Tribunal in numerous rulings accumulates control benchmarks, treating dignity as a model, which accompanies the charge of infringement of another right.

4.2. Normative contents of freedom of conscience.

4.2.1. Since, in the present case, the constitutional control benchmark was undoubtedly this part of the provision of Article 53 para. 1 of the Constitution, which refers to freedom of conscience, it would be unnecessary to engage in a deeper deliberation over the significance of replacement by the Polish legislator of the traditional formula "freedom of conscience and religious confession" with the formula "freedom of conscience and religion". The Tribunal is relieved from the obligation to analyse, if the statement included in Article 53 para. 1 of the Constitution is in its content identical to the one adopted in the Act of 17 March 1921 – Constitution of the Republic of Poland (Dz. U. Nr 44, item 267, as amended) as well as acts of international law. What draws attention, however, is that according to certain authors, since "freedom of religious confession" becomes replaced with "freedom of religion", the semantic capacity of the first of freedoms listed in Article 53 para. 1 of the Constitution is enhanced, for "freedom of conscience" must now encompass also freedom not to profess any religion, which, what is not disputed, is guaranteed at the same level as freedom to profess any faith. Invoking freedom of conscience, one may "exercise not only « freedom to religion » in its constitutional meaning, but also « freedom from religion »" (P. Winczorek, *Wolność wyznaniowa,* "Państwo i Prawo" z. 4/2015, s. 7). What follows, is that the idea of conscience in the Constitution is it its essence separated from religion. The orders of conscience may thus result from various systems of values. A closer analysis of this question clearly confirms this observation.

4.2.2. The idea of "conscience" appeared for the first time in Christian ethics. It dates back to Saint Jerome, who, in 4th century, began to use the notion of *synderesis* meaning inherent human ability to distinguish between good and evil. For Saint Thomas Aquinas, *"con-scientia"* ("with-knowledge"), that is, conscience, is the ability to intellectually evaluate one's own deeds as good or evil. The basis for this ability is the mind, which enables to distinguish between good and evil at the level of particular actions. In spite of its undoubtedly "Christian origin", conscience, as a philosophical category, in its further historical development separated from its roots and entered the canon of ideas considered important in isolation from theological theories. By 18th century philosophers it was considered an element of moral sense, wherewith each human being is equipped from the moment of birth; conscience is not the voice of god, but of nature. David Hume, in his *Treatise of Human Nature,* claimed that the source of a man's moral convictions are his emotions, not the reason. "Conscientious objection" is an emotional rebellion against the binding standards of behaviour. 19th century thinkers questioned the inherent human ability to distinguish between good and evil; they derived it rather from education and, more precisely, from the pressure exerted by the pedagogue (James and John Stuart Mill, Aleksander Bain). The 20th century brought the modification of that image, indicating the society as the source of pressure exerted on the individual and, as a consequence, shaping one's (Emil Durkheim). For Sigmund Freud, conscience was a disposition to assess oneself according to the criteria imposed under the pressure of "culture", especially self-condemnation and self-torment. "Conscientious objection" is a signal that norms, which the social environment intends to "imprint" in the thoughts and actions of the individual, are incoherent (see A. Szostek, *Kategoria sumienia w etyce,* [w:] *Sprzeciw sumienia w praktyce medycznej – aspekty etyczne i prawne,* red. P. Stanisz, J. Pawlikowski, M. Ordon, Lublin 2014, s 15 i nast.; W. Chańska, *Klauzula sumienia jako wyraz moralnego kompromisu,* "Prawo i Medycyna" nr 3–4/2013, s. 31–33). The cited opinions concerning conscience prove that this category "separated from its Christian roots already long ago and became a thoroughly secular idea" (W. Chańska, *Klauzula…,* s. 33).

4.2.3. "Conscience" is not subject to legal definition. Notably, in most Indo-European languages the intellectual etymology of the Polish term "conscience" is preserved, i.e. the reference to with-knowledge "*con-scientia*" has been maintained (see.A. Szostek, *Kategoria sumienia w etyce…*, s. 19). Nowadays, the foundation to establish the scope of this notion is provided by the results of analyses in other areas of knowledge, especially philosophy (ethics), anthropology, psychology and theology, therefore, it is necessary to acknowledge the necessity to define "freedom of conscience" separately from "freedom of religion". According to one of the views presented in contemporary German science, conscience is shaped in social communication and constitutes the basis to form coexistence in the society, in isolation from religious and philosophical values (see E. Tuora-Schwierskott, *Pojęcie…*, s. 94). In P. Winczorek's opinion, the notion of conscience may refer to "opinions and actions whose scope extends beyond the religious dimension, in particular to opinions of non-religious or anti-religious nature" (P. Winczorek, *Wolność…*, s. 7). Conscience constitutes an imperative to act according to such values as "good" and "evil", "truth" or "false", the choice of which is considered as binding and unconditionally obligatory, providing for the true development of human personality, constituting at the same time the basic structure of his psycho-social personality. According to *Słownika języka polskiego* (red. M. Szymczak, Warszawa 1995) conscience is: "psychological attribute, ability to appropriately assess one's own actions as consistent or inconsistent with the adopted ethical norms". Conscience as the attribute of individual sovereinty is, therefore, speaking in the most general terms, moral consciousness and ability to "pass judgement concerning the moral value of human actions, in particular the subject's own behaviour" (K. Kosior, *Sumienie*, [w:] *Mała encyklopedia filozofii: pojęcia, problemy, kierunki, szkoły*, red. S. Jedynak, Bydgoszcz 1996, s. 448–449). According to P. Winczorek "conscience may be understood as the ability of a person to experience moral orders to behave in a particular manner not only in relations with others, but also with oneself" (P. Winczorek, *Wolność…*, s. 7). According to B. Chyrowicz, "conscience is moral self-consciousness of man". Since it directly concerns his moral autonomy, "protection of the autonomy of conscience is, in its essence, protection of our moral identity" (B. Chyrowicz, *Moralna autonomia i klauzula sumienia,* „Medycyna Praktyczna" nr 1/2014, s. 120).

As observed by the Tribunal in its decision of 15 January 1991 (sygn. U 8/90, OTK w 1991, item 8), freedom of conscience does not solely mean the right to represent a particular worldview, but, above all, the right to act in accordance with one's conscience, to freedom from coercion to act against one's conscience. The institution guarding this freedom is the so-called conscience clause, understood as the possibility not to perform an action being one's lawful duty, which is at the same time contrary to one's worldview (ideological or religious beliefs) of a given person. In its ethical dimension, this construct may prove the primacy of conscience over the requirements of the stature law, while on the juridical level it ensures the exercise of freedom of conscience and eliminates the collision between the norms of the statute law with ethical norms norm, thus providing the individual with a possibility to act fair, in consistence with one's beliefs.

4.2.4. What has been hitherto established, substantiates the thesis that although we do not dispose of a legal definition, it is possible to indicate conditions necessary to speak of respect of freedom of conscience by the legal system. On the one hand, it is the guarantee of one's freedom to adopt a set of moral, philosophical, religious and social opinions and rules and to act in accordance with them; coercion to undertake actions contrary to one's conscience would constitute an infringement of inalienable human dignity. On the other hand, the condition to exercise freedom of conscience is a guarantee that no one will coerce others to be subject to orders, which, in their conscience, each of these persons considers as binding. What is indicated in the discussion about conscience clause, is the danger related with the discrepancy of assessments; the same behaviour may be judged differently by different subjects depending on the manner according to which their conscience is shaped. Although in a democratic state the axiology of the Constitution, and consequently of the entire legal system should by definition correspond with values accepted by the citizens (the law is, after all, made by their representatives), it is obvious that discrepancies within this scope will take place. If we assume that, in ace of conflict, conscience clause allows to refrain from undertaking actions expected by the legal system, this may result in infringement of the law and chaos. Therefore, it is argued that "(…) judgements and actions resulting from them based on conscience may not aspire to be considered as universal moral truths"; not every invocation of conscience is morally justified and not every action dictated by conscience may lawfully be accepted (see W. Chańska, *Klauzula…*, s. 35).

Aware of the problems related with the determination of consequences of freedom of conscience, in particular the danger related with acceptance of relativism in the domain of ethics, which could be the consequence of the subjective nature of conscience, the Tribunal indicates that the subject matter of the present case did not require a general statement with reference to these questions. What mattered in the case, was, however, the scope of use of the conscience clause by doctors, whose legal status enables the elimination of numerous uncertainties and the limitation of the risk of subjectivism.

4.3. Freedom of conscience, the legal status of doctors and their fundamental obligations.

4.3.1. Legal status of a doctor is shaped by a number of legal acts, of which the most important ones are the Acts of Parliament: Medical Profession Act and Act on Medical Activity of 15 April 2011 (Dz. U. z 2015 item 618, as amended; hereinafter: Act on Medical Activity or AMA). The first of these acts in Article 2 para. 1 states as follows: "Practice of the medical profession consists of providing (…) healthcare services, in particular: examination of the health condition, identification and prevention of illnesses, treatment and rehabilitation of patients, providing medical advice, as well as issuing of medical opinions and judgements"; in Article 2 para. 3 the Act envisages also practice of the profession in the form of conducting research, teaching the medical profession or managing a healthcare entity. Pursuant to Article 4 of AMP: "Doctor is obliged to practice his profession according to the current medical standards, methods and means of prevention, diagnose and treatment of illnesses being at his disposal, in accordance with the principles of professional ethics and on the basis of best efforts". According to Article 30 of AMP, opening chapter 5 of AMP regulating "rules for the practice of medical profession": "The doctor is obliged to provide medical assistance in any case, wherein the delay in their provision could result in a danger for the patient's life, serious injury to his body or grave health disorder as well as in other urgent cases". Article 38 para. 1 of AMP stipulates the conditions for the doctor to refrain from treatment or to withdraw from treating the patient. Whereas Article 15 of AMA states that: "The healthcare entity may not refuse to provide healthcare service to a person requiring immediate provision of such service due to danger to life or health". The last two provisions, referring to the doctor and the healthcare entity, impose statutory obligations, the fulfilment of which is independent from the existence of any other obligation (whether of contractual or administrative nature) towards a specific person in need. Infringement of the obligation to provide assistance by a doctor or failure to provide a healthcare service by a hospital to a person in a situation of danger to life or health involves liability (in the doctor's case even criminal liability, see M. Nesterowicz, N. Karczewska-Kamińska, *Prawa pacjenta w kontekście odmowy udzielenia świadczeń medycznych przez lekarza lub szpital (w związku z klauzulą sumienia)*, [w:] *Sprzeciw sumienia…*, s. 118). Correlated with the provisions establishing obligations of doctors and healthcare entities is Article 7 para. 1 of the Act of 6 November 2008 on Patients' Rights and Patient Rights Ombudsman (Dz. U. z 2012 item 159, as amended; hereinafter: PRA), which states the following: "The patient has right to immediate provision of healthcare services danger to life or health".

The Tribunal draws attention to the difference in the description of obligations conferred on the doctor and the healthcare entity. The Medical Profession Act does not burden the doctor *ex lege* with the obligation to perform healthcare services, although the practice of this profession may include the performance of such services (Article 2 para. 1 of AMP). The doctor's obligation involves "providing medical assistance" (Article 30 of AMP, correspondingly, Article 38 of AMP refers to failure to undertake treatment or withdrawal from treatment), whereas the hospital's obligation is to "provide healthcare services" (Article 15 of AMA). Also the patient's right refers to "healthcare service" (Article 7 PRA). It must be emphasised that, despite the broad scope of the notion of "healthcare service", defined in Article 2 para. 1 pt. 10 of AMA, the scope of statutory obligation binding the healthcare entity, as well as the right of the patient is clearly limited to situations, where immediate medical intervention is necessary with relation to danger to life or health.

4.3.2. From the perspective of the subject matter of the present case, it is necessary to note that doctors, as representatives of a liberal profession, are bound not only with the norms of universally binding law, which stipulates the principles for practicing their profession, but also corporative norms, adopted by them as a professional association and obliging themselves to comply with these norms. Doctors represent a profession, whose principles of ethics have been "codified", before all other codes or constitutions were created. The search for the ethical origins of morality and the unique ethos of the medical profession is attested by the content of the so-called Hippocratic Oath, attributed to the father of medicine. In his personal dimension, the doctor obliged himself to "maintain his life and his art unspoilt". In the fragment devoted to the relations with the patient the oath obliged the doctor to use medical procedures according to his ability and judgement for the benefit of the patients, protecting them from harm and injury. The contents of the oath leaves, furthermore, no doubts that the doctor's devotion is to protect life, from conception until death, for he obliged himself to "Neither will I administer a poison to anybody when asked to do so, nor will I suggest such a course. Similarly I will not give to a woman a pessary to cause abortion". Among the fundamental principles of medical ethics the oath listed also the obligation to maintain the secrecy of everything, what the doctor "shall see or hear in the course of my profession, as well as outside my profession in my intercourse with men, if it be what should not be published abroad, I will never divulge, holding such things to be holy secrets" (translation of the text of the "Hippocratic Oath" after: *Loeb Classical Library*. 147: 298–299. Polish translation: J. Gula, *Hipokrates a przerywanie ciąży*, [w:] *W imieniu dziecka poczętego*, red. J.W. Gałkowski, J. Gula, Rzym-Lublin 1991, s. 193 i nast.). These rules are listed in the so-called Hippocratic Oath, in a narrower or broader scope, are repeated in the contemporarily adopted legal acts, of different order and different binding force, whereas graduates of medical studies in the states of our cultural area before the award of the diploma, which entitles them to practice the medical profession take a pledge, the content of which is modelled after the Hippocratic Oath. In the Polish legal system, these rules are expressed in the Code of Medical Ethics (Resolution of 2nd Extraordinary National Medical Assembly of 14 December 1991, twice amended: in 1993 during 3rd National Medical Assembly and in 2003 during the 7th Extraordinary National Medical Assembly; hereinafter: the Code of Medical Ethics or CME). The Code of Medical Ethics, itself not constituting an act of the binding law, establishes a set of ethical norms independent of the law, which may be incorporated in the legal system and constitute binding norms of conduct for doctors (see ruling by the CT of 15 January 1991, sygn. U 8/90; see also decision by the CT of 7 October 1992, sygn. U 1/92, OTK w 1992, part 2, item 38).

According to Article 2 para. 1 of CME: "It is the doctor's vocation to protect human life and health, prevent illnesses, provide treatment to the ill and to bring relief for the suffering; the doctor may not apply his knowledge and medical skills for activities contrary to this vocation". Article 4 of CME states that: "In order to exercise his duties, the doctor shall maintain freedom of his professional activity, in accordance with his conscience and current medical standards". As can be easily noticed, the above quoted provisions of the Medical Profession Act clearly refer (even with their numbering) to the ethical principles adopted by the medical association. Also Article 30 of AMP has its prototype in the code of ethics, as Article 69 of CME states the following: "The doctor may not refuse to provide medical assistance in urgent cases (…)", while in Article 3 of CME it is stipulated that age, sex, race, genetic heritage, nationality, religion, social background, material situation, political opinions or other conditions may not constitute a reason to refuse assistance.

The Tribunal affirmed the fact of correspondence between the ethical principles adopted in the the Code of Medical Ethics and the doctors' obligations resulting from statutory regulations. The obligation to provide medical assistance, which results from Article 30 of AMP, together with the prohibition to refuse treatment or to withdraw therefrom, established in Article 38 para. 1 of AMP, are fully concordant with the provisions of the Code of Medical Ethics and express the so-called internal goals of medicine, which are derived from its very essence and decide of its ethos (see J. Pawlikowski, *Spór o klauzulę sumienia z perspektywy celów medycyny*, [w:] *Sprzeciw sumienia…*, s. 154–156). The

Tribunal concluded, furthermore, that Article 4 of AMP directly establishes the doctor's obligation to practice his profession in accordance with the principles of professional ethics, thereby making a reference to the Code of Medical Ethics, including its Article 4, which orders the doctors to practice their profession in accordance with their conscience. As a consequence, acting in accordance with one's conscience constitutes the doctor's statutory obligation.

4.3.3. From the analysis of provisions, which regulate the principles for practicing the medical profession it may be concluded that the fundamental obligations and ethical rules for Polish doctors are recognised and accepted by the medical circles. With relation to them arise none of the uncertainties indicated above which concern the excessively subjective nature of assessments, in particular the danger of moral relativism (see part III, pt. 4.2.4 of the substantiation). Every doctor in Poland solemnly vows to "serve human life and health" (medical oath, second indent). He undertakes the responsibility to fulfil this obligation according to the best standards of knowledge towards all patients, regardless of their race, religion, nationality, political opinions and material status, with the sole objective of their good and showing them the necessary respect (third indent). There is, thus, no room for moral relativism, as far as the fundamental commandment of medical ethics is concerned, which is the "protection of human life and health, prevention of illnesses, treatment of the ill and bringing relief to the suffering" (Article 2 para. 1 of CME). As observed in the literature, "conscientious objection by a doctor results more often from the Hippocratic ethical tradition than from religious beliefs" (J. Pawlikowski, *Prawo do wyrażania sprzeciwu sumienia przez personel medyczny – problemy etyczno-prawne*, „Prawo i Medycyna" nr 3/2009, s. 36, z odesłaniem do wypowiedzi J.K. Mason).

In view of the established facts, what shall be considered as definitely misleading, are the examples, quoted in the literature, of white doctors who refuse invoking the conscience clause, to provide healthcare services to dark-skinned patients (and vice versa), which are supposed to indicate the inadmissibility of making medical practices dependent on the conscience of persons who exercise this profession (see. W. Chańska, *Klauzula*..., s. 36). These examples, at least against the background of the Polish law, are unrealistic. The Tribunal declared that the conclusion by the Supreme Medical Council surely does not aim at granting the doctors the possibility to infringe upon the ethical rules expressed in the Code of Medical Ethics while invoking conscience clause. On the contrary, the applicant recalls these universally accepted rules in order to strengthen the arguments addressed against the contested provisions.

4.3.4. The source of ethical problems is, on the contrary, extension of the doctors' obligations beyond the fulfilment of the internal goals of medicine derived from the Code of Medical Ethics, and also from Article 30 and Article 38 of AMP, which, to use the expression from the Medical Profession Act, may be described as the obligation to provide medical assistance. This extension results from Article 2 para. 1 of AMP, which, describing wherein consists practicing the medical profession, points to the provision of "healthcare services" and not medical assistance. Standard medical activities are in the aforementioned provision listed as examples of healthcare services ("in particular"). According to the legal definition, found in Article 2 para. 1 pt. 10 of AMA, as a "healthcare service" one shall understand: "actions aimed at preserving, saving, restoring or improving health, as well as other medical activities resulting from the process of treatment or separate provisions regulating the rules of their application". The Tribunal concluded that the linguistic interpretation of this provision fails to indicate that the defined concept of healthcare service is extended beyond the medical goals. The legislator, applying in the final part of the provision the pronoun "their", imposes the assumption that "separate provisions" shall refer to the rules governing the performance of actions listed in the first part of the provision, thus, to medical activities. Despite such wording of the provision, it is widely assumed that "healthcare services" include also activities with non-curative purposes. What is more important, the legislator himself makes use of the broad meaning of this concept, listing, among healthcare services, activities whose purposes extend beyond "actions aimed at preserving, saving, restoring or improving health". A proof that the "separate provisions" exist, in the meaning of Article 2 para. 1 pt. 10 of AMA, is the Act of 27 August 2004 on Healthcare Services Financed from Public Funds (Dz. U. z 2015 item 581, as amended; hereinafter: Act on Healthcare Services), as well as implementing acts issued on the basis thereof by the Minister responsible for health, which, in the lists of the so-called guaranteed services, envisage also the financing of activities with non-curative purposes.

The Tribunal concluded that the subject matter of the application in the adjudicated case is exactly the margin of the doctors' professional activity, encompassing actions qualified in separate provisions as healthcare services, which, however, expand beyond the doctor's fundamental obligation, specified in Article 30 of AMP, which is to provide the patient with medical assistance. Although both the allegations raised in the application and the positions adopted by the participants in the procedure have been formulated in a general manner, as concerning all situations, wherein the doctor may refuse to provide medical services for reasons of conscientious objection, what can be clearly discerned in the background of the case, are the nowadays vividly discussed services related with human procreation, and in particular termination of pregnancy. While failing to refer to these questions, at the current stage of analysis, the Tribunal draws attention only to this aspect of the problem, which is directly related with the concerns of excessive subjectivism of the doctors' conscience. The Tribunal concluded, namely, that the maintenance of the fundamental moral imperative, obligatory for all doctors, i.e. the requirement to protect human life and health, leaves no freedom of action dictated by conscience of individual representatives of the profession. There is no room for moral relativism here. The problem is, however, the settlement of the fundamental anthropological question, i.e. the beginning of life (see. B. Chyrowicz, *Moralna autonomia…*, s. 121).

4.4. The primary nature of conscience clause with reference to doctors.

4.4.1. As heretofore established, in a democratic state based on the rule of law an expression of the right to act in accordance with one's conscience, and, in consequence, also an expression of freedom from coercion to act against one's conscience, is the conscience clause (see J. Pawlikowski, *Prawo do wyrażania sprzeciwu sumienia…*, s. 29). For freedom of conscience must manifest itself also in the possibility of refusal to perform an obligation imposed in accordance with the right to invoke one's scientific, religious or moral convictions. The view that the right to conscientious objection is grounded in freedom of conscience and religion expressed in Article 53 para. 1 of the Constitution, is shared almost universally in the doctrine (see m.in. K. Szczucki, *Klauzula sumienia – uwagi de lege lata i de lege ferenda*, „Studia Iuridica" nr 50/2009, s. 168–169; R. Kubiak, *Prawo medyczne*, Warszawa 2014, s. 155–156, M. Skwarzyński, *Sprzeciw sumienia w adwokaturze*, [w:] *Standardy bezstronności światopoglądowej władz publicznych*, red. A. Mezglewski, A. Tunia, Lublin 2013, s. 219; A. Zoll, *Charakter prawny klauzuli sumienia*, „Medycyna Praktyczna" nr 1/2014, s. 100–101). It is also shared by Rzecznik Praw Obywatelskich (see wystąpienie Rzecznika Praw Obywatelskich z 21 July 2014 skierowane do Ministra Zdrowia, nr I.812.8.2014. AM; hereinafter: pismo RPO z 21 July 2014). W. Johann and B. Lewaszkiewicz-Petrykowska state that "what guards this freedom [of conscience] is the right to invoke conscience clause and to refuse the performance of an action which is contrary to one's conscience. (…) It is impossible to effectively protect inalienable rights of man, without the protection of his conscience, as freedom of conscience constitutes a reflection of human dignity. Its protection is necessary to guarantee the essential content of certain fundamental rights, such as freedom to express one's ethical, philosophical or religious beliefs. (…) The possibility to invoke the conscience clause is considered a fundamental right, whose limitation may only take place as an absolute exception" (see W. Johann, B. Lewaszkiewicz-Petrykowska, *Wolność sumienia i wyznania w orzecznictwie konstytucyjnym…*,

p. 21). Individual freedom to invoke "conscience clause" guards, therefore, not only freedom of conscience, but also dignity of the human person, which is an inherent and inalienable right.

4.4.2. Nevertheless, what is presented in the doctrine, is also the opinion, which gives rise to the stance adopted by the Public Prosecutor General and the Minister of Health in the adjudicated case, pursuant to which the possibility to invoke conscience clause is an exceptional situation, and the contested Article 39 first sentence of AMP establishes only a doctors' "privilege" (see E. Dyttus, *Klauzula sumienia – przywilej lekarza, problem pacjenta*, [w:] *Lege artis: problemy prawa medycznego*, red. J. Haberko, R. D. Kocyłowski, B. Pawelczyk, Poznań 2008, p. 148; E. Zielińska, [w:] *Ustawa o zawodach lekarza i lekarza dentysty. Komentarz*, red. E. Zielińska, Warszawa 2008, p. 554; W. Brzozowski, *Uzewnętrznianie przynależności religijnej. Zagadnienia systemowe*, [w:] *Prawne granice wolności sumienia i wyznania*, red. R. Wieruszewski, M. Wyrzykowski, J. Kondratiewa-Bryzik, Warszawa 2012, s. 278 i nast.). The above view was also adopted in the position of the Bioethics Committee at the Presidium of Polish Academy of Sciences (PAN – Polska Akademia Nauk) nr 4/2013 of 12 November 2013 concerning the so-called conscience clause. Adoption of the above opinion would mean that the legislator enjoys full freedom to shape such "privilege" with reference to doctors.

4.4.3. In the view of the Tribunal, this opinion lies in apparent contradiction with the above quoted standards elaborated on the basis of acts of international law, as well as with the status, which is commonly attributed to freedom derived from Article 53 para. 1 of the Constitution. In their light thereof, the right to conscientious objection shall be considered a primary right with regard to its limitations. Such interpretation was, moreover, presented hereto in the case law of the Constitutional Tribunal, which had acknowledged the existence of conscience clause in the Polish legal system, with reference to doctors obliged to issue a statement of admissibility to terminate pregnancy and to perform the procedure of termination of pregnancy, already before it was officially codified in the primary level legislation (see the ruling of the TK z 15 January 1991, sygn. U 8/90; see. Also the decision by the CT of 7 October 1992, sygn. U 1/92). In the ruling of the Tribunal with the sygn. U 8/90, the existence of such clause with relations to doctors is derived both from Article 82 para. 1 of the Constitution z 1952 (guaranteeing the citizens freedom of conscience and religion), and from Article 18 of the ICCPR. In the light of the explanation provided by this decision, there remain no doubts that Article 39 of AMP does not create a privilege for the doctor, since freedom of conscience of every human being is a primary and inalienable category, which the constitutional law and international regulations only guarantee. Freedom of conscience, including conscientious objection, which is its element, must, therefore, be respected regardless of the existence of statutory provisions confirming it.

4.4.4. Against the presented view of the conscience clause as a general clause derived directly from the Constitution, on occasion the argument is raised, whose sense may be formed as the question why the right to conscientious objection, supposedly enjoyed by all subjects, is regulated with reference to doctors. The lack of appropriate legal framework for numerous other professions is supposed to prove that it is the act, and not the Constitution, which is the source of the doctors' privilege. Rejecting this allegation, the Tribunal stated that the legislator's decision to articulate the conscience clause in the act, which regulates the practice of medical profession, has its deep justification. It may not be denied that representatives of this profession are on the daily basis confronted with situations which require to take decisions, whose consequences may even lead to the patient's death. As was rightly observed: "Taking into account the nature of dilemmas resulting from the development of medical science and techniques, conflicts of conscience, to which the representatives of medical professions are exposed, appear as particularly crucial, for they touch upon the most fundamental values, also from the perspective of the state based on the rule of law" (O. Nawrot, *Prawa człowieka, sprzeciw sumienia i państwo prawa*, [w:] *Sprzeciw sumienia...*, s. 109). Apart from indicating the practical dimension of statutory regulation of conscience clause with reference to doctors, what must especially be emphasised, is the legal significance of this regulation. As indicated above (see pt. III, pt. 4.3.2 of the substantiation), acting in accordance with one's conscience is, in case of doctors is not only their exercise of a constitutional freedom and fulfilment of a moral duty, but a statutory obligation, derived from Article 4 of AMP with relation to Article 4 of CME. As a consequence, the doctor may find himself in his professional in a situation of conflict between two statutory obligations that bind him: on the one hand, the obligation to perform a healthcare service, on the other, acting in accordance with his conscience. This conflict is resolved by a specific regulation stipulated in Article 39 of AMP, thereby protecting the doctor from liability for the infringement of this obligation.

4.4.5. In conclusion, the Tribunal stated that the doctor's right to invoke the conscience clause within the domain of medical law stems not from Article 39 of AMP, but directly from the constitutional provisions and acts of international law. There is, therefore, no ground to formulate a separate right to "conscience clause", and, consequently, it is beyond doubt that the legislator cannot arbitrarily shape this "privilege" or to abolish it, but must respect the constitutional conditions for the introduction of limitations to freedoms and rights of man and of the citizen (Article 30 and Article 31 para. 3 of the Constitution).

The Tribunal decidedly rejected, therefore, the stance adopted by the Public Prosecutor General and the Minister of Health, supported by a few scientific works, whose authors assume that the possibility of refusal to provide a health-care service by a doctor constitutes a privilege of the latter. In the opinion of the Tribunal, the right of the doctor, as well as of any other person to refrain from actions contrary to one's conscience is derived directly from the freedom guaranteed by the Constitution, and thus, even without the regulation found in Article 39 of AMP, the doctor could refuse to perform a service invoking conscientious objection. However, the statutory obligation to act in accordance with his conscience rests upon the doctor; without Article 39 of AMP, the possibility to be relieved from this obligation would not be obvious.

4.5. Conclusions regarding constitutional control.

Before embarking on the constitutional assessment of the norms contested in the application by the SMC, the Tribunal found it useful to make a few initial assumptions with reference to all allegations in order to avoid repetition and to provide order in the further analysis. Thus, despite the discrepancy of views concerning the status of conscience clause discussed before (part III, pt. 4.4 of the substantiation), the Tribunal stated that the participants in the procedure do coincide in certain questions.

First, freedom of conscience, being the principal constitutional control benchmark in the adjudicated case, is perceived by all participants in the procedure as a fundamental freedom, grounded not only in the Constitution, but also in acts of international law.

Secondly, the participants in the procedure agree that the provisions of AMP contested in the application introduce limitations to the use of freedom of conscience by doctors.

Thirdly, all of them, it is assumed, accept limitations to this freedom. Furthermore, in the adjudicated case the problem of indication of the source for the clause limiting freedom of conscience generally fails to appear, although, in theory, two provisions could be considered here, i.e. Article 31 para. 3 of the Constitution and Article 53 para. 5 of the Constitution. The Tribunal draws attention to the fact that Article 53 of the Constitution consisting of 7 sections contains its own limitation clause, namely, in para. 5 it stipulates the conditions for an acceptable limitation to the "freedom to manifest one's religion". This provision to a large extent reiterates the content of Article 31 para. 3 of the Constitution. Nonetheless, it accepts limitation of freedom "on the one hand in a somewhat narrower scope than in Article 31 para. 3 (formal inadmissibility of limitations related with «environment protection» (…), and on the other hand, apparently broader, for example, through lack of necessity for proportionality of the introduced limitations or formal admissibility to destroy also the «nature» of these freedoms)" (P. Sarnecki, commentary to Article 53 of the Constitution, [w:] *Konstytucja…*, pt. 16, s. 9–10). In the adjudicated case, differently as it was in the case settled by the judgement by TK of 10 December 2014, sygn. K 52/13 (part III, pt. 7 of the substantiation), there arises no necessity to decide upon the relations of both quoted provisions, as their possible conflict may only be discussed with reference to limitations of freedom to manifest one's religion. In view of the unequivocal determination in Article 53 para. 5 of the Constitution of the scope of its use with reference to only one of two freedoms referred to in Article 53 para. 1 of the Constitution, i.e. freedom of religion (in its external aspect), it may hardly be assumed that this specific limitation clause refers also to freedom of conscience. In particular it must be emphasised that the applicant alleges the infringement of Article 53 para. 1 with relations to Article 31 para. 3 of the Constitution (and not Article 53 para. 5 of the Constitution). Freedom of conscience, according to all participants in the procedure, may be limited while maintaining the principle of proportionality expressed in Article 31 para. 3 of the Constitution. The applicant claims, however, that in a certain scope limitations are entirely inadmissible (Article 53 para. 7 of the Constitution). Nonetheless, among the control benchmarks indicated with relations to the third and fourth allegation, Article 31 para. 3 of the Constitution is also recalled, which, on the ground of Polish law, constitutes the basis for a proportionality test, indispensable for the assessment of constitutional admissibility of compromises introduced in the field of protection of freedoms and rights introduced by the legislator.

The clear discrepancy between the stances: on the one hand, adopted by the applicant, on the other, by the Marshal of the Sejm and the Public Prosecutor General, refers to the results of the proportionality test. In the applicant's view, the contested provisions "fail to pass the test with a positive result", which was decisive for the application to the Constitutional Tribunal. However, other participants claim that limitations indicated in the application are, for different reasons, necessary, therefore, they do not exceed the scope of admissible limitations to constitutional rights and freedoms. Thus, the Tribunal focused on the examination, whether the unquestionable limitations to freedom of doctors' conscience are acceptable in a democratic legal system.

5. Assessment of compliance with the Constitution of Article 39 **first sentence** with relation to Article 30 of AMP (the doctor's obligation to provide healthcare service in urgent cases).

5.1. Scope of examination of the allegation.

5.1.1. The normative content of Article 39 of AMP is the declaration of the possibility enjoyed by the doctor to refrain from the performance of a health-care service contrary to his conscience, which is, in legal terminology, shortly referred to as conscience clause. One could seemingly assume that from this provision, the doctor's right of refusal to undertake actions against his conscience is derived. However, from the perspective of facts established above, the Tribunal concluded that Article 39 first sentence of AMP constitutes an exemplification ("fulfilment"), with relation to doctors, of freedom of conscience (see part III, pt. 4.4 of the substantiation) expressed in Article 53 para. 1 of the Constitution. Maintaining the same perspective, the Tribunal further decided that the principal normative significance is not enjoyed by the possibility to refuse an action contrary to the doctor's conscience declared in Article 39 first sentence of AMP, but by limitations to this freedom derived from the provision under assessment.

5.1.2. The first of these limitations, and undoubtedly the most pronounced one, is to determine situations, in which the doctor, regardless of conscientious objection, is obliged to perform the service. From the list in Article 39 from Article 30 of AMP it may be concluded that the doctor may not refrain from the performance of healthcare services contrary to his conscience, if the delay in their provision could result in a danger for the patient's life, serious injury to his body or grave health disorder, as well as in other urgent cases. Exclusion of the doctor's possibility to invoke conscience clause in situations of danger to the patient's life or health, thus, in the first three cases stipulated in the quoted norm, is not covered by the application submitted by the SMC. Imposition of the obligation for the doctor to provide a healthcare service to a person, whose life or health face direct and serious danger, the applicant considers as justified in the light of medical ethics and the nature of profession practiced by the doctor. It may be added that it is also substantiated by the hierarchy of constitutional values, as situations of danger to life or serious danger to health may be regarded as cases, wherein one good (the doctor's freedom of conscience) is limited for the sake of good of other subjects (life and health of patients). The Supreme Medical Council questions the obligation to perform a healthcare service, contrary to the doctor's conscience, only in such a scope, in which it encompasses "other urgent cases".

5.1.3. The applicant alleges that the presented norm violates Article 2, Article 53 para. 1 and Article 65 para. 1 with relation to Article 30 and Article 31 para. 3 of the Constitution, while, as far as the first benchmark is concerned, in the

SMC's view, not only the principle of correct legislation and definiteness of legal provisions derived from Article 2 was infringed, but also the principle of democratic state based on the rule of law became violated. According to the SMC, "the protection of freedom of conscience belongs undoubtedly to fundamental values of a democratic society and state". The allegation of being contrary to Article 30 of the Constitution has only been substantiated in the application with the statement that "[c]ompulsion to actively act against one's religion or conscience (…) is often identified with violation of human dignity (Article 30 of the Constitution)". From Article 65 para. 1 of the Constitution the applicant derives the prohibition to shape working conditions in such a manner, so that for ideological reasons certain professions become formally or practically inaccessible for certain legal entities. The compulsion to provide medical assistance in the situation of conflict of conscience is, according to the applicant, incompatible with the nature of freedom to practice the medical profession. The consequence of disobeying the statutory obligation by the doctor could even be criminal liability for unintentional crime.

5.1.4. The Constitutional Tribunal assumed that the applicant's substantiation of allegations: infringement of the principle of democratic state based on the rule of law principle of correct legislation) and of human dignity established in Article 30 of the Constitution, which is in fact a reiteration of arguments for its incompatibility with the principal control benchmark, that is, Article 53 para. 1 of the Constitution, does not provide for their separate adjudication. One may agree with the applicant that, generally speaking, every act of violation of freedom of conscience, due to its anchorage in human dignity, constitutes, thereby, an assault against the dignity of the human person. In turn, by virtue of the fundamental significance of protection of dignity in the system of a democratic state based on the rule of law, every act of violation of freedom of conscience is an assault on the foundation of this state. Nevertheless, the legislative distinction of freedom of conscience and religion in the Constitution (Article 53 of the Constitution), requires that the assessment of provisions limiting freedom of conscience is conducted from the perspective of this particular, "specialised" provision. Derivation of this freedom from human dignity and indication of its fundamental significance for the democratic system is aimed at emphasising the legislator's duty to provide for its protection. This does not mean, however, that in any case of limitation of freedom of conscience, while failing to provide further arguments, there exists ground to adjudicate non-conformity with Article 2 of the Constitution (principle of democratic state based on the rule of law) and Article 30 of the Constitution.

In the case law of the Tribunal, against the background of Article 47 of the Constitution (establishing the right to privacy), it is assumed that if the violation of every right and freedom is identified with infringement of dignity, the guarantees found in Article 30 of the Constitution would be deprived of their independent scope of use (see rulings by the CT of: 5 March 2003, sygn. K 7/01, OTK ZU nr 3/A/2003, item 19; 4 November 2014, sygn. SK 55/13, OTK ZU nr 10/A/2014, item 111). Referring these norms respectively to freedom of conscience, the Tribunal in the present composition ruled that allegations of violation of Article 30 and of the principle of democratic state based on the rule of law expressed in Article 2 of the Constitution require a separate substantiation extending beyond the arguments invoked to support the allegation that a specific freedom was violated. Adoption of a different position would necessarily lead to the assumption that every disproportionate limitation to freedom of conscience in its external aspect is a violation of dignity and also of the principle of democratic state based on the rule of law. Since the substantiation of the application submitted by the SMC failed to include a separate substantiation of allegations referring to Article 2 and Article 30 of the Constitution, the procedure concerning the analysis of compatibility with the principle of democratic state based on the rule of law (Article 2 of the Constitution) and with Article 30 of the Constitution was terminated on the basis of Article 39 para. 1 pt. 1 of the Act of 1 August 1997 on the Constitutional Tribunal (Dz. U. Nr 102, item 643, as amended; hereinafter: Act on CT of 1997), with relation to Article 134 pt. 3 of the Act of 25 June 2015 on the Constitutional Tribunal (Dz. U. item 1064; hereinafter: Act on CT of 2015).

5.1.5. Consequently, the Tribunal assessed the contested provision from the perspective of constitutional control benchmark, which is the principle of correct legislation derived from Article 2 of the Constitution and distinguished in the application by the SMC (part III, pt. 5.2 of the substantiation) and from the perspective of Article 53 para. 1 with relation to Article 31 para. 3 of the Constitution (part III, pt. 5.3 of the substantiation). The Tribunal also related to other control benchmarks indicated in the application (part III, pt. 5.4 of the substantiation).

5.2. Constitutionality assessment – allegation of violation of the principle of correct legislation (Article 2 of the Constitution).

5.2.1. Both in the application by the SMC, and in the positions of the participants in the procedure, significant emphasis is put on the issue of legislative correctness to use in Article 39 of AMP, by reference to Article 30 of AMP, the wording "other urgent cases". The applicant alleges that the legislator failed to determine when such situations do occur, nor provided at least an exemplary catalogue, which could be useful in their determination. From the content of Article 30 of AMP it may only be concluded that these situations are different from those, wherein delay to provide a healthcare service could result could result in a danger for the patient's life, serious injury to his body or grave health disorder.

As noted in the doctrine, the present wording generates numerous interpretative difficulties and may lead, as a result of its general nature and semantic capacity, to inadmissible interference in freedom of conscience enjoyed by the doctor (see K. Szczucki, *Klauzula sumienia…*, s. 171). Failure to provide in the Medical Profession Act even an exemplary catalogue of situations which could be treated as "urgent" results in postulates by the representatives of the doctrine to the legislator for further clarification of the question what urgent preclude the use of conscience clause (see m.in. A. Zoll, *Prawo lekarza do odmowy udzielenia świadczeń zdrowotnych i jego granice*, „Prawo i Medycyna" nr 13/2003, s. 19–20; R. Kubiak, *Prawo medyczne…*, s. 157).

On the one hand, in the doctrine one may find views indicating the need for a broad interpretation of this notion, including those that would oblige the doctor to provide assistance to the patient even in situations, when "urgency" is only justified by the patient's immediate departure or elapsing validity of the latter's insurance (see E. Zielińska, *Odpowiedzialność zawodowa lekarza i jej stosunek do odpowiedzialności karnej*, Warszawa 2001, s. 352; A. Jacek, *Stosowanie klauzuli sumienia przez lekarza – aspekty etyczne i prawne*, [w:] *Etyczne aspekty decyzji medycznych*, red. J. Hartman, M. Waligóra, Warszawa 2011, s. 107). On the other hand, in the doctrine on occasion the opinion is voiced, to which refers the stance adopted by the Marshal of the Sejm, that these are: "circumstances, wherein delay to provide the patient with a healthcare service due to the doctor's invocation of conscience clause would directly result in negative consequences for the patient's health" (M. Żelichowski, *Obowiązek leczenia – przypadek niecierpiący zwłoki*, „Medycyna Praktyczna" nr 2/2007, s. 171–172).

Difficulties to interpret the contested wording of the act are besides noticed by the Marshal of the Sejm, who mentions that the norm found in Article 30 of AMP, due to its scope may be considered "as overly radical and excessively rigorous, thus, subject to criticism" (p. 34 of the letter). The Marshal assumes, however, that this opinion is only justified, if we analyse the wording "other urgent cases" from a general point of view, in separation from the doctor's obligations. Nonetheless, if we read it in the context of these obligations, its meaning becomes unequivocal.

5.2.2. The Tribunal shared the applicant's views and quoted opinions by the representatives of the doctrine with reference to Article 39 of AMP, in which it is rightly reiterated that the legislator applied an imprecise wording leaving a broad margin to freedom of assessment. The Tribunal points to the fact that the source of difficulties related with the determination of the normative content of the contested provision is not the formula: "in other urgent cases" itself, but its application in two different normative contexts, namely Article 30 and Article 39 of AMP. This thesis requires an explanation.

The Constitutional Tribunal generally shared the observation by the Marshal of the Sejm that the allegation of imprecision concerning the wording "other urgent cases" is substantiated only then, if the formula is analysed from a general point of view, in separation from the doctor's obligations. Read in the context of these obligations, according to the Marshal of the Sejm, the statutory wording becomes unequivocal. This argument is legitimate against the background of Article 30 of AMP, establishing a fundamental, derived directly from the act, obligation for the doctor, which consists of providing medical assistance. In the context of this provision it should be assumed that "other urgent cases" refer to situations related with the patient's health condition, wherein he is, admittedly, not in danger of death, serious injury to his body or grave health disorder, but still requires immediate medical assistance.

The analysed statutory wording, transmitted into the domain of Article 39 of AMP, gains, nonetheless, a different meaning, which is difficult to clarify, as Article 39 of AMP speaks, contrary to Article 30 of AMP, not of providing medical assistance, but of "performance of healthcare services". With reference to the heretofore established facts, (part III, pt. 4.3.4 of the substantiation) the Tribunal reiterates that, first, the notion of healthcare service encompasses not only provision of medical assistance, but also services with non-curative purposes regulated in separate provisions, and secondly, the Medical Profession Act does not consider "performance of (the entirety of) healthcare services" as the doctor's statutory obligation. Obligation to perform these services, which fail to display curative nature, may result from a contract. The legislator, provided, however, Article 39 of AMP with a wording indicating enhancement of the doctor's obligations (resulting from Article 30 of AMP) so that these include performance of all healthcare services. The wording: "other urgent cases" applied in the provision concerning the obligation to provide medical assistance (Article 30 of AMP) and repeated in another editing unit, which includes in its scope the entirety of healthcare services (Article 39 of AMP), completely loses its clarity. Consequently, against the background of Article 39 first sentence of AMP it is impossible to determine in which specific "urgent" situations, the doctor would be obliged to perform a healthcare service against his conscience.

5.2.3. In conclusion, the Constitutional Tribunal states that the application in Article 39 first sentence of AMP of a reference to another provision (Article 30 of AMP), which includes an imprecise wording, leads to uncertainties which cannot be removed concerning the scope, in which the legislator limits the doctors' freedom of conscience. Therefore, the allegation of violation of the principle of correct legislation derived from Article 2 of the Constitution is justified.

5.3. Constitutionality assessment – allegation of violation of Article 53 para. 1 in relation with Article 31 para. 3 of the Constitution.

5.3.1. In the view of the Tribunal, the applicant's allegation against the doctor's obligation to perform, against his conscience, a healthcare service in urgent cases is undoubtedly characterised by the greatest specific gravity. Limitation to freedom of conscience is most severe for a person, whom it concerns, as it means compulsion to perform an action one considers "evil" (i.e., immoral, unethical) and consequently leads to a deep psychological discomfort ("pangs of conscience"). On the one hand, being permanently or even repeatedly subject to coercion to act against oneself may result in serious disorders both mentally as physically with all of its further consequences. On the other hand, a doctor, who, against the obligation derived from Article 39 first sentence with relation to Article 30 of AMP, would give priority to his conscience thus refusing to perform a healthcare service, would expose himself to disciplinary measures, including redundancy, as well as legal liability and criminal liability for an unintentional crime. This gave rise to the applicant's obvious conclusion that due to the doctor's obligation to undertake actions contrary to his conscience, though urgent, freedom of conscience becomes limited. As mentioned above, all participants in the procedure agree with regard to this matter. The Marshal of the Sejm and the Public Prosecutor General represent the opinion that the contested limitation is necessary in a democratic state, thus considering that it does not exceed the framework resulting from the principle of proportionality, expressed by the Constitution in Article 31 para. 3. As rights which may be in conflict with the doctor's freedom of conscience and for the sake of which the legislator, in the view adopted by the Marshal of the Sejm and the Public Prosecutor General, has rightly "sacrificed" the doctor's freedom conscience, they indicate rights of others, namely right to protection of health (Article 68 para. 1 of the Constitution) and protection of private life (Article 47 of the Constitution). The applicant does not share this view.

5.3.2. Following international regulations and the universally accepted interpretation of provisions of the Constitution, the Tribunal assumed that freedom of conscience expressed in Article 53 para. 1 of the Constitution may be subject to limitations, which must, however, be proportional, i.e. meet the criteria (premises) of Article 31 para. 3 of the Constitution. In view of a uniform and solidified understanding of this provision in the jurisprudence of the Tribunal it is enough to recall that the principle of proportionality enables to decide in situation of collision between a few rights protected by the constitution or when the legislator's interference in order to protect one constitutional value results in excessive limitation of the other value belonging to that category. Article 31 para. 3 of the Constitution stipulates universal criteria, the fulfilment of which is necessary to introduce constraints on constitutional rights and freedoms of the individual. The principle of proportionality is perceived in two aspects. The formal aspect consists of the requirement for statutory form of the introduced limitation to a subjective right. The material aspect concerns the assessment, if the limitation of individual rights, formally correct, is substantiated by at least one purpose of these enumerated in the content of Article 31 para. 3 of the Constitution. If the same legislative purpose possible to be achieved with another norm, which imposes lesser limitations to rights and freedoms, the application by the legislator of a regulation which is more bothersome for the subject of these rights extends beyond what is necessary from the constitutional perspective (see ruling by the CT of 23 November 2009, sygn. P 61/08, OTK ZU nr 10/A/2009, item 150, oraz powołane tam orzecznictwo). The assessment of proportionality requires to analyse the norm from the following perspectives:

- the criterion of its usefulness, namely, if it can generate the effects intended by the legislator,
- the criterion of its necessity, namely, if it is indispensable for the protection of public interest with which it is related,
- the criterion of its proportionality *sensu stricto*, namely, if its effect remain in the right proportion to the burdens or limitations it imposes on the citizens.

5.3.3. The Tribunal assumes that the first step to be taken for the proportionality test to be possible and purposeful, is to establish the value, for the sake of which the assessed limitation to constitutional freedom or right was introduced by the legislator. From Article 31 para. 3 of the Constitution it follows that only specifically enumerated values may be taken into account, namely: public safety and order, environment protection, health and public morality, freedoms and rights of others. Only when it has been established that the assessed limitation to a constitutional right or freedom indeed serves to protect one of these values, further analysis may be continued, i.e. to establish, whether the limitation was useful and necessary to achieve the given purpose and if the proportionality *sensu stricto* was maintained, i.e. if the benefit achieved by sacrificing the first of these goods is greater than the sacrificed good itself.

In the adjudicated case, assessing the undoubtable limitation to the doctor's freedom of conscience from the perspective of the proportionality principle, one should first question the purpose of this limitation. According to the legislator's assumption, advocated by the Marshal of the Sejm and the Public Prosecutor General, this purpose is indicated by reference to Article 30 of AMP. Consequently, the doctor is obliged to perform a medical service contrary to his conscience "in any case wherein delay in their provision could result in a danger for the patient's life, serious injury to his body or grave health disorder as well as in other urgent cases". As long as the statutory wording referred to the case of "danger for the patient's life, serious injury to his body or grave health disorder" allows to identify the right for the sake of which the legislator forces the doctor to undertake actions against conscience, the wording: "in other urgent cases" is excessively general from the perspective of requirements of the proportionality test. The Tribunal has already acknowledged that this formula violates the principle of correct legislation, for it does not enable to unequivocally determine in what situation, for different reasons, the "urgent" case does occur. The general character of this formula results, however, in a further consequence, namely, does not enable to identify constitutional values or rights, indicated in Article 31 para. 3 of the Constitution, whose exercise could justify the limitation to freedom of conscience. Assessment of the provision limiting the constitutional freedom does not consist of the analysis of specific situations (factual cases), wherein the collision of values occurs or may possibly occur, but is performed at the level of a legal text, which should provide for an unequivocal determination of conflicting values. Referring this assumption to Article 39 first sentence of AMP, the Tribunal stated that the aim is not that the doctor, in a specific factual situation, should perform the assessment whether the cause for which the patients intends to obtain immediate medical service, requires from the former to sacrifice his own conscience in the light of the Constitution, but to make it possible to establish on the basis of the provision the constitutional rights, for the sake of which the doctor's freedom of conscience shall be sacrificed. Only their unequivocal identification paves way for the weighing of constitutional values, which is the essence of the proportionality test conducted by the Constitutional Tribunal.

5.3.4. The Tribunal rejected thereby the stance by the Marshal of the Sejm and the Public Prosecutor General, in whose view the legislator had rightly "sacrificed" the doctors' freedom of conscience for the sake of rights of others, namely the right to medical care (Article 68 para. 1 of the Constitution) and protection of private life (Article 47 of the Constitution).

The fact that the legislator's purpose was not to protect the life and health of the patient, thus, values protected by Article 38 i Article 68 para. 1 of the Constitution, is best attested by the comparison between the norm constructed on the basis of Article 39 first sentence and Article 30 of AMP and the content of Article 15 of AMA and Article 7 PRA. In the last two regulations, concerning healthcare services, the legislator linked the patient's right to immediate healthcare service and the healthcare entity's obligation to perform it immediately with the danger to the patient's health or life. The obligation to act against his conscience, conferred on the doctor in Article 39 first sentence of AMP, goes still further, as it includes also "other" urgent cases.

What testifies against the assumption that the right protected in Article 39 first sentence of AMP it the patient's right to privacy, is the nature of this right. From Article 47 of the Constitution, establishing the right to privacy, otherwise referred to as freedom from interference, follows the guarantee of integrity of the private life, in a broad meaning. Commentators derive from this provision the obligation by the state to refrain from encroaching into private matters of the citizens and to protect the latter by the interference of other entities (see P. Sarnecki, komentarz do Article 47 of the Constitution, [w:] *Konstytucja…*, pt. 3, s. 1; B. Banaszak, *Konstytucja Rzeczypospolitej Polskiej. Komentarz*, Warszawa 2012, s. 297–298; J. Braciak, *Prawo do prywatności*, [w:] *Prawa i wolności obywateli w* of the Constitution *RP*, red. B. Banaszak, A. Preisner, Warszawa 2002, s. 277). In view of the Tribunal, the guarantee following from Article 47 of the Constitution "[m]eans that the state accepts the obligation, on the one hand, of non-interference in the constitutionally determined scope of individual lives of the citizens and, on the other hand, it provides appropriate protection in case when such actions have already been undertaken" (judgement of 2 April 2001, sygn. SK 10/00, OTK ZU nr 3/A/2001, item 52; similarly judgement of 26 February 2014, sygn. K 22/10, OTK ZU nr 2/A/2014, item 15). Even if, exceptionally, it is allowed for the state, on the basis of Article 47 of the Constitution, to impose the obligation of a certain activity, this obligation is conferred on the protected subject, in its own interest (see ruling of the CT of 9 July 2009, sygn. SK 48/05). Article 47 of the Constitution provides no ground for the legislator to confer, for the sake of protection of privacy of one group of persons (patients), an obligation to undertake actions contrary to their conscience on others (doctors). This would mean, according to the Tribunal, that the latter group is treated as objects.

5.3.5. The Tribunal admits that the application of the contested formula by the legislator may in certain situations serve to protect the patient's health, nonetheless, the assessed norm, for the reason of its general character, may with all certainty be applied in situations, wherein none of the rights or freedoms enjoying constitutional protection is in danger. As emphasised above, (part III, pt. 5.2 of the substantiation), the premise of "other urgent cases", in relation with a particularly broad definition of healthcare service, is characterised by an excessive degree of generality. The consequence of its imprecise form is that "it is impossible to determine the character of constitutionally protected values, for the sake of which the legislator decides to legalise the violation of another constitutional value" (wording included in the substantiation of the ruling of the CT of 28 May 1997, sygn. K 26/96, OTK ZU nr 2/1997, item 19), namely, in the adjudicated case, freedom of conscience. In practice this may result in factual contestation of the doctor's possibility to invoke conscience clause, especially in situation of subjective interpretation of an "urgent case", performed from the patient's perspective. Sacrifice of the doctor's freedom of conscience appears then as ungrounded, and, in any case, completely unjustified from the constitutional perspective and thus unacceptable.

Summarising this part of the constitutional assessment, the Tribunal stated that in the assessed Article 39 first sentence with relation to Article 30 of AMP the legislator applied an imprecise wording, which, being an instrument of limitation to freedom of conscience, renders the identification of protected values impossible; at the normative level is does not allow for the unequivocal determination of a situation, wherein the doctor may refuse to provide a medical service, but, above all, it confers on him the obligation działania to against his conscience also in cases, where no constitutional rights justify the sacrifice of the freedom he enjoys. Consequently, the Tribunal assumed that Article 39 first sentence with relation to Article 30 of AMP, in the assessed scope, is incompatible with Article 53 para. 1 with relation to Article 31 para. 3 of the Constitution.

5.3.6. Since it has been assumed that the assessed limitation to freedom of conscience may not be subject to the proportionality test due to the impossibility to establish what constitutional values the legislator intends to protect at the expense of the doctors' conscience, the Tribunal was relieved from the analysis of premises, which, pursuant to Article 31 para. 3 of the Constitution, substantiate limitations to enjoy constitutional freedoms. The need to perform the proportionality test would then become binding, if the provision was formulated in a manner providing for an unequivocal identification of the constitutional value, for which the legislator imposes a constraint on the doctors' freedom of conscience. Only on occasion of the constitutional assessment of Article 39 first sentence of AMP, the Tribunal drew attention to the fact that in the light of the hierarchy of constitutional values it can hardly be assumed that other rights of the patient, not related with his life or health, could enjoy the primacy before the value, which in a democratic state based on the rule of law, is freedom of conscience derived directly from human dignity. The Tribunal emphasises that maintenance of Article 31 para. 3 of the Constitution is inextricably related with the internal hierarchy of constitutional values. Thus, the more valuable is the limited good and the higher the degree of its limitation, the greater must be the value which justifies sich limitations. Already in the ruling of the Tribunal of 26 April 1995, sygn. K 11/94 (OTK w 1995, part 1, item 12) it was rightly observed that the stricter standards for assessment are applied in case of limitation of personal and political rights. Moreover, Article 31 para. 3 second sentence of the Constitution prohibits to infringe the "essence of freedoms and rights", since in the contents of each constitutional right or constitutional freedom certain fundamental elements (often described as the "core") may be found, whose existence is the necessary premise for the given right or freedom to preserve its constitutional identity. Violation thereof should thus be considered an disproportionate encroachment into the domain of rights enjoyed by the given individual (see rulings of the CT of: 20 March 2006, sygn. K 17/05, OTK ZU nr 3/A/2006, item 30 and of 25 July 2013, sygn. P 56/11, OTK ZU nr 6/A/2013, item 85).

5.4. Other control benchmarks.

The Tribunal assumed that declaration of unconstitutionality of Article 39 first sentence of AMP with relation to Article 30 of AMP with the principle of correct legislation derived from Article 2 of the Constitution and from Article 53 para. 1 with relation to Article 31 para. 3 of the Constitution, renders it unnecessary to perform control from the perspective of other benchmarks, i.e. Article 18 para. 1 and para. 2 of the ICCPR and Article 65 para. 1 of the Constitution, pursuant to which: " Everyone shall have the freedom to choose and to pursue his occupation and to choose his place of work. Exceptions shall be specified by statute". Only on occasion of of this ruling does the Tribunal reiterate its earlier position, pursuant to which interference in the freedom to choose a profession and a workplace by an individual is admissible, and its scope is broader than what would follow from Article 31 para. 3 of the Constitution, what is clearly indicated by second sentence Article 65 para. 1 of the Constitution (see ruling of the CT of 19 March 2001, sygn. K 32/00, OTK ZU nr 3/2001, item 50). Regardless of the general legal consideration concerning limitation to freedom of work, the Tribunal assessed that the situation, displayed by the applicant, of the doctor who faces the choice: either to personally provide the patient with a medical service which is against his conscience, or to guarantee its performance to the patient, or to abandon practicing his profession, usually fails to find sufficient justification in the facts. The relations between limitations derived from the contested legal norm and freedom of conscience and the doctors' freedom of work is too distant, to speak of the infringement of the latter. In view of the Tribunal, the suggestion by the SMC, that with the contested provision the legislator supposedly introduced factual limitation to freedom to practice the medical profession, limitation unrelated to the talent and qualifications the doctor possesses, fails to find sufficient reflection in the reality.

The procedurę within the scope of analysing compatibility with Article 18 para. 1 and para. 2 of the ICCPR as well as with Article 65 para. 1 of the Constitution was, therefore, terminated on the basis of Article 39 para. 1 pt. 1 Act on CT of 1997 with relation to Article 134 pt. 3 Act on CT of 2015

5.5. Effects of declaration of unconstitutionality.

The Constitutional Tribunal emphasises that the effect of the ruling on unconstitutionality of the scope of the norm created on the basis of Article 39 first sentence of AMP with relation to Article 30 of AMP is not the limitation of the doctor's statutory obligations, derived from Article 30 of AMP. Thus, the obligation to provide medical assistance still encompasses "other urgent cases". The ruling of the Tribunal settles only the scope of limitation to the doctor's right to invoke conscience clause, specified by Article 39 first sentence of AMP. The doctor, as heretofore, will not be entitled to invoke it in situations, wherein delay to perform such service could result in for the patient's life, serious injury to his body or grave health disorder. However, in other cases, for different reasons considered urgent, he shall be able to refuse to perform the healthcare service (not consisting of the performance of medical assistance) contrary to his conscience.

6. Assessment of the compatibility of **Article** 39, first sentence, of the Act on Professions of Doctor and Dentist (doctor's obligation to indicate a real possibility of obtaining the service from another doctor or in another medical entity) with the Constitution.

6.1. The scope of the assessment of the allegation.

6.1.1. The second allegation formulated by the Supreme Medical Council concerns Article 39, first sentence, of the Act on Professions of Doctor and Dentist, in so far as it imposes on a doctor refusing a medical service the obligation to indicate a "real possibility of obtaining that service from another doctor or in another medical entity." In the light of the law that requirement compels a doctor to actively, substantially and really help the patient to obtain a medical service, which – in that doctor's opinion – is incompatible with his conscience (cf. A. Zoll, *Charakter prawny...*, p. 103 and O. Nawrot, *Sumienie lekarza a prawa człowieka w świetle standardów Rady Europy*, "Medycyna Praktyczna" no 1/2014,, p. 116). Therefore in practice, invoking the clause of conscience he cannot avoid the obligation to "help" the patient in receiving that service from another doctor or in another entity. Thus the literal understanding of the contested provision makes the doctor – by virtue of the Act – an actual helper in terms of achieving the goal that he considers morally wicked (cf. J. Pawlikowski, *Prawo do wyrażania sprzeciwu sumienia...*, p. 39; M. Świeca, *Klauzula sumienia – jako rozwiązanie kolizji norm prawa stanowionego z normami światopoglądowymi*, "Prawo i Medycyna" no 3–4/2013, p. 56; A. Zoll, *Charakter prawny...*, p. 103).

6.1.2. The applicant alleges that this provision infringes Article 2, Article 53 para. 1 and Article 65 para. 1 in connection with Article 30 and Article 31 para. 3 of the Constitution. Contradiction with Article 2 of the Constitution, according to the Supreme Medical Council, consists in imposing on a doctor an obligation impossible to fulfil, which is equivalent to creating "a kind of trap for a citizen". In addition, that provision, in the disputed scope, is "grossly dysfunctional and disproportionate". The violation of Article 53 para. 1 of the Constitution lies in the fact that, as a result of the imposing on a doctor an unconditional obligation of notification when the medical service is incompatible with the doctor's conscience, the ability to refrain from executing that service – declared in Article 39 of the Act on Professions of Doctor and Dentist – becomes "a game of appearances". According to the applicant, the obligation to provide information reveals the "deceptive nature" of the clause of conscience; as a result of its enforcement "the set of situations, in which a doctor may successfully invoke the constitutionally guaranteed freedom of conscience, is empty" (p. 32 of the Application). Enforcement of that obligation in the long run leads to excluding persons, who want to invoke it, from the profession, and to undermining the foundation of a pluralist and democratic State.

6.1.3. Both the Marshal of the Sejm and the Public Prosecutor General, although disregarding the weight of moral responsibility incurred by a doctor providing information about the real possibility of obtaining a service, nevertheless they admit that also in that field Article 39, first sentence, of the Act on Professions of Doctor and Dentist limits doctors' conscientious objection. For the assessment of the constitutionality they apply the test of proportionality. They deem necessary the limitation of the freedom of conscience in a democratic State by imposing the duty of notification.

The Marshal of the Sejm states that "the lack of the contested by the Supreme Medical Council obligation would mean that broken is the patient's right to information guaranteed by Article 9 of the Act on Patient's Rights", which "does not provide for exceptions or limitations"(p. 42 of the Position). The same provision is invoked by the Public Prosecutor General to justify imposing the obligation of notification upon the doctor.

6.1.4. The Constitutional Tribunal assumed that – as has been the case with regard to the first allegation – the applicant had not separately substantiated an infringement of Article 30 of the Constitution (Part III, point 5.1.4 of the Justification). Therefore, the procedure was so closed in that respect. A similar decision concerns the allegation of infringement of the principle of correct legislation and the principle of trust to the State and constituted by it, stemming from Article 2 of the Constitution. On the basis of superficial justification for those allegations it was difficult to determine in what the applicant identifies ambiguity of the assessed provision and why that provision would establish "a trap for the citizen". Proceedings concerning the assessment of the compatibility of the provision in question (in the assessed scope) with Article 2 of the Constitution were terminated on the basis of Article 39 para. 1 point 1 of the Act on CC of 1997 in connection with Article 134, point 3 of the Act on CC of 2015.

6.2. The constitutional assessment.

6.2.1. The Constitutional Tribunal started the constitutional assessment of the examined portion of the provision, the from describing the actual situation in which its hypothesis comes to realisation. On the background of the current wording of Article 39, the first sentence, in conjunction with Article 30 of the Act on Professions of Doctor and Dentist, it can occur when there is no need to rescue the patient's health or life, nor any urgent circumstance, in which the doctor must act. Since he must, even contrary to his conscience grant a medical service, the obligation of providing information does not arise, because the doctor himself meets the expectation of the patient. *A contrario*, that obligation arises when the doctor refuses to grant a medical service. Since the Tribunal deems the provision unconstitutional in so far as it imposes on the doctor the obligation to act contrary to his conscience, when there occur "other cases of urgency", grows the set of situations in which the doctor may refuse to provide a medical service. In that way, at least in theory (cf. Part III, Point 7 of the Justification), expands the scope of applying the evaluated obligation of information. Another issue is to determine the scope of the obligation, which under Article 39, first sentence, of the Act on Professions of Doctor and Dentist rests with the doctor. The Constitutional Tribunal estimated that the indication required by the legislator of the "real possibility" means that the doctor, who refuses to provide a service invoking the clause of conscience, should indicate another doctor or entity, as to whom he might have justified by circumstances certainty, that will perform the given service. Due to the clear wording of the provision, it should be presumed, that the doctor cannot exempt himself from that obligation by directing the patient to the National Health Fund (cf. L. Bosek, *Prawo osobiste do odmowy działania sprzecznego z własnym sumieniem – na przykładzie lekarza*, "Forum Prawnicze" nr 1/2014, p. 25). The provision understood just in that way is subject to constitutional assessment. The Tribunal – like the applicant and the parties to the proceedings – is of the opinion that the imposition on a doctor the obligation to indicate a real possibility of obtaining a service incompatible with his conscience constitutes a limitation of the freedom of conscience.

The constitutional guarantee of the freedom of conscience, in fact, protects an individual not only against coercion to harm directly the protected good, but also against such practices incompatible with the individual's conscience, which lead indirectly to ethically unacceptable effect, and in particular against coercion to collaborate in achieving a reprehensible purpose (cf. decision of the CC from 15 January 1991, File U 8/90). In that situation, the constitutional assessment depends on the outcome of the test of proportionality.

6.2.2. The Tribunal started conducting it from indicating a constitutional value, for which – in that case – was sacrificed the doctor's freedom of conscience. From the wording of the provision it can be inferred that the right was the right to information. However, it should be pointed out that Article 9 of the Act on Patient's Rights – granting patients the right to information and indicated by the Minister of Health as the source of the values for which the legislator had restricted the freedom of conscience – is not sufficient as a justification for that limitation. It should rather be indicated that the right to information has its foundation in Article 61 para. 1 of the Constitution. That provision, constituting the citizen's right, basically refers to information about the activities of public authorities and persons performing public functions. However, it also includes "getting information about the activities of the (…) organisational units to the extent that they perform tasks of public authority and administer the municipal property or state-owned assets " . The Tribunal assumes that the right constituted in Article 61 para. 1. the Constitution includes also obtaining information about medical services financed from public funds. That is strictly connected with the obligation of public authorities to ensure that all citizens "have equal access to health care services financed from public funds", provided for in Article 68 para. 2 of the Constitution. In that context, the patient's right to information should be treated as a measure necessary to accomplish a task imposed on public authorities by the Constitution. The quoted Article 68 para. 2 of the Constitution states that "the conditions and extent of the provision of services is prescribed by the act". As it was indicated above (Part III, para. 4.3 of the Justification), the currently existing provisions, in particular the acts: on Healthcare Services (along with its implementing regulations); of 8 September 2006 on the National Medical Rescue Service (OJ of 2013, item 757, as amended); of 19 August 1994 on the Protection of Mental Health (OJ of 2011 no. 231, item 1375, as amended); of 7 January 1993 on Family Planning, Protection of the Human Foetus and Conditions for the Admissibility of Abortion (OJ No. 17, item 78, as amended), provide for public funding not only medicinal services, but also non-medicinal services fitting in a broader concept of health services, including services which are "sensitive" in the sense that executing them can most often provoke medical personnel's conscientious objection.

In the light of Article 68 para. 2 of the Constitution, the legislator decides about the range of medical services financed from public funds. The Tribunal underlines that their range – designated by provisions currently in force – is not the subject of the present case. Consequently, it must be held that the State's constitutional responsibility is to provide access to those services. As long as the State cannot – for the purpose of fulfilling that obligation – force doctors to act contrary to their conscience, it should organise information about doctors, or rather medicinal entities, which carrying out those services. Therefore, the Tribunal assumed, that maintaining the public order of the Republic of Poland, understood as a set of rules which ensure the functioning of the society and its institutional system (cf. judgment of the CC of 10 April 2002 File K 26/00, Rulings of the Constitutional Tribunal ZU no. 8/A/2002, item. 18, Point VI of the Justification), in the present case: the functioning of the system of medical services financed from public funds (Article 68, para. 2, of the Constitution) requires adequate organizing of an information system for citizens (Article 61, para. 1, of the Constitution).

Identification of the constitutional values, indicated in Article 31 para. 3 of the Constitution, competing with the doctor's freedom of conscience, opens the possibility to carry out the test of proportionality. Therefore the following questions should be answered: whether imposing the obligation to provide information about the real possibilities of obtaining a medical service "from another doctor or medicinal entity" upon a doctor, who exercises the right to refuse performance of a medical service, is useful, necessary and proportionate to achieving the legislator's purpose, i.e. enabling the patient to obtain a service as soon as possible.

6.2.3. The Tribunal found that assessing whether challenged by the applicant restricting doctors' freedom of conscience remains within the limits of proportionality, is facilitated by the widespread criticizing Article 39, first sentence, of the Act on Professions of Doctor and Dentist, as expression of the legislator's ineffectiveness in shaping the information system on medical services financed from public funds. The defectiveness of the provision has long been mentioned in the literature, but – above all – that defectiveness was indicated to the authorities responsible for the organisation of health services by the public authorities responsible for the protection of the citizens' rights. As written by M. Nesterowicz and N. Karczewska-Kaminska, "the formulation of [that] provision is faulty, that obligation should concern the entity, and not the doctor" (M. Nesterowicz, n. Karczewska-Kaminska, *Prawa pacjenta…*, p. 123). At the same time the authors point to unsuccessful attempts of correct formulation of that issue in the Ministry of Health regulations and complain, that the obligation of informing is still based solely on Article 39 of the Act on Professions of Doctor and Dentist, and consequently burdens only the doctor. E. Zielińska, referring to the present obligation to provide information, notes like other authors: "that such a requirement is often unrealistic for an individual doctor, as for example a doctor practicing privately have no such possibility" (E. Zielińska, *Klauzula sumienia*, "Prawo i Medycyna" no. 13/2003, p. 30; likewise R. Kubiak, *Prawo medyczne…*, p. 158). However, more important than doctrinal assessment Article 39 of the Act on Professions of Doctor and Dentist (in the questioned scope) is the position of state functionaries, whose job is to protect the rights of citizens.

The lack of effectiveness of the current regulation was pointed out by the Government Plenipotentiary for Equal Treatment A. Kozłowska-Rajewicz, who, pronounced the opinion that a doctor invoking the clause of conscience in practice does not fulfil the obligation of informing, "because he has no knowledge which doctor does not apply that clause"; that obligation should rest upon the entity, "which has a contract with the National Health Fund," (*Kozłowska-Rajewicz wants changes to the clause of conscience*, journal "Rzeczpospolita" of 15 September 2012, the source: PAP).

The most important seems that the Ombudswoman took a firm position on that issue in a letter to the Minister of Health, of 21 July 2014, emphasising that, in accordance with the Constitution and international law, "no one can be held liable or discriminated because of a refusal to provide various types of services, invoking the clause of conscience". At the same time the Ombudswoman underlined that the responsibility "for ensuring patients access to legitimate medical services without undue delay falls on the State" (p. 4 of the letter). Such state of affairs is due, inter alia, the Council of Europe's resolution of 7 October 2010 (cf. Part III, para. 3.2.4 of the Justification). Referring to the standards arising from the Constitution and the obligations of Poland as a member of the Council of Europe, the Ombudswoman pointed out that there is a need for "urgent amendment to the Act on Professions of Doctor and Dentist, in order to shift the obligation of ensuring the real possibility of obtaining by the patient a service, from an individual doctor onto public entities, which institutionally carry out medical services on behalf of the State and funded from public funds" (p. 4 of the letter). The Ombudswoman added that, in accordance with Article 5. 68 para. 2 of the Constitution, the public authorities have the obligation to ensure equal access to healthcare services. A clear confirmation of the lack of rationality of the legislative solution questioned by the Supreme Medical Council is included in the Minister of Health stance of August 20, 2014, which explains that the doctor, who refuses a service invoking the clause of conscience, "should refer to a person responsible for the organisation of services in the same entity" in order to obtain the required information (p. 22 letter). The Minister of Health assumes, therefore, that there are persons, who because of their functions in the organisational entities of healthcare financed by public funds, should have the information, who (what entity) performs certain types of services, guaranteed by the National Health Fund.

Similar "advice" was given to doctors by the Marshal of the Sejm, according to whom: "a doctor can fulfil the obligation by asking the National Health Fund for relevant information". The Marshal assumed that: "its acquisition will be simple and can be compared to acquiring and upgrading by the doctor information about reimbursable drugs (…)" (p. 43 of the letter). Also the Public Prosecutor General, referring to numerous statements in the doctrine, pointed out in what ways a doctor could obtain information that he is obliged to provide to a patient.

6.2.4. The Tribunal found that the proposed by the participants in the proceeding and the Minister of Health manner of getting by a doctor information is the best proof that: firstly, there are different ways to inform the patient about the availability of a service, and secondly, the way put forward in Article 39 the first sentence of the Act on Professions of Doctor and Dentist lengthens the patient's route to information and thus delays in time his getting the desired service. If in fact it is so, as the Marshal of the Sejm and the Minister of Health maintain, that is to say, the National Health Fund or a person responsible, in the subject, have information about doctors or other organisational entities providing "sensitive" medical services, then the only reasonable and effective legislative solution would be to direct patients to get the information immediately from those institutions and their employees, that is, from the source of information.

6.2.5. Therefore the provision, according to which an individual doctor is obliged to give the patient information about real possibilities of getting a medical service, turns out to be an inadequate tool to achieve the purpose pursued by the legislator: to ensure that the patient gets as quickly as possible a medical service guaranteed by the health service financed form public funds. As the evocated defenders of citizens' interest rightly point out, a doctor simply does not have, and in any case needs not to have, the necessary knowledge to provide such information; in many cases, getting it would require infringement of the applicable law by a doctor.

Possibilities of obtaining that knowledge, indicated by the Marshal of the Sejm and the Minister of Health, only make longer the way to obtain that information and simultaneously ignore the valid principles of protecting personal data. In the Tribunal's estimation, the legal order of the Republic of Poland contains no provision that would impose on doctors the obligation to possess information about medical providers, including doctors, performing certain medical services. Obligating them to gain knowledge in that domain may raise concerns from the point of view of the provisions of the Act of 29 August 1997 on the Protection of Personal Data (Journal of laws from 2014, item 1182, as amended), as well as from the point of view of Article 53 para. 7 of the Constitution. In the light of that provision, having knowledge about which medical providers are ready to perform "sensitive" services can even suggest the use of illegal means to obtain such information. For those reasons, the Tribunal strongly objects to equating by the Marshal of the Sejm the doctors' obligation of becoming familiar with the list of reimbursable drugs with the alleged obligation to acquire and update knowledge about potential service providers. Its fulfilment presumes the state of a doctor's permanent encroachment on the sphere of other doctors' freedom of conscience, violating medical secrecy and rules governing the protection of personal data.

6.2.6. At the same time the Tribunal stated that the assessed regulation is not necessary to guarantee patients' access to public information and to preserve public order in a democratic rule of law. The legislator could and should use alternative, more efficient ways of informing the patient about a real possibility of obtaining a medical service. The Tribunal assumed, that if the aim (in that case – ensuring a medical service to a patient) is achievable using different means, imposing lesser constraints on rights and freedoms, then the application by the legislator of a more bothersome measure goes beyond what is necessary, and therefore violates the Constitution (cf. judgments of the CC: of 12 January 2000, File P 11/98, OTK ZU no. 1/2000, item. 3 and of 23 June 2009, File K 54/07, OTK ZU no. 6/A/2009, item 86). The legislator's duty to form in a different way the obligation of information arises from the fact, that the legal solution adopted in Article 39 the first sentence of the Act on Professions of Doctor and Dentist is not the right tool to achieve the objective established by the legislator, and in no case is the optimal tool. Much more effective way to ensure patients equal and quick access to medical services would be the imposition of the duty of informing on the " the authorised public institutions" providing medical activities on behalf of the State.

6.2.7. Summarising, the Tribunal concludes that the restriction of doctors' freedom of conscience by obligating them to inform the patient about the possibility of obtaining a service remaining in conflict with their moral principles, resulting from Article 39 the first sentence of the Act on Professions of Doctor and Dentist, does not pass the proportionality test. Not only it is an inefficient tool for achieving the objective established by the legislator, but in addition, it is not indispensable to achieve it. Consequently, the provision in question, in so far as it imposes on a doctor refraining from the performance of medical services incompatible with his conscience the obligation to indicate the real possibility of obtaining such provision from another doctor or in another entity, is incompatible with Article 53 para. 1 in connection with Article 31 para. 3 of the Constitution.

6.2.8. Because of finding that Article 39 the first sentence of the Act on Professions of Doctor and Dentist in the assessed area is incompatible with Article 53 para. 1 in connection with Article 31 para. 3 of the Constitution, the Tribunal deemed unnecessary to make its assessment from the point of view of another control standard pointed out in the Application, i.e. Article. 65 para. 1 of the Constitution. The proceedings in that regard were discontinued on the basis of Article 39 para. 1 point 1 of the Act on the CC in 1997 in connection with Article 134, point 3 of the Act on the CC of 2015.

7. Assessment of the compatibility with the Constitution of Article 39 the second sentence of the Act on Professions of Doctor and Dentist (the doctors' obligation to notify their supervisor).

7.1. The scope of examination of the **allegation**

7.1.1. Article 39 the second sentence of the Act on Professions of Doctor and Dentist obligates the doctors practicing their profession on the basis of employment or service, who exercise their right to refuse executing medical services that are incompatible with their conscience, to give their supervisor prior notification in writing. According to the applicant, that provision contains "a legal constraint to reveal one's moral and religious views to one's employer in writing" and as such is directly contrary to Article 53 para. 7 of the Constitution, while the cited the control standard is not subject to any restrictive clause (neither from Article 53, para. 5, nor from Article 31, para. 3, of the Constitution). Moreover, the provision is contrary to Article 53 para. 1 in connection with Article 31 para. 3 of the Constitution, since notifying the employer is not indispensable for the achievement of the objectives of the legislator. The Supreme Medical Council Returns also indicates, that the contested regulation may cause the so called deterring effect. A person, who would like to invoke the clause of conscience, may refrain from it for the reason that it will require providing his/her supervisor with that information in writing. Also in that respect, real can be a doctor's apprehension of revealing his/her worldview to the supervisor and of the negative consequences connected with that fact, which can affect him. That leads the applicant to formulate the allegation of infringement of Article. 2 of the Constitution, since the provision introducing "direct discrimination on grounds of religion in labour relations, violates the foundation of the democratic rule of law" (p. 34 of the Application). However the Tribunal points out, that the applicant has not referred to the Article 65 para. 1 of the Constitution as a control standard in that respect. Although it could be considered whether obligating the doctors to inform about their use of the clause of conscience affects their right to work, nevertheless the quoted sentence does not justify the allegation of violating the principle of the democratic rule of law.

7.1.2. The principal control standard of the assessed provision was made by the applicant the Article 53 para. 7 of the Constitution, which states: "no one may be compelled by organs of public authority to disclose his philosophy of life, religious convictions or belief". The quoted provision establishes the right to silence and is an example of a standard providing for the so-called constitutional "freedom from interference". In that case, it's about ensuring that the public authority will not interrogate about one's views and will not interfere with them. For the state should not be interested in its citizens' convictions (cf M. Pietrzak, *Stosunki państwo – kościół w nowej Konstytucji*, "Państwo i Prawo" no. 11–12/1997, p. 179). According to the applicant, the obligation to notify in writing the superior about executing the refusal of a medical service due to conscientious objection obliges the doctor, in an indirect way, to disclose his worldview. In addition, that obligation is imposed upon the doctor in a statutory way imposed, by public authorities. Moreover, the applicant alleges that the contested norm violates Article 53 para. 1 in connection with Article 31 para. 3 and Article 2 of the Constitution.

7.1.3. The Tribunal is of the opinion that Article 53 para. 7 of the Constitution does not constitute a proper control standard for the provision imposing on doctors the obligation to notify a supervisor about their use of the clause of conscience. Such a stance is supported by several reasons.

Firstly, the formulation of Article 53 para. 7 of the Constitution indicates that it refers to the *forum internum*. I means, after all, the prohibition of compelling to "disclose one's philosophy of life, religious convictions or belief", that is, pulling out what is hidden in the human consciousness. Meanwhile, the use of the clause of conscience is explicit by nature; a doctor invoking the conscientious objection acts on the *forum externum*. Notifying the superior, as provided for in Article 39, second sentence, of the Act on Professions of Doctor and Dentist, does not require to indicate the existing in the doctor's conscience causes of failing to perform specific medical services, but only to provide information, what medical services he does not perform, which refers to the external sphere of freedom of conscience.

Secondly, although a common cause of doctors' invoking the clause of conscience are religious motivations, the doctors' refusal of medical services should not be equated with religious reasons, as it results from earlier findings (cf. Part III, point 4.3.3 of the Justification). In particular, the doctors' refusal to perform abortion cannot be equated with their confession of a specific faith, as in those cases their conscientious objection stems most frequently from the Hippocratic ethical tradition, and not from religious beliefs.

Thirdly, doubts whether the situation regulated in Article 39 the second sentence of the AMP is within the scope of the subject of the prohibition resulting from Article. 53 para. 1. 7 of the Constitution, which literally refers to "public authorities". Meanwhile, vote now fragment clearly employee relations and work provision.

Thirdly, it is doubtful whether the situation regulated by Article 39, second sentence, of the Act on Professions of Doctor and Dentist stays within the subject scope of the prohibition resulting from Article 53 para. 7 of the Constitution, which literally refers to "public authorities", while the herewith assessed fragment clearly refers to employment and service relations.

Consequently the Tribunal estimated that Article 53 para. 7 of the Constitution is not an adequate control standard for the questioned provision in the scope under the present assessment.

Notwithstanding the accomplished assessment, the Tribunal indicates, that the applicant's standpoint referring the prohibition, imposed on public authorities in Article 53 para. 7 of the Constitution, is of absolute nature and not subject to restrictions set forth in Article 31 para. 31 of the Constitution, cannot be shared. The argument derived from the scheme Article 53 of the Constitution, used by the applicant in support of its position, is not convincing, and its use is inconsistent. The applicant indicates that, since the clause limiting the freedom of conscience is in Article 53 para. 5 of the Constitution, it cannot be applied to the limitation of the "freedom from interference" regulated in a further editorial unit, i.e. in Article 53 para. 7 of the Constitution. According to the applicant, "it would be absurd" to deprive that "deliberate legislative tactic" of the legal importance by referring to Article 31 para. 3 of the Constitution. The Tribunal assumed that the herewith invoked norm has importance for the determination of the acceptable limits of all constitutional rights and freedoms, including the freedom expressed in Article 53 para. 7 of the Constitution (cf. P. Sarnecki, commentary to Article 53 of the Constitution, [in:] *The Constitution* ..., point 16, pp. 9–10 and W. Sobczak, *Wolność myśli, sumienia...*, p. 555). We deal with a particular situation, when a provision, constituting the freedom or right, contains its own limitation clause, as it is the case – for example –regarding the freedom to manifest one's religion. There arises a question, whether that particular limitation clause excludes the application of Article 31 para. 3 of the Constitution. As the Tribunal have stated above (Part III, point 4.5 of the Justification), in the assessed matter, however, that issue does not appear, as Article 53 para. 5 of the Constitution does not refer to the freedom of conscience.

The applicant's incongruity consists in that – despite the lack of the special restrictive clause relating to the freedom of conscience in Article 53 of the Constitution, declared in its first para. – the applicant treats Article 31 para. 3 of the Constitution as a provision, which designates constitutional admissibility of restricting that freedom (the applicant actually appeals to Article 53, para. 1, in connection with Article 31, para. 3, of the Constitution as the control standard). Whereas the freedom expressed in Article 53 para. 7 of the Constitution, precisely because of the lack of a specific provision referring it, would not be – as stated by the applicant – subject to restrictions due to a general limitation clause, and that would decide about recognizing it as absolute freedom.

7.1.4. Proceedings for the assessment of the compliance of the contested norm with Article 2 of the Constitution, both as regards the allegation of infringement of the democratic rule of law and the principle of valid legislation resulting from it, is terminated on the basis of Article 39 para. 1 point 1 of the Act on the CC of 1997 in connection with Article 134, point 3 of the Act on the CC of 2015, due to the lack of sufficient justification. The applicant's statement, that the obligation to inform the superior "by introducing directly immediate discrimination on the grounds of religion into labour relations, violates the foundation of the rule of law, and by that is contrary to Article 2 the Constitution"(p. 34 of the Application), cannot be considered a sufficient argumentation for the allegation.

7.1.5. As follows from the above, out of several provisions indicated by the applicant as the constitutional control standard for Article 39 the second of the Act on Professions of Doctor and Dentist, in so far as it imposes on the doctor remaining in employment or service relationship the obligation to inform the supervisor of the use of the clause of conscience, only Article 53 para. 1 in connection with Article 31 para. 3 of the Constitution can be such standard. For the Tribunal deemed that the execution of that obligation may in some cases lead to the limitation of the freedom of conscience, especially when the employer is interested in hiring only the doctor who performs all medical services. In that situation, the doctor applying for employment, in order to increase the chances of admission, indeed could refrain from exercising the freedom of conscience. Recognizing the "deterring effect" of the obligation to notify the employer, the Tribunal found that the acceptability of the assessed provision is determined by the proportionality test in accordance with Article 31 para. 3 of the Constitution.

7.2. Evaluation of constitutionality.

7.2.1. The Tribunal recognised that the formulation of the controlled provision may bring about some interpretational questions concerning the time and content of the "notice", which the doctor (working professionally on the basis of the employment or service relationship) is obliged to deliver to his superior. For the Act does not precise whether such a declaration should be general and preceding, and include a statement that the doctor will not perform particular medical services at all (in the future), or it should be a declaration concerning the refusal to provide a service for an individual patient (see A. Zoll, *Prawo lekarza do odmowy…*, p. 24 and A. Jacek, *Stosowanie klauzuli sumienia…*, p. 108). According to the Tribunal, a recourse to that provision requires to adopt as appropriate the first interpretation. Associating the obligation of notification with a specific case of refusing a medical service would be essentially significant if providing the patient with information were the superior's duty. Since, however, the analysed provisions stipulate no superior's obligation in that regard, it should be held that the notification is rather a priori, addressed to the superior in principle at the time of establishing the employment relationship or service, or possibly – in the course of the relationship – when due to changes of his opinion the doctor wants to refrain from the exercise of services, which previously he was able to perform in accordance with his conscience. If we consider the mechanism of performing medical services financed from public funds, which was presented by the Minister of Health in the letter to the Tribunal, the purpose of such notification is quite clear. The basis for the financing of medical services is a contract between a healthcare provider and the National Health Fund, in which the operator (service provider) assumes the obligation to perform specified services for the benefit of the insured persons in exchange for certain remunerations. By signing a contract with the National Health Fund, "the provider undertakes to provide all services referred to as guaranteed in the relevant implementing regulations of the Act, in the range and type of services for which the contract was concluded" (letter of the Minister of Health, p. 20). A healthcare provider may also be held responsible for the material injury resulting from the non-performance of the contract. In the light of that information it seems obvious that a person, who negotiates and concludes a contract with the National Health Fund on behalf of a medicinal entity, should have knowledge of the capability of that entity to perform defined services. That capability, in turn, depends on the scope of services provided by the employed doctors. That is why the doctors-employees' superior – to manage rationally the entity, and in particular to be able to apply for public funding – should be aware that some or all of the employed doctors do not perform defined services.

In conclusion, according to the Tribunal some relevant arguments are in favour of considering the doctor's informing his superior about his use of the clause of conscience, required by Article 39 the second sentence of the Act on Professions of Doctor and Dentist, as single in principle and submitted in parallel with the establishment of the employment or service relationship (with the possibility of change of views), constituting a statement of prospective nature. At the same time, however, according to the Tribunal, the result of the subsequent assessment of the constitutionality of the obligation to inform the superior does not in principle depend on whether it is a single and a priori, or refers to every specific case of the refusal of medical service.

7.2.2. The Tribunal assumed that the value, for which the implementation of Article 39 the second sentence of the Act on Professions of Doctor and Dentist in the evaluated scope restricts the doctors' freedom of conscience, is public policy. As it has already been mentioned (Part III, para. 6.2.2 of the Justification), Article 68 para. 2 of the Constitution imposes on public authorities a duty to provide citizens with equal access to healthcare services financed from public funds. Although – in accordance with Article 68 para. 2 the Constitution – establishing the conditions and the scope of those services is left to the legislator (in contrast to Article 68 para. 1 of the Constitution, which grants the right to health protection to "everyone"), nevertheless, the health services granted by laws (their implementing acts) should be realised and available to citizens. A democratic state must have legal instruments enabling it to fulfil the obligations it has assumed. The Tribunal points out that the scope of health services financed from public funds is not questioned in the Supreme Medical Council's application and is not subject to the constitutional control in the present proceedings. Consequently, it must be assumed that public authorities are obliged to organise such a system of medical entities, that will make available all services financing of which by the National Health Fund is guaranteed by the valid normative acts. The obligation of the public authorities in this area also includes such medical services, the performance of which raises many doctors' moral objection (in particular the termination of pregnancy).

7.2.3. In the Tribunal's assessment, the purpose of the legislator, which is to ensure the availability of healthcare services financed from public funds, cannot be achieved without imposing on doctors-employees the obligation of notifying their supervisors, which is questioned by the Supreme Medical Council. The Tribunal does not find another way to determine which organisational entities provide specific services of, or rather – another possibility to exclude those entities, in which the doctors do not perform certain medical services.

7.2.4. According to the Tribunal, notifying the superior that an employed doctor will not perform defined services, does not affect the essence of the freedom of conscience. As it was noted above, the fact of invoking the clause of conscience is always a public act. Notifying the superior about the intention to apply it moves in time the disclosure of the doctor's moral principles, but does not change the nature of that act.

In conclusion, the Constitutional Tribunal decided that the assessed obligation to notify the superior is the means necessary for the implementation of the value indicated in Article 31 para. 3 of the Constitution, still it is a measure which does not unduly interfere with the doctors' freedom of conscience. Consequently, the questioned Article 39 the second sentence of the Act on Professions of Doctor and Dentist, in so far as it provides for obligating a doctor, working on the basis of the employment or service relationship, to notify his supervisor about his use of the clause of conscience, is compatible with Article 53 para. 1 in association with Article 31 para. 3 of the Constitution.

7.2.5. The Tribunal emphasises here, that the conducted assessment of the constitutionality of the contested regulation does not repeal for the doctor the provisions of the Act of 26 June 1974 – the Labour Code (Journal of laws of

2014, item 1502, as amended; hereinafter: LC) protecting the principle of equal treatment in employment, and in particular its Article 11^3 and the provisions of the Section I, Chapter IIa (Article 18^{3a} et seq. of the LC). That applies in particular to protecting the doctor as regards the establishment and termination of his employment relationship, conditions of his employment and promotion, e.g. because of his religion or belief.

7.3. Consequences of the doctor's obligation to inform his superior about his application of the right to refuse performing a medical service.

7.3.1. The Tribunal points out that the maintenance of the contested by the Supreme Medical Council obligation in spite of its effect criticised in the application, has also effects beneficial for doctors and in line with the applicant's expectations.

Firstly, the doctors who in advance inform their employers about their intention to apply the clause of conscience, should not be confronted with the necessity to refuse providing a service for a particular patient. Their supervisors should only turn to them when the performance of the service is indispensable to save the patient's life or health. Thereby, the doctor's obligation to inform the patient about the real possibilities of getting the service, found unconstitutional (Part III, point 6 of the Justification), in principle should not be put into practice.

Secondly, in practice, as a rule the doctor using the clause of conscience should not be subject to another obligation, which is the fourth ground of appeal, namely the obligation to make an appropriate annotation in the patient's medical record (Part III, point 8 of the Justification).

Thirdly, if all doctors employed by a medical entity notify their superior that – due to the incompatibility with their conscience – they do not perform specific medical services, there exists a basis to provide the public with the relevant information about the limited range of services provided by that entity. In such a case we do not deal with a so called collective conscience clause, but with facts. An entity which employs only staffs who do not perform certain services should not undertake to provide them in the contract with the National Health Fund, unless – on the basis of civil law contracts – it has, however, the possibility of providing them.

7.3.2. Therefore, the Tribunal found that the public authorities should shape the scope of contracts for medical services offered and concluded with medical entities in such a way, as not to include in them obligatorily non-therapeutic services that in practice most frequently give rise to doctors' invoking the conscience clause, and not force the contractors to undertake services which they cannot assume because of the lack of doctors. The National Health Fund, " contracting" health services, should not, by imposing the obligation to perform specified services as a condition *sine qua non* of concluding that contract, enforce the performance of "morally sensitive" services by medical entities and hence should not compel to shape the medical staff of those entities according to the criterion of conscience. It seems purposeful to contract those services separately and to maintain by the National Health Fund current information about performing them entities, because it is the public administration bodies, and not to the doctors or even medicinal entities, that are obliged to ensure, that services financed from public funds are available on an equal basis.

8. Assessment of the compatibility with the Constitution of Article 39 the first sentence of the Act on Professions of Doctor and Dentist (doctor's obligation to note and justify the fact of invoking the conscientious objection in the medical documentation).

8.1. The scope of the recognition of the allegation.

8.1.1. Article 39 the first sentence of the Act on Professions of Doctor and Dentist obligates the doctor, who refrains from executing a medical service because of conscientious objection, to note and justify the fact in the patient's medical documentation. The applicant alleges that that provision leads directly to disclosing the doctor's sensitive data, and therefore to a violation of Article 53 para. 7 of the Constitution, and the infringement is persistent due to the 20-year retention period of medical documentation. Since – according to the applicant – Article 53 para. 7 of the Constitution institutes a prohibition of an absolute character, the non-compliance with this constitutional control pattern is evident. By formulating a allegation of an infringement of Article 53 para. 1 of the Constitution, the applicant indicates that "self- accusation," which is required by the disputed provision, is not justified in the light of the principle of proportionality (Article 31, para. 3, of the Constitution). In addition, according to the applicant, Article 39 of the Act on Professions of Doctor and Dentist within the evaluation scope, striking the very essence of the freedom of conscience, violates the foundation of the democratic rule of law, and therefore Article 2 of the Constitution.

According to the Marshal of the Sejm, the allegations are based on a misunderstanding. The Marshal perceives much more narrowly than the Supreme Medical Council the disputed obligation of the doctor to document his own behaviour; that obligation does not comprise "justification of one's belief" (p. 46 of the application; that view was also repeated at the hearing before the Constitutional Tribunal). The doctor should write that he refrained from performing the service due to the conflict with his ethical beliefs and should explain that there do not occur any of the indicated in Article 30 of the Supreme Medical Council circumstances, which would require – as the Marshal of the Sejm verbalises it – "an absolute obligation of medical assistance" (p. 46 of the application).

According to the Public Prosecutor General, the purpose of the contested provision is to allow to distinguish an "ordinary", quite unjustified refusal of performance, from cases where the refusal is dictated by conscientious objection. The Public Prosecutor General considers so understood obligation as not only natural but also necessary to ensure that the institution of conscientious objection shall not be misused.

Moreover the participants of the proceeding underline also the importance of the obligation in question from the point of view of the patient's right to information about provided him services (Article 23 para. 1 of the Act on Professions of Doctor and Dentist).

8.1.2. The Tribunal, similarly as in the case of the allegation analysed before, adopts the view that Article 53 para. 7 of the Constitution is not an adequate benchmark of control. Within the currently analysed norm, unlikely to the previously considered case (cf. Section 7 of the Justification), undoubtedly we deal with the obligation of information concerning a specific, already existing refusal to perform a service by the doctor. In that situation apparently there has already occurred a doctor's disclosure of the fact, that the performance of a specific medical service is contrary to his conscience. In the Tribunal's assessment, it is not possible to simultaneously use the clause of conscience and keep secret the fact that the doctor uses it – according to the Roman principle *protestatio facta contraria non valet*. As long as one can imagine that as regards the obligation to notify prospectively a supervisor about using the clause (Part III, section 7 of the Justification), that without it the supervisor would never get acquainted with the doctors ethical outlooks (e.g., if during the period of employment of the doctor was never confronted with the necessity to perform contrary to his conscience), there is no way to imagine the secrecy in the case, when the doctor found himself in a situation of the conflict of conscience, and refused to provide a service, relying on Article 39 of the Act on Professions of Doctor and Dentist. The obligation to annotate that fact in the medical documentation is purely technical, reporting, but – above all – it is secondary in relation to the demonstrated by the doctor attitude of preserving his fidelity of conscience. Therefore the Tribunal concluded that Article 53 para. 7 of the Constitution is not an adequate standard of the constitutional control for Article 39, second sentence, of the Act on Professions of Doctor and Dentist, in so far as that provision imposes on the doctor the obligation to annotate the fact of refraining from performance of a service due to conscientious objection, in the medical documentation.

8.1.3. Moreover the Tribunal decided that the examination of the application in relation to the allegation of infringement of Article 2 the Constitution – due to the lack of sufficient grounds – shall be terminated on the basis of Article 39 para. 1 point 1 of the Act on the Constitutional Tribunal of 1997 in connection with Article 134 point 3 of the Act on the Constitutional Tribunal of 2015.

8.2. The constitutional assessment

8.2.1. The assessment of the conformity of the questioned norm with the standard, which was Article 53 para. 1 in connection with Article 31 para. 3 of the Constitution was started by the Tribunal with the presentation of the questioned obligation to document the refusal of executing a service by a doctor. The doctor's obligation to conduct an individual patient's medical record derives directly from Article 41 para. 1 of the Act on Professions of Doctor and Dentist. Every patient has the right to access medical documentation concerning his health and granted medical services (Article 23, para. 1, of the Act on patient's rights), which is correlated with the obligation of the entity granting medical services to carry, store and share medical documentation (Article 24, para. 1, of the Act on patient's rights). A natural consequence of those provisions is the obligation to annotate the a refusal to provide a service in the patient's medical record. The patient and the entities specified in Article 26 of the Act on patient's rights can demand written information about those cases. Such information may be necessary for example to demonstrate a deficiency in a doctor's performance in possible compensation proceedings.

The Tribunal sees no grounds for exclusion of the obligation to annotate the refusal to provide a medical service in the medical documentation in cases when that refusal is determined by the use of the clause of conscience by the doctor. The Tribunal does not see either, in what would consist an infringement of the doctor's freedom of conscience, guaranteed in Article 53 para. 1 of the Constitution in connection with the principle of proportionality expressed in Article 31 para. 3 of the Constitution. Constitutional concerns may raise only the obligation to "justify" a refusal, which – according to the applicant – leads to the disclosure of the doctor's worldview and can have a so called deterrent effect, meaning his renouncement from using his rights to protect his conscience in its external aspects out of the fear of disclosing his worldview and suffering possible negative consequences which can be connected with that fact.

8.2.2. The Tribunal notes that – in connection with the above mentioned considerations (Part III, para. 7.3 of the Justification) – the need to document the refusal of executing a service should in practice occur extremely rarely. Deemed compatible with the Constitution, the obligation to notify the supervisor of the use of the clause of conscience should serve – according to the Tribunal – i. a. a correct and efficient work organisation of medical entities. Correct organisation of work means that the supervisor directs patients to right doctors i.e. to doctors who are not only professionally prepared to perform a service (appropriate professionals), but also are ready to perform a specific medical service. Consequently, the Tribunal assumes that at least doctors practising under an employment or service relationship should not be, as a rule, confronted with the necessity to refuse performing contrary to their conscience. Therefore the disputed obligation will not arise for them. That obligation may occur when the doctor does not share the patient's or his superior's conviction that "the delay [in performing the service] would cause the danger of the loss of life, severe personal injury or serious health disorder", i.e. that the circumstances specified in Article 30 of the Act on Professions of Doctor and Dentist, which – after the Tribunal's judgment – will be the only ones claiming the doctor's duty to perform a service contrary to his conscience. In that case, giving a comprehensive justification of the reasons for refusal is necessary and lies primarily in the doctor's interest, because the consequences of the lack of justification can later be converted into his civil and disciplinary liability.

8.2.3. The Tribunal acknowledges that the contested provision does not specify what the required "justification" should contain. That allows different interpretations, including the one that obligates the doctor to indicate thoroughly the moral principle on which is based his refusal (as e.g., the position of the Bioethics Committee at the Presidium of the Polish Academy of Sciences no. 4/2013 of November 12, 2013 concerning the so-called clause of conscience and M. Boratyńska, *Free choice. Guarantees and limits of patients' right to self-determination*, Warsaw, 2012, p. 361) or simultaneous comprehensive discussion of that principle, its sources and its relation to the specific circumstances of patients' claims (cf. L. Bosek, *Klauzula sumienia – czy ustawa o zawodzie lekarza jest zgodna z konstytucją*, "Medycyna Praktyczna" no. 1/2014, p. 108 and A. Jacek, *Stosowanie klauzuli sumienia…*, p. 110; see also J. Pawlikowski, *Prawo do wyrażania sprzeciwu sumienia…*, pp. 38–39 and E. Zielińska, [in:] the Act on Professions of Doctor and Dentist…, p. 562). Hence, in the doctrine there appears the postulate to clarify the content of Article 39 para. 1 of the Act on professions of doctor and dentist (cf. A. Jacek, *Stosowanie klauzuli sumienia…*, p. 110).

The Tribunal did not concur with the indicated doubts, and in any case did not consider that their rank determined the incompatibility with the Constitution, even if the relevant control pattern were designated and justified – the principle of correct legislation, ensuing from Article 2 of the Constitution. Having in mind the purpose of the provision, the Tribunal found that the required by Article 39 the first sentence of the Act on Professions of Doctor and Dentist justification of the reasons for refusal of executing a service should be of medical character, and not serve to clarify the doctor's belief or to indicate the moral principles underlying his behaviour. The purpose of making medical documentation is not to perpetuate in writing doctors' views on philosophy and law, but to preserve medical data (for example, the results of health examinations, analyses or measurements) attesting that at the time of the refusal of executing a medical service there was no danger of the loss of the patient's life, or of a severe bodily injury, or of a serious health disorder. It is a misunderstanding to oblige a doctor to explain in medical documentation by what worldview he is guided in his life and professional work.

8.2.4. Referring to the allegation that the requirement of justifying the refusal to perform a service in the patient's medical documentation may have a deterring effect, i.e. may force doctors to act against their conscience for fear of the consequences of a refusal, the Tribunal found no grounds for that kind of concern. Again, the actual circumstances, in which the obligation to make appropriate annotation in the medical documentation is found, should be reassembled: they concern the situations, when the doctor refused to perform a medical service and, therefore, had the courage to take advantage of the clause of conscience, despite the obligation to annotate that fact. Therefore the assessed duty, contained in Article 39, the first sentence, of the Act on Professions of Doctor and Dentist, had not created " a deterring effect". As far as the "deterring effect" could be stated in case of the obligation to prospectively notify one's supervisor (Part III, section 7 of the Justification), the allegation of " deterring" doctors by demanding to annotate their already performed actions (omissions) in medical documentation is irrelevant. Consequently, the Tribunal stated that Article 39, the first sentence, of the Act on Professions of Doctor and Dentist does not infringe Article 53 para. 1 in connection with Article 31 para. 3 of the Constitution in the assessed scope.

For the above reasons, the Constitutional Tribunal decided as set forth in the conclusion hereof.

Dorinda C. Bordley & Nikolas T. Nikas

Conscience and Science: Why a Conscientious Objection to Forced Prescription or Dispensation of Abortifacient Drugs Is Reasonable

In the world today, there is an ongoing struggle for the soul of Western civilization. "Reason," once understood as the essence of law because it pointed to justice, is now replaced by human "will," effectively codifying as law human passions regardless of justice, in an attempt to normalize self-serving behaviors that neither benefit the good of the human person nor the common good. Acts once considered inherently evil for millennia are now routinely claimed to be essential for the protection of some newly asserted human "right," unknown throughout human history until creatively manufactured and asserted by legislative bodies and courts over the last several decades.

Unfortunately, the medical and allied health professions have not escaped this "culture war." The pressure on physicians, nurses and pharmacists (and students studying to enter these noble professions) to participate directly or indirectly in these newly conceived, albeit objectively immoral, "rights" mounts daily.

Abortion, euthanasia, physician-assisted suicide and provision of abortifacient drugs, to name but a few of the asserted "necessary goods" of the brave new world, are all claimed by some medical and health activists as the essence of good medical care. Consequently, the exercise of conscientious objection to these sacred cows of modernity is increasingly seen as rank heresy to the prevailing progressive, relativistic, materialistic orthodoxy being relentlessly and intolerantly imposed.

One particular case of note has reached the doorstep of Supreme Court of the United States. Pharmacists licensed in the State of Washington attempted to conscientiously object to a state regulation that required them to dispense abortifacient contraceptive drugs, that is, drugs that have the possibility of causing the destruction of a developing human being at the embryonic stage of existence.

The heart of their conscientious objection rests on two reasonable claims: (1) the result of human conception is a new human being and (2) that certain so-called "contraceptive" drugs have the known capacity on occasion to end the life of a developing human being rather than preventing its conception. While a claim of conscientious objection does not necessarily have to rest on a scientific basis to be honored, in this case modern embryology and pharmacology demonstrate that the pharmacists' objections are reasonable and consistent with uncontroverted medical science.

The attached *amicus curie* brief supporting a petition for review, filed recently in the United States Supreme Court on behalf of certain medical associations by the Bioethics Defense Fund and others, sets forth in great detail the science buttressing the conscience claims of the Washington state pharmacists. This brief was submitted to the United States Supreme Court, and now to the readers of this article, to demonstrate that science and morality are not in opposition when it comes to the nature and effect of certain abortifacient drugs. Indeed, in this case, science and morality demonstrate that conscientious objection to dispensing abortifacient drugs is deeply rooted in reason and therefore just. Consequently, this exercise of conscience should be respected by the medical profession, and recognized by courts of law. For more details, see below the attached amicus curie.

Dorinda C. Bordley & Nikolas T. Nikas

Brief Amicus Curiae to US Supreme Court Case *Stormans Inc v. John Wiesman*

In The
Supreme Court of the United States

--------------------------------♦--------------------------------

STORMANS INC., doing business as Ralph's Thriftway, *et al.*,
Petitioners,
v.
JOHN WIESMAN, Secretary of the Washington State Department of Health,
et al.,
Respondents.

--------------------------------♦--------------------------------

BRIEF *AMICUS CURIAE* OF AMERICAN ASSOCIATION OF PROLIFE OBSTETRICIANS & GYNECOLOGISTS, ASSOCIATION OF AMERICAN PHYSICIANS & SURGEONS, CATHOLIC MEDICAL ASSOCIATION, CHRISTIAN MEDICAL ASSOCIATION, AND CHRISTIAN PHARMACISTS FELLOWSHIP INTERNATIONAL IN SUPPORT OF PETITIONERS

--------------------------------♦--------------------------------

NIKOLAS T. NIKAS DORINDA C. BORDLEY - Bioethics Defense Fund

"QUESTION PRESENTED"

Whether the Petitioner-Pharmacists' belief that it is immoral to participate in the taking of human life is informed by the objective medical science establishing that a new, distinct, human being comes into existence at the moment of sperm-egg fusion, and that the objectionable drugs, Plan B and *ella*, have the capacity to end the life of a new human being at the embryonic stage of development.

SUMMARY OF THE ARGUMENT

Petitioner-Pharmacists believe that they have a religious and moral duty to refrain from the taking of human life. Informing this sincerely held religious belief and moral conviction that forms the basis of their conscientious objection is objective medical science establishing that a unique, individual human being comes into existence at the moment of sperm- egg fusion (known as conception or fertilization), and that the objectionable drugs, Plan B and *ella*, have the capacity to end the life of a new human being.

More specifically, the Petitioner-Pharmacists conscience objections are based on their sincerely held religious beliefs that each individual human being is entitled to dignity and protection from the moment of conception/fertilization until natural death. The Ninth Circuit erred by failing to recognize the distinction between the *objective* scientific facts that inform Petitioner-Pharmacists' conscience objections and their religious beliefs about the moral value of every human life from the moment that life begins, as determined by the scientific facts. This led the Ninth Circuit to erroneously reject the Pharmacists' asserted "right to refrain from taking human life" as not "objectively" established. *Stormans v. Wiesman*, 794 F.3d 1064, 1086 (9th Cir. 2015).

This brief on behalf of *Amici* medical associations presents the objective and scientifically supportable facts that inform the religious objections by the Petitioner-Pharmacists in regard to the stocking and dispensing of drugs that have the capacity to terminate the life of a human being at the embryonic stage of development as one possible mechanism of action – specifically the so-called "emergency contraceptive" drugs known as Plan B and *ella*.

The amicus brief begins by presenting a concise survey of human embryology and establishing that the biological humanity of a new embryonic human being begins at the moment of sperm-egg fusion (fertilization). The next section includes a review of the medical literature, FDA directives, and FDA- approved labeling on Plan B and ella – all of which Petitioner-Pharmacists reasonably rely on to conclude that these drugs have the capacity to destroy the life of a human being at the earliest stages of development.

The Ninth Circuit erred in disregarding the district court's factual findings and adopting an exceptionally narrow interpretation of the Free Exercise Clause that upsets the longstanding national consensus on the issue of conscience protections in health- care. *Amici* respectfully urge this Court to grant the petition for writ of *certiorari*.

ARGUMENT

The Pharmacists' Conscience Objections Regarding "Emergency Contraceptives" Are Consistent with Objective Scientific Evidence

As established in the district court, the Petitioner-Pharmacists are Christians who inform their con- sciences with objective scientific facts establishing that every individual human being comes into existence at the moment of fertilization, when the female ovum and male sperm unite to begin the unique and separate life of an individual human embryo. Their sincerely held religious belief in the inherent dignity of every human life thus leads them to ascribe moral value to pre-implantation human beings, such that their cooperation with the dispensation of drugs capable of destroying those early human lives would be considered a grave evil.[1]

The Pharmacists' conscience objections that dispensing the so-called "emergency contraceptives" Plan B or *ella* constitutes immoral direct participation in the destruction of human life is based on the Pharmacists' objective review of the medical literature, FDA directives, and FDA-approved labeling on Plan B and *ella* – all of which confirm that Plan B and *ella* are known to have the capacity to prevent a new human being whose life began at fertilization from implanting in the uterine lining, thus causing the death of the new human embryo.

Despite the objectivity of the facts undergirding the Pharmacists' sincere religious beliefs and moral convictions, the Ninth Circuit disregarded the district court's factual findings and adopted an exceptionally narrow interpretation of the Free Exercise Clause that upsets the longstanding national consensus on the issue of conscience protections in healthcare.

More specifically, the Ninth Circuit failed to recognize the distinction between the "objective" scientific facts that inform Petitioner-Pharmacists' conscience objections and the Pharmacists' religious beliefs about the moral value of every human life from the moment that life begins, as determined by the scientific facts. This led the Ninth Circuit to disregard the Pharma- cists' asserted fundamental liberty interest in the "right to refrain from taking human life," and to erroneously dismiss it as not "objectively" established. *Stormans v. Wiesman*, 794 F.3d 1064, 1086 (9th Cir. 2015).[2] If left standing, this new standard would eviscerate the ability of Christian pharmacists and other healthcare providers

---

1 The district court found that the pharmacists "are Chris- tians who believe that all of human life is uniquely and inherently precious because it is created by God in His image" and that "dispensing Plan B or *ella* constitutes direct participation in the destruction of human life." *Stormans v. Selecky*, 854 F.Supp.2d 925, 962 (W.D. Wash. 2012) (Finding No. 149). For that reason, the Pharmacists' "religious beliefs prevent them from stocking or delivering Plan B or *ella*." *Id.*

2 *See generally*, Brief *Amicus Curiae* of Christian Legal So- ciety in support of Petitioners (to be filed Feb. 5, 2016) setting forth the argument that courts in free exercise cases do not second-guess the truth of the claimant's belief, and that at any rate the belief in this case is based on a reasonable conclusion from objective scientific evidence.

to serve others via their vocations in accord with their sincerely held religious beliefs and moral convictions that respect the sanctity of human life.

A Embryology establishes that the life of a new human being begins at fertilization, and that implantation is simply a later but necessary event instituted by the new human organism for the pur- pose of nourishment

To clearly understand the basis of the Pharmacists' conscientious objection to dispensing the objectionable drugs, it is necessary to distinguish "fertilization" (which marks the beginning of an individ- ual human life) from uterine "implantation" (a later event in the self-directed life of the human embryo that is the standard marker for determining that a woman is pregnant).

In their filings in the Ninth Circuit, the Respondents and Intervenors entangled and interchanged these two separate phases of development in the life of the individual human being in their attempt to cast the Pharmacists' conscience objections as unreasonable. To be clear, Petitioner-Pharmacists' religious beliefs and moral convictions attach to the moral status of the human life that comes into existence at the moment of fertilization, with the later event of implantation of the human embryo into the uterine wall simply being a necessary condition of that human being's continued life cycle.

1 *Fertilization*

As universally stated in medical embryology text- books used in United States medical schools, each individual human life has its origin at the moment of fertilization. For example:

"Human development begins at fertilization when a male gamete or sperm (spermatozoon) unites with a female gamete or oocyte (ovum) to produce a single cell – a zygote. This highly specialized, totipotent cell marked the beginning of each of us as a unique individual."

Keith L. Moore and T.V.N. Persuad, THE DEVELOPING HUMAN: CLINICALLY ORIENTED EMBRYOLOGY 11 (10th ed. 2015) (emphasis added).

"Fertilization, the uniting of egg and sperm, takes place in the oviduct. After the oocyte finishes meiosis, the paternal and maternal chromosomes come together, resulting in the formation of a zygote containing a single diploid nucleus. Embryonic development is considered to begin at this point."

Schoenwolf, G.C., LARSEN'S HUMAN EMBRYOLOGY 14 (5th ed. 2015) (emphasis added).

"Although life is a continuous process, fertilization [...] is a critical landmark because, under ordinary circumstances, **a new genetically distinct human organism is formed** when the chromosomes of the male and female pronuclei blend in the oocyte."

O'Rahilly, R. and Miller, F., HUMAN EMBRYOLOGY AND TERATOLOGY 8 (3rd ed. 2001) (emphasis added).

The universally accepted scientific fact about the beginning of each individual human life is also recognized in a myriad of peer-reviewed scientific literature. *See, e.g.*, Wilding, M., et al., *Maternal non-Mendelian inheritance of a reduced lifespan? A hypothesis*, 31(6) Journal of Assist. Reprod. Genet. 637–43 (Jun. 2014) ("**Since a new individual** is derived from the fusion of a single sperm and egg, we tested.") (emphasis added); Gadella B.M., Boerke A., *An update on post-ejaculatory remodeling of the sperm surface before mammalian fertilization*, 85(1) Theriogenology 113–24 (Jan. 1, 2016) ("The fusion of a sperm with an oocyte to form **new life** is a highly regulated event.") (emphasis added).[3]

Therefore, the objective scientific observation that "a unique individual" begins his or her life "at fertilization" is the factual foundation of the Pharmacists' religious objection to dispensing a drug that has the capacity to halt the natural processes involved in the ongoing nourishment and development of the newly formed human embryo. The Petitioner- Pharmacists are simply acting in accord with the objective fact that "[b]ased on universally accepted scientific criteria" every human being begins his or her life "as a new cell, the human zygote, which comes into existence at the moment of sperm-egg fusion, an event that occurs in less than a second."[4]

While no one objects to the destruction of ordinary human cells for biomedical research or any other purpose, the destruction of *human beings* to obtain

3 *See also*, Kashir, J., Nomikos, M., Swann, K., Lai F.A., *PLCζ or PAWP: revisiting the putative mammalian sperm factor that triggers egg activation and embryogenesis*, 21(5) MOL. HUM. REPROD. 383–88 (May 2015) ("In mammals, egg activation is initiated by multiple cytosolic Ca(2+) transients (Ca(2+) oscillations) that are triggered following delivery of a putative sperm factor from the fertilizing sperm. The identity of this 'sperm factor' thus holds much significance, not only as a vital component in creating a new life, but also for its potential therapeutic and diagnostic value in human infertility.") (emphasis added)

4 Condic, M.L., *When Does Human Life Begin? A Scientific Perspective* ix (Westchester Institute 2008), *available at* http://bdfund.org/wordpress/wp-content/uploads/2012/06/wi_whitepaper_life_print.pdf. All internet citations throughout this brief were last checked January 28, 2016.

biological material for research is a matter of grave moral and legal consequence.[5] As a matter of logic, there must be some non-arbitrary scientific criteria to determine when living human gamete cells give rise to a new individual human being.

These criteria are cogently presented in a white paper authored by Maureen Condic, Ph.D., *When Does Life Begin: A Scientific Perspective* (2008),[6] and updated in 2014.[7] The Condic white paper provides a concise yet comprehensive survey of the foundational question of when, as a matter of developmental biology, the life of a new human being begins. The conclusions unambiguously support the factual premise underlying Pharmacists' conscience objections. After all, their objection to the challenged requirement to stock and dispense Plan B and *ella* are coherent only if the drugs are capable of taking the life of a human being and not a mere collection of human cells.

Specifically, the review of modern embryology found in the Condic white paper provides this Court with the objective conclusions of two central questions regarding the biological beginning of human life: (1) in the course of sperm-egg interaction, when is a new cell formed that is distinct from either sperm or egg? and (2) is this new cell a distinct individual human organism (i.e., a new human being), or merely a new kind of human cell?[8]

Based on universally accepted scientific criteria, the white paper sets forth the unequivocal conclusion that a new single-cell organism, the human zygote, comes into existence at a precise moment of sperm- egg fusion, an event that occurs in less than a second.

---

5 *See* YUVAL LEVIN, IMAGINING THE FUTURE: SCIENCE AND AMERICAN DEMOCRACY (2008); Robert P. George and Christopher Tollefson, EMBRYO (2008); *see also* Albert R. Jonsen, THE BIRTH OF BIOETHICS 90–100 (1998), recounting the history of the 1974 legislation that created the National Commission for the Protection of Human Subjects of Biomedical and Behavioral Research. The Commission was charged to conduct a "comprehensive study of the ethical, legal, and social implications of advances in biomedical research" involving human subjects. The Commission ultimately produced *The Belmont Report*, which became the basis for federal regulations at 45 C.F.R. 46, Subpart A "to cover all biomedical researchers who received federal funds for their work" including protection for human fetuses.

6 *Supra*, n.5.

7 *See also*, Condic, M.L., *When Does Human Life Begin? The Scientific Evidence and Terminology Revisited*, 8 UNIV. OF ST. THOMAS JOURNAL OF LAW AND PUBLIC POLICY 44, 46 (2014), *avail- able at* <https://www.stthomas.edu/media/schooloflaw/pdf/jlpp/volume 8no1/CondicArticle.pdf.>

8 *Id.* at 5.

Upon formation, the human zygote immediately initiates a complex sequence of events that establish the molecular conditions required for its own self-directed development. The behavior of the one-cell human embryo and its molecular composition are radically unlike that of either sperm or egg separately, and are characteristic of a human organism.[9]

As the human embryo matures over the next hours and days, it continues to meet the distinguishing feature of an organism or being: self-directed interaction of parts in the context of a coordinated whole.[10] In contrast, collections of human cells (such as skin cells) carry on the activities of cellular life, yet fail to exhibit the coordinated interactions directed towards any higher level of organization that are unique to a human organism. Unlike a human embryo, collections of skin or other somatic cells do not establish the complex, interrelated cellular structures (tissues, organs, and organ systems) that exist in a whole, living human being.[11]

Thus, from the beginning, "the human embryo is a living, individuated human being. The unique behavior and molecular composition of embryos, from their initiation at sperm-egg fusion onward, can be readily observed and manipulated in the laboratory using the scientific method. Thus, the conclusion that a human zygote is a human being (i.e., a human organism) is not a matter of religious belief, societal convention or emotional reaction. It is a matter of observable, objective, scientific fact."[12]

In addition to scientists and developmental biologists, other prominent Jewish and Christian theologians, philosophers and scholars have recognized that a human embryo from the moment of fertilization is indeed a *human being*:

"The embryo is a being; that is to say, it is an integral whole with actual existence. The being is human; it will not articulate itself into some other kind of animal. Any *being* that is *human* is a human being. If it is objected that, at five days or fifteen days, the embryo does not look like a human being, it must be pointed out that this is precisely what a human being looks like – and what each of us looked like – at five or fifteen days of development. Clarity of language is essential to clarity of thought."[13]

---

9 *Id.* at 7.

10 *Id.* at 6.

11 *Id.*

12 13 Expert Report of Maureen L. Condic, as quoted in *Planned Parenthood of Ind. v. Comm'r*, 794 F.Supp.2d 892, 916–17 (S.D. Ind. 2011).

13 Ramsey Colloquium, *The Inhuman Use of Human Beings: A Statement on Embryo Research*, 49 FIRST THINGS 17, 18 (1995), *available at* <http://www.firstthings.com/article/1995/01/001-the- inhuman-use-of-human-beings>.

2 *Implantation*

Approximately five to six days *after* the human embryo's life has begun at fertilization, the human embryo (now at the "blastocyst" stage of development) begins the self-directed process of attaching to the uterine lining.[14] Uterine implantation is necessary for the human embryo's continued development because it provides nourishment from surrounding maternal tissues.[15]

Thus, if a human embryo is unable to attach to the uterus due to the mechanism of the objectionable drugs, the human embryo, now one week old, will not have the environment necessary to provide for continued nourishment and growth. Just as a newly born human infant left alone in an environment without human milk or formula is no less human, neither is a human being at the embryonic stage of development any less human when a drug prevents the embryo's nourishment that can only be received in the environment of uterine implantation.

The Pharmacists' offer of proof in the district court included an expert report of Bruce M. Carlson, M.D., Ph.D., a University of Michigan medical professor and author of two widely used textbooks on embryology. Dr. Carlson's report provides rebuttal to Intervenors' expert report of Dr. David Grimes, whose statements focused on whether emergency contraception causes post-*implantation*

The Ramsey Colloquium signatories include Leon R. Kass, M.D., who was at that time with the University of Chicago, Committee on Social Thought, as well as Hadley Arkes, Amherst College; Matthew Berke, First Things; Gerard Bradley, Notre Dame Law School; Fr. James T. Burtchaell, Congregation of the Holy Cross; Fr. Francis Canavan, Fordham University; Rabbi David G. Dalin, West Hartford, CT; Midge Decter, Institute on Religion and Public Life; Thomas S. Derr, Smith College; Fr. Ernest Fortin, Boston College; Jorge Garcia, Rutgers University; Rabbi Marc Gellman, Dix Hills, NY; Robert P. George, Princeton University; Mary Ann Glendon, Harvard Law School; Stanley Hauerwas, Duke University; John Hittinger, Professor of Phi- losophy, CO; Russell Hittinger, Catholic University of America; Rev. Robert W. Jenson, St. Olaf College; Ralph McInerny, University of Notre Dame; Fr. Richard John Neuhaus, Institute on Religion and Public Life; Rabbi David Novak, University of Virginia; Michael Novak, American Enterprise Institute; James Nuechterlein, First Things; David Singer, American Jewish Committee; George Weigel, Ethics and Public Policy Center; and Robert L. Wilken, University of Virginia. Institutional affilia- tions given for identification purposes only.

14 *See* embryology textbooks cited in Section A(1), *supra*.

15 *See, e.g.*, Burton, G.J., et al., *Nutrition of the human fetus during the first trimester – a review*, PLACENTA, Suppl. A:S70-7 (Apr. 2001).

abortion.[16] Dr. Grimes' statements were found by Dr. Carlson to "miss the point of the plaintiffs' [Petitioner-Pharmacists'] case, namely that from the time of fertilization the human embryo deserves full protection":

"Because the plaintiffs believe that human life should be protected from the time of fertilization, the discussion of pregnancy's be- ginning upon implantation is irrelevant, because at the time of implantation the embryo has already been worthy of protection for approximately six days."[17]

Therefore, as explained by Dr. Carlson, "Regard- less of the mechanism of action of Plan B, the plain- tiffs' concerns would only be assuaged if the scientific evidence showed that in no case does Plan B act by preventing implantation of an existing embryo."[18]

B Plan B and *ella* have the capacity to end the life of a human being at the embryonic stage of development in the event fertilization has occurred

Drugs and devices with post-fertilization mechanisms of action are properly considered by Petitioner- Pharmacists to be life-ending since embryology establishes that a unique human life begins at fertilization. Although these drugs or devices have the capacity to end a distinct human being's life either before or after uterine implantation, they are labeled by the FDA as "contraception," a term that connotes simply preventing fertilization/conception.

This is because the FDA's relevant criterion is whether the drugs can work by preventing "pregnancy" – a term that describes the state of the woman – which they define as beginning at "implantation," not fertilization.[19]

Moreover, as will be discussed below, with the approval of the drug *ella* in 2010, the FDA definition of "contraception" now encompasses a drug or device that has the capacity to end the life of a human em- bryo even *after* implantation.

---

16 17 Expert Report of Dr. David A. Grimes (Sept. 26, 2008) (Intervenors' Offer of Proof, Doc. 493-1, at 2-9).

17 Expert Report of Dr. Bruce Coleman (Oct. 30, 2008) (Plaintiffs' Offer of Proof Regarding Mechanism of Action of Emergency Contraceptives Related to their Religious Beliefs, Doc. 495 at 18–26).

18 *Id.* at 18.

19 For an overview of how the definition of pregnancy has changed, *see* Christopher Gacek, *Conceiving Pregnancy: U.S. Med- ical Dictionaries and Their Definitions of Conception and Preg- nancy*, FRC INSIGHT PAPER (Apr. 2009), *available at* <http://downloads.frc.org/EF/EF09D12.pdf.>

In his recent study on "emergency contraception," Dr. James Trussell, whose research concerning "contraception" has been cited by the FDA, states: "To make an informed choice, women must know that [emergency contraception pills] may at times inhibit implantation."[20] In other words, Dr. Trussell, although an advocate of "emergency contraception,"[21] understands that the scientific difference between a drug that prevents fertilization/conception of a new human embryo and one that may also prevent implantation of that human embryo into the uterine lining is significant enough that it must be disclosed to a potential user.

Strikingly, Dr. Warren Wallace, a physician at Northwestern University Medical School who has prescribed "emergency contraceptives," and who was called to testify in support of a law restricting rights of conscience pertaining to the prescription of "emergency contraception," testified under oath that "there is a new unique human life before" implantation of an embryo.[22]

Moreover, a relatively new drug classified by the FDA as an "emergency contraception" – Ulipristal Acetate (*ella*) – is actually an abortion-inducing drug, because it can cause the death of a human embryo after implantation, the accepted marker for the be- ginning of pregnancy. The mechanisms of action of each common type of "emergency contraception" are discussed in more detail below.

1 *Plan B can end the life of a human embryo by preventing implantation.*

In 1999, the FDA first approved the distribution of "emergency contraception," specifically "Plan B," by prescription. In 2006, the FDA extended the drug's approval to over-the-counter sales for women 18 years of age and over.[23]

---

20 J. Trussell et al., *Emergency Contraception: A Last Chance to Prevent Unintended Pregnancy*, Office of Population Research at Princeton University (Jun. 2010).

21 *See* Profile of Dr. James Trussell, *available at* <https:// www.princeton.edu/~trussell/> (Trussell "has actively promoted making emergency contraception more widely available").

22 Transcript of Bench Trial at 91–92, 111, *Morr-Fitz, Inc. v. Quinn*, 2012 IL App. (4th) 110398 (Ill. App. Ct. Sept. 20, 2012).

23 In 2013, the Food and Drug Administration approved Plan B as a nonprescription drug for women who have the potential to bear children, pursuant to a federal court ruling in a suit brought by the Center for Reproductive Rights that was not appealed by the Obama administration. This ruling meant that teenagers could purchase Plan B over the counter, without a prescription. Before this ruling, women under age 17 needed a prescription to buy Plan B. FDA News Release, *FDA Approves Plan B One-Step emergency contraception for use without a pre- scription for all women of child-bearing*

Although called "contraception," the FDA's labeling acknowledges that Plan B can prevent implantation of a human embryo.[24] 25 Further, the FDA states on its website:

"Plan B acts primarily by stopping the release of an egg from the ovary (ovulation). It may prevent the union of sperm and egg (fertili- zation). **If fertilization does occur, Plan B may prevent a fertilized egg[25] from attaching to the womb (implantation).**"[26]

On its website, the same explanation is provided by Duramed Pharmaceuticals, the manufacturer of Plan B One-Step:

HOW "PLAN B ONE-STEP"® WORKS

It works mainly by:

Stopping the release of an egg from the ovary

It is possible that Plan B One-Step® may also work by:

Preventing fertilization of an egg (the uniting of sperm with the egg)

Preventing attachment (implantation) to the uterus (womb)[27]

2 Ella *can end the life of a human embryo by preventing implantation or by causing an implanted human embryo to lose sustenance from the uterine lining*

In 2010, the FDA approved the drug Ulipristal Acetate (*ella*) as another "emergency contraceptive." Importantly, *ella* is not a variant of Plan B; instead, the chemical make-up of *ella* is similar to the abortion drug RU-486. Like RU-486, *ella* is a selective progesterone receptor modulator (SPRM) – "[t]he mechanism

potential (Jun. 20, 2013), *available at* <http://www.fda.gov/NewsEvents/Newsroom/PressAnnouncements/ucm358082.htm.>

24 Plan B Approved Labeling, 12.1 *available at* http://www. accessdata.fda.gov/drugsatfda_docs/label/2009/021998lbl.pdf (Plan B "may inhibit implantation (by altering the endometrium).").

25 *Amici* medical associations emphasize that "fertilized egg" is a non-scientific euphemism for the early human embryo.

26 FDA, *FDA's Decision Regarding Plan B: Questions and Answers* (updated Apr. 30, 2009), *available at* http://www.fda. gov/cder/drug/infopage/planB/planBQandA.htm (emphasis added).

27 Duramed Pharmaceuticals, *How Plan B One-Step Works* (2016), *available at* http://www.planbonestep.com/howitworks.aspx (emphasis added).

of action of ulipristal (*ella*) in human ovarian and endometrial tissue is identical to that of its parent compound mifepristone."[28]

This means that though labeled as "contraception," *ella* works the same way as RU-486. By blocking progesterone – a hormone necessary to build and maintain the uterine wall during pregnancy – an SPRM can either prevent a human embryo from implanting in the uterus, or it can abort a human embryo that has already implanted in the uterine lining by essentially starving it to death. Therefore, *ella* has the capacity to abort a pregnancy even under a definition that limits abortion to the time after the human embryo implants in the uterus.[29]

i FDA labeling and directives

The FDA's own labeling notes that *ella* may "af- fect implantation,"[30] and advises against the use of *ella* in the case of known or suspected pregnancy. A study funded by *ella*'s manufacturer, HRA Pharma, explains that SPRMs (drugs that block the hormone progesterone) "including ulipristal acetate" can "impair implantation."[31] While the study theorizes that the dosage used in its trial "might be too low to inhibit implantation,"[32] it states affirmatively "an additional

28 D.J. Harrison & J.G. Mitroka, *Defining Reality: The Po- tential Role of Pharmacists in Assessing the Impact of Progesterone Receptor Modulators and Misoprostol in Reproductive Health, 45 ANNALS PHARMACOLOTHERAPY 115, 115–19 (2011).*

29 *See* Gacek, C., *Conceiving Pregnancy, supra* note 19. Be- cause the semantics of what constitutes an "abortifacient" or "abortion-inducing" drug differ based on the underlying moral value ascribed to the pre-implantation human embryo, this brief focuses on the more precise question of when the life of the human embryo begins and how Plan B and *ella* end the life of the human embryo, whether before uterine implantation or after.

30 *ella* Labeling Information, 12.1, *available at* http://www. accessdata.fda.gov/drugsatfda_docs/label/2010/022474s000lbl.pdf.

31 32 Glasier et al., *Ulipristal acetate versus levongestrel for emergency contraception: a randomized non-inferiority trial and meta-analysis*, 375 THE LANCET 555, 555–62 (2010).

32 *Id.* In the Glasier study, "follow-up was done 5–7 days after expected menses. If menses had occurred and a pregnancy test was negative, participation [in the study] ended. If menses had not occurred, participants returned a week later." *Id.* Con- sidering that implantation must occur before menses, the study could not, and did not attempt to, measure an impact on an embryo prior to implantation or even shortly after implantation. *Id. ella* was not given to anyone who was known to already be pregnant (upon enrollment participants were given a pregnancy test; pregnant women were excluded from the study). *See id.* The only criterion for *ella* "working" was that a woman was not

postovulatory mechanism of action," for example, impairing implantation, "cannot be excluded."[33]

And according to a commentary by a professor of molecular pharmacology in the *International Journal of Women's Health*, "[w]hen unprotected intercourse and the administration of ulipristal occur at or within 24 hours of ovulation, then ulipristal has an abortifacient action."[34]

In fact, *ella*'s deadliness is confirmed by its high rate of "effectiveness." Notably, at the FDA advisory panel meeting for *ella*, panelist Dr. Scott Emerson, a professor of biostatistics at the University of Washington, raised the point that the low pregnancy rate for women taking *ella* four or five days after intercourse suggests that the drug must have an "abortifacient" quality.[35]

In short, the FDA-approved "contraceptive" *ella* can work by ending an established pregnancy – meaning a pregnancy as defined by the stage of embryonic development in which the embryo implants by its own self-directed, self-organizing action into the uterine lining.[36]

---

preg- nant in the end. *See id.* Whether that was achieved through blocking implantation, or even ending implantation, was not determinable. *See id.*

33 *Id.*

34 Ralph P. Miech, *Immunopharmacology of Ulipristal as an Emergency Contraceptive*, 3 INT'L J. WOMEN'S HEALTH 391–97 (2011).

35 *See* Transcript, Food and Drug Administration Center for Drug Evaluation and Research (CDER), Advisory Committee for Reproductive Health Drugs 157–58 (Jun. 17, 2010), *available at* http://www.fda.gov/downloads/AdvisoryCommittees/Committees MeetingMaterials/Drugs/ReproductiveHealthDrugsAdvisoryCommittee/ UCM218560.pdf.

36 Despite the objective science as established by both the manufacturers and other supporters of "emergency contraceptive," the ideological denial of the drugs' mechanisms of action persist. For example, the 2012 opening brief of the Intervenors at the appellate level suggested that the Pharmacists' conscience objections are unreasonable, stating: "Plaintiffs refuse to dispense Plan B because they believe, *contrary to the scientific evidence*, that Plan B can cause a fertilized egg to fail to implant in the uterus, which they consider the taking of a life." Opening Brief of Intervenors-Appellants Judith Billings et al., at 14 n.1 (emphasis added).
Intervenors leveled this accusation based on a *New York Times* article which itself admits that the Federal Drug Administration (FDA) requires the drugs' product packaging materials to reveal the capacity of "emergency contraception" to prevent implanta- tion in the event fertilization occurs. For a rebuttal of the claims made in the *New York Times* article, *see* Donna Harrison, *The Times's Convolution of Facts on Abortifacients*, National Review Online (Jun. 6, 2012), *available at* http://www.nationalreview.com/corner/301980/timess-convolution-facts-abortifacients-donna-harrison.

ii Peer-reviewed medical literature

Studies confirm that ella is toxic to a human embryo.[37] Beyond review articles, there are four important original research articles examining the effects of dose- and time-specific provision of *ella* (also known as UPA, and CBD-2914 in the medical literature), all confirming that *ella* is toxic to a human embryo.[38]

These studies, which were cited by the manufacturer in its own FDA application, demonstrate that *ella* is capable of interfering with progesterone production by the ovary, needed for the woman's body to sustain the conditions needed for the human embryo's continued life. The studies confirm that *ella* interferes with the action of progesterone on the lining of the uterus, causing human embryos who have not yet implanted to be unable to do so, and further causing the death of human embryos who have implanted.[39]

---

37 *See, e.g.*, European Medicines Agency, *Evaluation of Med- icines for Human Use: CHMP Assessment Report for Ellaone*, at 16 (2009), *available at* http://www.ema.europa.eu/docs/en_GB/ document_library/EPAR_-_Public_assessment_report/human/001027/WC500023673.pdf.

38 Stratton, P., Hartog, B., Hajizadeh, N., Piquion, J., Suther- land, D., Merino, M., Lee, Y.J., and Nieman, L.K., *A Single Mid- Follicular Dose of CDB-2914, a New Antiprogestin, Inhibits Folliculogenesis and Endometrial Differentiation in Normally Cycling Women*, 15(5) HUMAN REPRODUCTION 1092–99 (2000); Passaro, M., Piquion, J., Mullen, N., et al., *Luteal phase dose re- sponse relationships of the antiprogestin CDB-2914 in normally cycling women*, 18(9) HUMAN REPRODUCTION 1820–27 (2003); Brache, V., Cochon, L., Jesam, C. et al., *Immediate Pre-Ovulatory Administration of 30 mg Ulipristal Acetate Significantly Delays Follicular Rupture*, 25(9) HUMAN REPRODUCTION 2256–63 (2010); Stratton, P., Levens, E., Hartog, B., et al., *Endometrial Effects of a Single Early Luteal Dose of the Selective Progesterone Receptor Modulator CDB-2914*, 93(6) FERTILITY AND STERILITY 2035–41 (Apr. 2010). CDB-2914 is a selective progesterone modulator similar in structure and function to UPA. *See* Passaro, et al., 2003, at 1821.

39 For a more in depth analysis of these studies, *see* Brehany, J., Ph.D., *No consensus on ella*, 41(2) ETHICS & MEDICS (Feb. 2016), *available at* http://ncbcenter.org/document.doc?id=923 ("Be- low I question whether a relevant consensus exists and argue that the scientific evidence militates against, rather than in favor of, use of UPA/*ella* by Catholic providers.").

Annex: National Laws in EU Member States on Freedom of Conscience and Conscientious Objection

Member State	Relevant Law		Provision	Details
AUSTRIA	**General:**	Staatsgrundgesetz	Art. 14	'Everyone is guaranteed complete freedom of conscience and creed. The enjoyment of civil and political rights is independent of religious belief. Nevertheless duties incumbent on nationals may not be prejudiced by religious beliefs. No one can be forced to observe a ritual act or to participate in an ecclesiastical ceremony in so far as he is not subordinate to another who is by law invested with such authority.'
	Specific:	Austrian Constitution	Art. 9a(3) and (4)	'(3)Every male Austrian is liable for military service… (4) Conscientious objectors who refuse the fulfillment of compulsory military service and are exonerated therefrom must perform an alternative service. The details are settled by law.'
		Austrian Criminal Code	Art. 97(2)	'No physician is required to perform an abortion or to participate in it, unless an abortion without delay is necessary to save the pregnant woman from an imminent, not otherwise preventable death. This is also true for those working in the nursing profession, in medical-technical services, and for people employed in auxiliary medical services.'
			Art. 97(3)	'No one shall be in any way whatever disadvantaged due for refusing to participate in or to perform a non-criminal abortion.'

		Reproductive Medicine Act 1992 (Fortpflanzungsmedizingesetz, BGB1. No. 275/1992) s 6(1)	S 6(1)	'No doctor is obliged to perform a medically assisted procreation or to participate in it. This also applies in the upper services for health and nursing, medical and technical services or people working in emergency medical services.'
			S 6(2)	'No person shall be in any way whatever disadvantaged as a result of refusing to perform or participate in medically assisted reproduction in accordance with this Act.'
Belgium	**General:**	Belgian Constitution	Art. 19	'Freedom of worship, its public practice and freedom to demonstrate one's opinions on all matters are guaranteed, but offences committed when this freedom is used may be punished.'
	Specific:	The Belgian Act on Euthanasia 2002	Ch VI, s 14	'The request and advance directive referred to in Sections 3 and 4 of this Act are not compulsory in nature. No physician may be compelled to perform euthanasia. No other person may be compelled to assist in performing euthanasia. Should the physician consulted refuse to perform euthanasia, then he/she must inform the patient and the persons taken in confidence, if any, of this fact in a timely manner, and explain his/her reasons for such refusal. If the refusal is based on medical reasons, then these reasons are noted in the patient's medical record.'

(*continued on next page*)

Member State	Relevant Law		Provision	Details
		Belgian Penal Code	Art. 350	'Neither a physician, nor a nurse, nor a medical assistant is obliged to cooperate with the termination of a pregnancy. The physician is obliged to inform a patient interested in abortion, during the first visit, of his refusal.'
Bulgaria	**General:**	Bulgarian Constitution (adopted 12 July 1991)	Art. 37(1)	'Freedom of conscience, thought, and choice of religion or religious or atheistic beliefs are inviolable. The state shall assist the keeping up of tolerance and respect among believers of different faiths as well as between believers and nonbelievers.'
			Art. 37(2)	'Freedom of conscience and religion may not be detrimental to national security, public order, public health and morality, or the rights and freedoms of other citizens.'
			Art. 58(2)	'Religious or other beliefs are not grounds for refusing to fulfill the obligations imposed by the Constitution and laws.'
Croatia	**General:**	Constitution of the Republic of Croatia (consolidated and confirmed 6 July 2010)	Art. 17	'Even in cases of clear and present danger to the existence of the state, no restrictions may be imposed upon the provisions of this Constitution stipulating the right to life, prohibition of torture, cruel or unusual treatment or punishment, and concerning the legal definitions of criminal offences and punishment, and the freedom of thought, conscience and religion.'
			Art. 40	'Freedom of conscience and religion and the freedom to demonstrate religious or other convictions shall be guaranteed.'

Specific:		Art. 47	'Conscientious objection shall be allowed to all of those who, based on religious or moral conviction, are not willing to perform military duties in the armed forces. Such persons are obliged to perform other duties as specified by law.'
	Law on Nursing (Zakon o sestrinstvu, pročišćenitekstzakona NN 121/03, 117/08, 57/11), Art. 3	Art. 3	'Because of their ethical, religious or moral beliefs or beliefs, nurses have the right to assert conscientious objection and refuse to conduct medical / nursing care if doing so does not conflict with the rules of the profession, and if it does not cause permanent damage to the patient's health or endanger the patient's life. Nurses must promptly inform the patient and parent or responsible person about such objections.'
	Law on Medical Practice (Zakon o liječništvu, pročišćenitekstzakona, NN 121/03, 117/08)	Art. 20	'Because of their ethical, religious or moral beliefs or beliefs, doctors have the right to assert a conscientious objection and refuse to conduct diagnosis, treatment and rehabilitation of the patient, if doing so does not conflict with the rules of the profession, and if it does not cause permanent damage to the health of or threaten the life of a patient.

(*continued on next page*)

Member State	Relevant Law	Provision	Details
			Doctors must promptly inform patients about their objections and refer them to another physician of the same profession. In the case of doctors employed in a medical institution, a company, or other legal entity that performs health services, or who work with another doctor in a private practice, they must notify their supervisor or employer of their objection.'
CYPRUS	**General:** Constitution of the Republic of Cyprus	Art. 18(1)	'Every person has the right to freedom of thought, conscience and religion.'
		Art. 18(6)	'Freedom to manifest one's religion or belief shall be subject only to such limitations as are prescribed by law and are necessary in the interests of the security of the Republic or the constitutional order or the public safety or the public order or the public health or the public morals or for the protection of the rights and liberties guaranteed by this Constitution to any person.'
	Specific: Doctors (Council, Discipline and Pension Fund) Law of 1967 & 1970	Art. 8	'…a doctor may refuse medical treatment to a patient except in cases of emergency or humanitarian duty; this general provision may be relied upon, in principle, where the motivations for refusing to provide a medical treatment are religious or ideological.'

Czech Republic	**General:**	Charter of Fundamental Rights and Freedoms (incorporated as part of the Constitution of the Czech Republic	Art. 15(1)	'The freedom of thought, conscience, and religious conviction is guaranteed. Everyone has the right to change her religion or faith or to have no religious conviction.'
	Specific:	under Art. 112(1) of the Constitution, both adopted 16 December 1992)	Art. 15(3)	'No one may be compelled to perform military service if such is contrary to his conscience or religious conviction. Detailed provisions shall be laid down in a law.'
	Specific:	Code of Ethics of the Czech Medical Chamber	§ 2 para. 5	'a doctor cannot be forced to take medical performance or participation on him, which is contrary to his conscience.'
	Specific:	Act 372/2011 Coll of the Act on the Healthcare Services	Section 50(2)	'Healthcare worker may refuse to provide medical services to the patient if providing them would be contrary to his conscience or religious belief. He is obliged to immediately inform the provider (of health services) that provides the patient another healthcare worker. If the provider cannot provide another health worker, he must ensure the patient another provider that will provide him with medical services; the patient can refuse ensuring another healthcare worker or another provider. Record of refusal of ensuring another healthcare worker or another provider is part of the medical documentation; the record is signed by patient and healthcare worker.

(*continued on next page*)

Member State	Relevant Law		Provision	Details
				Healthcare worker cannot refuse to provide health services to the patient for the reason mentioned in the first sentence, should the rejection endangers the patient's life or causes a serious threat to his health and the provider is unable to provide (ensure?) health services with another health professional. The sentences first to fourth are similarly used when a healthcare provider refuses to provide health services.'
DENMARK	**Specific:**	Consolidated Act on Induced Abortion (LovbekendtgÃ¸relse, 2006-10-16 nr. 541)	Section 10(2)	'…doctors, nurses, midwifes and social and health assistants, or students in these professions, for whom it is contrary to their ethics or religious beliefs to perform or assist in induced abortion, can apply for and be granted exemption.'
ESTONIA	**General:**	Constitution of the Republic of Estonia	Section 40	'Everyone is entitled to freedom of conscience, freedom of religion and freedom of thought.'
FINLAND	**General:**	Finnish Constitution 1999	Section 11	'…Freedom of religion and conscience entails the right to profess and practice a religion, the right to express one's convictions and the right to be a member of or decline to be a member of a religious community. No one is under the obligation, against his or her conscience, to participate in the practice of a religion.'
FRANCE	**General:**	Declaration of Human and Civic Rights of 26 August 1789	Art. 10	'No one may be disturbed on account of his opinions, even religious ones, as long as the manifestation of such opinions does not interfere with the established Law and Order.'
		Act of 9 December 1905 on the separation of Church and State	Art. 1	'The Republic shall ensure freedom of conscience. It shall guarantee the free practice of religion, subject only to restrictions imposed in the interests of public order.'

Specific:	Code of Public Health (Code de la santé publique)	Art. L.2212-8	Allows medical physicians to invoke a 'conscience clause' on the basis of which they may refuse to perform an abortion. However, they are obliged to inform the woman seeking abortion without delay of their intention to invoke the clause.
	CC decision no. 2001-446DC, June 27, 2001, Rec 74, [14]-[17] (Fr)	-	This decision of the French Constitutional Court recognized the principle that conscientious objection is a right afforded to individuals, not institutions, and upheld the repeal of paragraphs of the Code of Public Health, removing the possibility that departments heads of public health establishments could refuse to allow the provision of abortion services in their departments.
	Loi No 2013-404 du 17 Mai 2013 ouvrant le mariage aux couple de personnes de meme sexe; Circulaire du 13 Juin 2013	-	This recent French statute modified the French Code Civil to achieve marriage equality in France. A regime of sanctions imposable on officials who refuse to perform same-sex marriages was summarised by a circulaire of 13 June 2013. The Conseil Constitutionnel dismissed a challenge by seven mayors alleging that the statute failed to provide a conscience clause and thus interfered with their freedom of conscience. The matter has moved to Strasbourg as of 24 February 2014. See further D Marrani, 'France: no conscientious objection defence for mayors refusing to marry same-sex couples' [2014] PL 337.

(*continued on next page*)

Member State	Relevant Law		Provision	Details
GERMANY	**General:**	Basic Law for the Federal Republic of Germany (Grundgesetz) (adopted 8 May 1949)	Art. 4(1)	'Freedom of faith and of conscience, and freedom to profess a religious or philosophical creed, shall be inviolable.'
	Specific:		Art. 4(3)	'No person shall be compelled against his conscience to render military service involving the use of arms. Details shall be regulated by a federal law.'
			Art. 12a(2)	'Any person who, on grounds of conscience, refuses to render military service involving the use of arms may be required to perform alternative service…'
		Judgment of the Bavarian Higher Administrative Court of 03/07/1990, BayVGH DVB1. 1990, 880-82 (FRG); *Judgment of the Federal Administrative Court of 12/13/1991*, BVerwGE 89, 260-70 (FRG)		The Bavarian High Administrative Court and the Federal Administrative Court of Germany ruled that a municipality's job advertisement for a chief physician in a women's hospital, which included a requirement that the physician in a women's hospital, which included a requirement that the physicians be willing to perform abortions, was not in violation of a law providing that no one is obligated to perform abortions. *Judgment of the Federal Administrative Court of 12/13/1991*, BVerwGE 89, 260-70 (FRG '14 a) According to Article 2 para. 1 of the 5th StrRG no one is obliged to participate in an abortion, unless the participation is necessary to prevent an avoidable, death or serious damage to women's health (Article 2 para. 2 supra).

				This provision exempted, as already unmistakably clear from its wording, anyone from the legal obligation to participate in an abortion, if it is not medically indicated. It thus serves to protect the conscience and so concretized in Article 4, Section 1 of the Basic Law guaranteed the freedom of conscience. Anyone, who's conscience forbids participation in medically indicated abortions is, can follow freely this legal prohibition.'
	Specific:	Schwangerschaftskonfliktgesetz	§ 12	'(1) No one is obliged to participate in an abortion. (2) Paragraph 1 shall not apply if the participation is necessary to avert an otherwise unavoidable danger of death or serious damage to health of the woman.'
	Specific:	Embryonenschutzgesetz	§3a Abs. 5	'No doctor is obliged to carry out a measure under paragraph 2 or to participate in it. No disadvantage may artise for the non-participating person in question.'
GREECE	**General:**	Constitution of Greece (revised 6 April 2001)	Art. 13(1)	'Freedom of religious conscience is inviolable. The enjoyment of civil rights and liberties does not depend on the individual's religious beliefs.'
			Art. 13(5)	'No person shall be exempt from discharging his obligations to the State or may refuse to comply with the laws by reason of his religious convictions.'
			Art. 16(2)	'Education constitutes a basic mission for the State and shall aim at the moral, intellectual, professional and physical training of the Greeks, the development of national and religious consciousness and at their formation as free and responsible citizens.'

(*continued on next page*)

Member State	Relevant Law		Provision	Details
	Specific:	Law 3418/2005	Art. 31	'Doctors can involve the principle of moral conscience and refuse to participate in artificial termination of pregnancy, unless inescapable risk to the life of the pregnant woman or risk of serious and permanent damage to health…'
HUNGARY	**General:**	Constitution of the Republic of Hungary 2011	Article VII	Every person shall have the right to freedom of thought, conscience and religion. This right shall include the freedom to choose or change religion or any other persuasion, and the freedom for every person to proclaim, refrain from proclaiming, profess or teach his or her religion or any other persuasion by performing religious acts, ceremonies or in any other way, whether individually or jointly with others, in the public domain or in his or her private life.
			Article XXXI (3)	'If armed service is incompatible with the conscience of any person obliged to perform military service, he shall perform unarmed service. The forms and detailed rules for military service shall be defined by a cardinal Act.'

	Specific:	Judgment 64/1991, (XII.17) AB - hatarozat		The Hungarian Constitutional Court recognized that medical practitioners have a right to religious conscientious objection, however it considered that certain restrictions to the freedom of religion which this right is derived from may be allowed unless they are unreasonable. Specifically, the Court considered that in any employment relationship, the employee may not object to the performance of duties which form a substantive part of the profession. It considered that only non therapeutic abortions – i.e., not medically prescribed – could be considered as not part of the normal activities of a gynecologist. 'The right to freedom of conscience evaluated in the context of this decision should be highlighted in the sense that the state cannot force anyone to a position which would take discord that is inconsistent with the person's (identity) fundamental convictions. The state has the duty to refrain from such constraints, but also to make it possible - within reasonable limits - the alternative behavior....'
IRELAND	**General:**	Constitution of Ireland (adopted 29 December 1937)	Art. 44(2)(1)	'Freedom of conscience and the free profession and practice of religion are, subject to public order and morality, guaranteed to every citizen.'

(*continued on next page*)

Member State	Relevant Law		Provision	Details
	Specific:	Protection of life during pregnancy Act 2013	Section 17	'…nothing in this Act shall be construed as obliging any medical practitioner, nurse or midwife to carry out, or to assist in carrying out, any medical procedure [including abortion] … to which he or she has a conscientious objection…'
ITALY	**Specific:**	Law No 194 of 22 May 1978 on the social protection of motherhood and the voluntary termination of pregnancy, Gazz. Ugg., Part I, 22 May 1978, No 140, 3642-46 (Italy)	Art. 9	Section 9 requires health care personnel to submit a written declaration of their conscientious objection to abortion to the medical director of their employer healthcare institution and to the regional medical officer.
				'Health personnel and allied health personnel shall not be required to assist in the procedures referred to in Sections 5 and 7 or in pregnancy terminations if they have a conscientious objection, declared in advance. Such declaration must be forwarded to the provincial medical officer and, in the case of personnel on the staff of the hospital or the nursing home, to the medical director, not later than one month following the entry into force of this Law, or the date of qualification, or the date of commencement of employment at an establishment required to provide services for the termination of pregnancy, or the date of the drawing up of a convention with insurance agencies entailing the provision of such services.

The objection may be withdrawn at any time, or may be submitted after the periods prescribed in the preceding paragraph, in which case the declaration shall take effect one month after it has been submitted to the provincial medical officer.

Conscientious objection shall exempt health personnel and allied health personnel from carrying out procedures and activities specifically and necessarily designed to bring about the termination of pregnancy, and shall not exempt them from providing care prior to and following the termination.

In all cases, hospital establishments and authorized nursing homes shall be required to ensure that the procedures referred to in Section 7 are carried out and pregnancy terminations requested in accordance with the procedures referred to in Sections 5, 7, and 8 are performed. The regions shall supervise and ensure implementation of this requirement, if necessary by the movement [mobilità] of personnel. Conscientious objection may not be invoked by health personnel or allied health personnel if, under the particular circumstances, their personal intervention is essential in order to save the life of a woman in imminent danger. Conscientious objection shall be deemed to have been withdrawn with immediate effect if the objector assists in procedures or pregnancy terminations provided for under this Law, in cases other than those referred to in the preceding paragraph.'

(*continued on next page*)

Member State	Relevant Law		Provision	Details
Latvia	**General:**	Constitution of Latvia (adopted 15 Feb 1922, significantly amended 1998)	Art. 99	'Everyone has the right to freedom of thought, conscience and religion. The church shall be separate from the State.'
Lithuania	**General:**	Constitution of Lithuania	Art. 26(1)	'Freedom of thought, conscience, and religion shall not be restricted.'
	Specific:		Art. 139(2)	'The citizens of the republic of Lithuania must perform military or alternative national defence service according to the procedure established by law."
		Law on national conscription: No 1593/1996 (amended 2015)	Art. 4	Substitute service available for 'those who due to religious or pacifist beliefs may not serve under arms.'
Luxembourg	**Specific:**	Law of 17 December 2014	Art. 13	'No doctor will be required to perform an abortion. Similarly no health professional will be required to contribute to such an intervention.'
Malta	**General:**	Constitution of Malta (adopted 21 September 1964)	Art. 40(1)	'All persons in Malta shall have full freedom of conscience and enjoy the free exercise of their respective mode of religious worship.'
Netherlands	**Specific:**	Constitution of the Kingdom of the Netherlands 2008	Art. 99	'Exemption from military service because of serious conscientious objections shall be regulated by Act of Parliament.'
		Law on the termination of pregnancy of 1 May 1981	Section 20	'No person shall be obliged to provide a woman with treatment intended to terminate pregnancy or to assist in providing such treatment…'

		Opinions 1997-46, 2000-13 and 2002-26 of the independent equality body (Commissie Gelikje Behandeling (CGB))	-	The CGH allowed the claim of the applicant, who was public servant who for religious reasons refused to celebrate a same-sex marriage and whose contract was not renewed on that ground. The CGB found that the Gender Equal Treatment Act had been violated as other public servants were available and prepared to perform same-sex marriage so that there were insufficient reasons to renew the contract of the applicant. The CGB observed that in preparing the Gender Equal Treatment Act, the legislator had acknowledged that conscientious objections on religious grounds do occur and that, in principle, they ought to be respected.
POLAND	**General:**	Constitution of the Republic of Poland (adopted 2 April 1997)	Art. 53.1	'Freedom of conscience and religion shall be ensured to everyone.'
	Specific:	Law on the professions of physician and dentist (1996)	Art. 39	'… a physician may refrain from applying medical treatment conflicting with his conscience, however [*he shall not be absolved of the duty to indicate actual possibilities of obtaining the treatment from another physician and/or another medical institution*]* and of the duty to state reasons and include this decision in the medical file …'

* The part of the Article 39 in italics was declared unconstitutional by Constitutional Tribunal in K12/14 Judgement.

(*continued on next page*)

Member State	Relevant Law		Provision	Details
PORTUGAL	**General:**	Constitution of the Portuguese Republic (7th revision, 2005)	Art. 41(1)	'Freedom of conscience, religion and worship shall be inviolable.'
			Art. 41(6)	'The right to be a conscientious objector, as laid down by the law, shall be guaranteed.'
		Law of Religious Freedom 2001 (Law n° 16/2001)	Art. 12(1)	'Freedom of conscience includes the right to object to the compliance of laws that contradict the imperative commands of one's own conscience, within the limits of the rights and duties imposed by the Constitution and under the terms of the law that may regulate the exercise of the conscientious objection.'
			Art. 12(2)	'The commands of conscience that are considered as imperative are those whose infringement involves a serious offence to one's moral integrity and, consequently, make any other behaviour as not mandatory.'
	Specific:		Art. 12(3)	'Conscientious objectors to military service, without excluding those who also invoke a conscientious objection to civil service, have the right to a civil service system, which respects the commands of their conscience, as long as it is compatible with the principle of equality.'
ROMANIA	**General:**	Constitution of Romania	Art. 29(2)	'Freedom of conscience is guaranteed; it must be manifested in a spirit of tolerance and mutual respect.

	Specific:	Medical Deontological Code of 30 March 2012 published in the Official Journal No. 298	Art. 33	'The refusal to offer medical service can be expressed under the strict conditions provided by the law, if the doctor is requested to perform acts which would infringe his professional independence, his image or his moral values or if the request is not in conformity with the fundamental principles of the goals and the social role of the medical profession.'
SLOVAKIA	**General:**	Constitution of the Slovak Republic	Art. 24(1)	'The freedoms of thought, conscience, religious creed and faith are guaranteed. This right also encompasses the possibility to change one's religious creed, or faith. Everyone has the right to be without religious creed. Everyone has the right to publicly express his thoughts.
	Specific:		Art. 25(2)	'No one may be forced to perform military service if it is against his conscience or religious creed. Details will be laid down by law.'
		Act no 578/2004 on healthcare providers, health workers and professional organizations in health	Annex, Health workers and the exercise of his/her profession, para. 3	'Health workers cannot be required to perform or to assist in performance of a procedure that is contrary to his or her conscience, except in cases where the life, health or rights of the patient are threatened.'

(*continued on next page*)

Member State	Relevant Law		Provision	Details
		Act 576/2004 on healthcare, and services related to healthcare	Para 12	'…Healthcare providers may refuse to enter into contracts for the provision of healthcare if…they are prevented on the grounds of personal conviction…. [This is] applicable only to abortion, sterilization and assisted reproduction technologies.'
SLOVENIA	**General:**	Constitution of the Republic of Slovenia	Art. 41	'Freedom of Conscience: Religious and other beliefs may be freely professed in private and public life. No one shall be obliged to declare his religious or other beliefs…'
			Art. 46	'The right of conscientious objection shall be permitted in such circumstances as are determined by statute, to the extent that the rights and freedoms of others are not affected.'
	Specific:	Health Services Act	Art. 56	'Healthcare workers may reject a medical intervention if they believe that it is not in accordance with their conscience and with international rules of medical ethics. Healthcare workers must notify the healthcare institute of their conscientious objections. Healthcare institutes must take these into consideration, but must ensure that patients' healthcare rights are exercised without disruption. Healthcare workers may not refuse to provide emergency medical assistance.'

Slovenian Code of Medical Deontology Practice	Art. 5	'In pursuing their profession physicians shall, within the limits of their professional capabilities, be fully independent and shall answerable to their own consciences, to their patients and to society for their work.'
	Art. 14	'Physicians shall be obliged to pursue their profession responsibly, professionally, conscientiously and precisely for every patient, irrespective of race, sex, ethnicity, religious persuasion, political convictions, and socio-economic position and irrespective of their personal relationship with the patient or the family thereof. Physicians shall be free to choose methods and means of treatment, whereby they shall be obliged to consistently take into consideration the achievements of medical science and the principles of professional behaviour. Physicians shall be obliged to reject any intervention that according to their professional convictions and conscience could be unethical or harmful to the patient.'
	Art. 42	'Physicians may refuse to carry out an abortion or sterilisation if it is not in accordance with their beliefs and conscience and it is not a case of emergency medical assistance. They shall be obliged to refer the patient to another capable physician, or must inform the healthcare institute of their refusal in order to ensure the execution of such interventions in accordance with the law.'

(*continued on next page*)

Member State	Relevant Law		Provision	Details
SPAIN	**General:**	Constitution of Spain (October 31 1978)	Div 2, s 16(1)	'Freedom of ideology, religion and worship is guaranteed, to individuals and communities with no other restriction on their expression than may be necessary to maintain public order as protected by law.'
	Specific:		Div 2, s 30(2)	'The law shall determine the military obligations of Spaniards and shall regulate, with all due guarantees, conscientious objection as well as other grounds for exemption from compulsory military service; it may also, when appropriate, impose a community service in place of military service.'
		Law 1/2003 of 28 January 2003 on the rights and information of the patient in the Community of Valencia (*Ley 1/2003, de 28 de enero, de la Generalitat, de Derechos e Información al Paciente de la CommunidadValenciana* (DOGV de 31 de enero))	Art. 17(2)	This specific legislation adopted by the Autonomous Community of Valencia recognizes the right for each patient to adopt a 'life will' according to which she may express the will not to be artificially kept alive in certain circumstances where life-saving medical treatment would have to be delivered. It allows for a conscientious objection clause benefitting health care practitioners, which they may invoke in order not to have to be instrumental in executing that will. But it also provides an obligation for the public authorities, where such conscientious objection is raised, to adopt the necessary measures to ensure that the will of the patient is respected. In practice, this means that another health care practitioner must be available to execute the will of the patient, and that it is the duty of the public administration to ensure this availability.

STC 53/1985, judgment of 26 August 1988	-	The Constitutional Court held that although the Organic Law 7/1980 on freedom of religion (*Ley Orgánica 7/1980, de 5 de julio, de libertadreligiosa* (BOE del 24 de julio)) does not refer to conscientious objection, this is without prejudice to the interpretation which could be given to Article 16 of the Constitution, which is to be interpreted in accordance with international and European human rights treaties. 'However, it should be noted, which refers to the right to conscientious objection, which exists and can be exercised regardless of whether such regulation has been issued or not. Conscientious objection is part of the fundamental right to ideological and religious freedom recognized in Article 16.1 of the Constitution and, as the Court has indicated on several occasions, the Constitution is directly applicable, especially in the field of fundamental rights.'
STC 19/1985, judgment of 13 February 1985	-	The Constitutional Court held that religious objection may not be invoked in order to modify unilaterally the existing contractual relationships with the employer.

(*continued on next page*)

Member State	Relevant Law		Provision	Details
		Auto del Juzgado Contencioso-Administrativo No 3 de Málaga, Piezaseparadamedidasprovisionales n° 12.1/2011. Pmto, Especial proteccióndererechos fundamentals n° 39/2011. 29 March, 2011.	-	A judge in Málaga held that the conscientious clause in the abortion law, allowing providers to refuse to provide services, applies only to the performance of a termination of pregnancy and not to the provision of information and referrals to non-objecting providers.
SWEDEN	-			
UNITED KINGDOM	**Specific:**	Abortion Act 1967, s 4	Section 4	'…no person shall be under any duty whether by contract or by statutory or other legal requirement, to participate in any treatment authorised by this Act to which he has a conscientious objection: Provided that in any legal proceeding the burden of proof conscientious objection shall rest on the person claiming to rely on it.'
		Human Fertilisation and Embryology Act 1990, s 38(1)	Section 38(1)	'No person who has a conscientious objection to participating in any activity governed by this Act shall be under any duty, however arising, to do so.' (**NB**: There is no definition of 'conscientious objection' in the Abortion Act 1967 or the Human Fertilisation and Embryology Act 1990.)

Marriage Act 1949 (as amended by the Gender Recognition Act 2004) s 5B(1)	Section 5B(1)	'A clergyman is not obliged to solemnise the marriage of a person if the clergyman reasonably believes that the person's gender has become the acquired gender under the Gender Recognition Act 2004.'
	Section 5B(2)	'A clerk in Holy Orders of the Church in Wales is not obliged to permit the marriage of a person to be solemnised in the church or chapel of which the clerk is the minister if the clerk reasonably believes that the person's gender has become the acquired gender under that Act.'

Bibliography

Articles and Books

Aquinas, T. Scriptum super Sententiis liber II a distinctione XXIII ad distinctionem XXIX. http://www.corpusthomisticum.org/snp2023.html. (11. Feb. 2019)

Arendt, H. *The Origins of Totalitarism*. New York: A Harvest Book, 1973.

Aristoteles, *Aristotelis opera*. Vol. 3. Berolini: Edidit Academia Regia Borusica, 1831.

Aristotle in 23 Volumes, Vol. 21. Trans. H. Rackham. Cambridge, MA: Harvard University Press; London: William Heinemann Ltd., 1944. http://www.perseus.tufts.edu/hopper/text?doc=urn:cts:greekLit:tlg0086.tlg035.perseus-eng1:1.1253a (24. Mar. 2018)

Aristotle, *The Nicomachean Ethics with an English Translation*. Trans. H. Rackham. Cambridge, MA, and London: Harvard University Press and William Heinemann Ltd., 1956.

Baewald, A. R., Walker, R. A. and Pierson, R. A. "Growth rates ovarian follicles during natural menstrual cycles, oral contraception cycles, and ovarian stimulation cycles." *Fertility and Sterility*, Vol. 91, 2009, pp. 443–444.

Bakircioglu, O. "The application of the margin of appreciation doctrine in freedom of expression and public morality cases." *German Law Journal*, Vol. 8, 2007, pp. 711–733.

Bąk, S. and Pawlikowski J. "Aspekty etyczne klauzuli sumienia dla farmaceutów w opinii pracowników aptek." *Farmacja Polska*, Vol. 69, No. 10, 2012, pp. 561–566.

Beard, F. H., Hull, B. P., Leask, J., Dey, A. and McIntyre, P. B. "Trends and patterns in vaccination objection, Australia, 2002–2013." *The Medical Journal of Australia*, Vol. 204, No. 7, 2016, pp. 275e1–275e6.

Beauchamp, T. L. and Childress, J. F. *Principles of Biomedical Ethics*, 7th edition. New York: Oxford University Press, 2013.

Biesaga, T. "Właściwe i niewłaściwe cele medycyny." *Medycyna Praktyczna*, Vol. 5, 2004, pp. 1–5.

Blackstone, W. *Commentaries on the Law of England*. Indianapolis: Liberty Fund, 2011 http://oll.libertyfund.org/titles/2140

Borrego, M. E. et al. "New Mexico pharmacists' knowledge, attitudes, and beliefs toward prescribing oral emergency contraception." *Journal of the American Pharmacists Association*, Vol. 46, 2006, pp. 33–43.

Bosek, L. "Prawo osobiste do odmowy działania sprzecznego z własnym sumieniem na przykładzie lekarza." *Forum prawnicze*, No. 1, 2014, pp. 14–25.

Bosek, L. "Problem zakresowej niekonstytucyjności art. 39 ustawy o zawodach lekarza i lekarza dentysty." In: *Sprzeciw sumienia w praktyce medycznej – aspekty etyczne i prawne*, eds. P. Stanisz, J. Pawlikowski, and M. Ordon. Lublin: Wydawnictwo KUL, 2014, pp. 96–100.

Broad, C. D. "Conscience and Conscientious Action." In: *Moral Concepts*, ed. Joel Feinberg. Oxford: Oxford University Press, 1970.

Brock, D. W. "Conscientious refusal by physicians and pharmacists: Who is obligated to do what, and why?" *Theoretical Medicine and Bioethics*, Vol. 28, No. 3, 2008, pp. 183–200.

Card, R. F. "Is there no alternative? Conscientious objection by medical students." *Journal of Medical Ethics*, Vol. 38, No. 10, 2012, pp. 602–604.

Cicero, M. T. *Librorum de Re Publica Sex*. Ed. C. F. W. Müller. Leipzig: Teubner, 1889.

Cicero, M. T. *The Political Works Comprising His Treatise on the Republic and His Treatise on the Laws in Two Volumes. Vol. 1: The Treatise on the Republic*. Trans. Francis Barham, London: Edmund Spettigue, 1841.

Cichoń, Z. "Klauzula sumienia w różnych zawodach." In: *Prawnik Katolicki a wartość prawa*. Kraków: D.Wyd. Ostoja, 1999, pp. 44–51.

Cogan, N. H., ed. *The Complete Bill of Rights*. New York: Oxford University Press, 1997.

Complak, K. "Uwagi o godności człowieka oraz jej ochrona w świetle nowej konstytucji." *Przegląd Sejmowy*, Vol. 6, No. 5, 1998, pp. 41–51.

Cornides, J. "Human Rights Pitted Against Man." *International Journal of Human Rights*, Vol. 12, No. 1, 2008, pp. 107–134.

Curlin, F. A., Nwodim, C., Vance, J. L., Chin, N. H., and Lantos, J. D. "To die, to sleep: US physicians, religious and other objections to physician-assisted suicide, terminal sedation, and withdrawal of life support." *American Journal of Hospice and Palliative Care*, Vol. 25, 2008, pp. 112–120.

Davidson, L. A. et al. "Religion and conscientious objection: A survey of pharmacists' willingness to dispense medications." *Social Science & Medicine*, Vol. 71, 2010, pp. 161–165.

Davis, S., Schrader, V., Belcheir, M. J. "*Influencers of ethical beliefs and the impact on moral distress and conscientious objection*." *Nursing Ethics*, Vol. 9, No. 6, 2012, pp. 738–749.

Dobrowolska, B. "Sprzeciw sumienia w zawodzie pielęgniarki i położnej – założenia i praktyka." In: *Sprzeciw sumienia w praktyce medycznej – aspekty etyczne i prawne*, eds. Piotr Stanisz, Jakub Pawlikowski, and Marta Ordon. Lublin: Wydawnictwo Naukowe KUL, 2014, pp. 197–209.

Downing, S. G. et al. "Emergency contraception over-the-counter: Practices and attitudes of pharmacists and pharmacy assistants in far North Queensland." *Australian and New Zealand Journal of Obstetrics and Gynaecology*, Vol. 51, 2011, pp. 527–531.

Duffy, M. E. "Good medicine: Why pharmacists should be prescribed a right of conscience." *Valparaiso University Law Review*, Vol. 44, 2010, pp. 509–564.

Edelstein, L. *The Hippocratic Oath: Text, Translation, and Interpretation*. Baltimore: Johns Hopkins Press, 1943.

Eliot, T. S. *Notes Toward the Definition of Culture*. London: Faber & Faber Ltd, 1948.

Evans, C. *Freedom of Religion under the European Convention on Human Rights*. New York: Oxford University Press, 2003, pp. 133–166.

Forte, D. F. "Religion and the Republic," Public Discourse blog, the Witherspoon Institute, 6 July 2015.

Franck, M. J. "After Hobby Lobby, the Struggle for Religious Freedom Continues," *Public Discourse*. <http://www.thepublicdiscourse.com/2014/07/13418>

Frankfurt, H. *Taking Ourselves Seriously and Getting It Right*. Stanford, CA: Stanford University Press, 2006.

Ganzini, L., Nelson, H. D., Lee, M. A., Kraemer, D. F., Schmidt, T. A. and Delorit, M. A. "Oregon physicians' attitudes about and experiences with end-of-life care since passage of the Oregon death with dignity act." *Journal of the American Medical Association*, Vol. 285, 2001, pp. 2363–2369.

Garlicki, L. "Komentarz do art. 9 EKPCz (Comments to Article 9 of the Charter of Fundamental Rights of the European Union)." In: *Konwencja o ochronie praw człowieka i podstawowych wolności. Komentarz do artykułów 1–18 (Convention on Protection of Human Rights and Fundamental Freedoms. Comments to Articles 1–18)*, eds. L. Garlicki, P. Hofmański, and A. Wróbel. Warszawa: C. H. Beck, 2010, Vol. I, pp. 550–583.

Garnett, A. C. "Conscience and Conscientiousness." In: *Moral Concepts*, ed. Joel Feinberg. Oxford: Oxford University Press, 1970, pp. 71–83.

Gawande, A. "When law and ethics collide: Why physicians participate in executions." *New England Journal of Medicine*, No. 354, 2006, pp. 1221–1229.

Gennarini, S. "The Diffusion of Sexual and Reproductive Rights through the UN Human Rights Framework." In: *Protection of Human Life in its Early Stage, Intellectual Foundations and Legal Means*, ed. Aleksander Stępkowski. Frankfurt ma Main: Peter Lang, 2014, pp. 255–263.

Greenawalt, K. *Private Consciences and Public Reasons*. New York: Oxford University Press, 1995.

Greene, J. P., ed. "Declaration and Resolves of the First Continental Congress." In: *Colonies to Nation, 1763–1789*. New York: Norton & Co., 1975.

Griggs, S. K., Brown, C. M. "Texas community pharmacists' willingness to participate in pharmacist-initiated emergency contraception." *Journal of American Pharmacists Association*, Vol. 47, No. 1, 2007, pp. 48–57.

Gryka, M. et al. *Stosunek polskich farmaceutów do tzw. klauzuli sumienia*, XXII Naukowy Zjazd Polskiego Towarzystwa Farmaceutycznego, streszczenia, 2013.

Hanson, M. J. and Callahan, D., eds., *The Goals of Medicine. The Forgotten Issues in Health Care Reform*. Washington: Georgetown University Press, 2000.

Harris, L. H., Cooper, A., Rasinski, A., Curlin, F. A. and Lyerly, A. D. "Obstetrician-gynecologists' objections to and willingness to help patients obtain an abortion." *Obstetrics and Gynecology*, Vol. 118, 2011, pp. 905–912.

Hobbes, T. *Leviathan*. ed. Edwin Curley. Indianapolis and Cambridge: Hackett Publishing Company, 1994.

Hobbes, T. *Leviathan*, ed. R. Tuck ed., Cambridge: Cambridge University Press, 1996.

Hołda, Z., Ostrowska, D., Hołda, J., Rybczyńska, J. A., *Prawa Człowieka, Zarys wykładu*. Warszawa: Wolters Kluwer, 2008.

Hopkins, D. and West, D. "Arkansas pharmacists' perceptions toward emergency contraception and nonprescription Plan B." *Pharmacy Practice*, Vol. 6, 2008, pp. 98–102.

Howell, J. H. and Sale, W. F., eds., *Life Choices. A Hastings Center Introduction to Bioethics*. Washington: Georgetown University Press, 2000.

Hume, D. A. *Treatise of Human Nature in Two Volumes*, Vol. 2. London and New York: Dent and Dutton, 1966.

Hunt, G. and Scott, J. B., eds. *Debates in the Federal Convention of 1787 Reported by James Madison*. New York: Oxford University Press, 1920.

Jedlecka, W. and Policiewicz, J. "Pojęcie godności na tle Konstytucji RP." In: *Z zagadnień teorii i filozofii prawa. Konstytucja*, ed. A. Bator. Wrocław: Wydawnictwo Uniwersytetu Wrocławsiego, 1999.

Jouvenal, B. de. *Sovereignty*. Indianapolis: Liberty Fund, 2001.

Kamiński, I. C. "Komentarz do Art. 10 KPP." In: *Karta Praw Podstawowych Unii Europejskiej. Komentarz*, ed. A. Wróbel. Warsaw: C.H. Beck, 2012.

Kant, I. Die Metaphysik der Sitten, J. H. v. Kirchmann Hrsg. Leipzig: Verlag der Dürr'schen buchhandlung, 1870

Kass, L. R. "The End of Medicine and the Pursuit of Health." In: *Toward a More Natural Science*, ed. L. R. Kass. New York: The Free Press, 1985.

Kato, Y. "Conscience in health care and the definitions of death." *Croatian Medical Journal*, Vol. 54, No. 1, 2013, pp. 75–77.

Keown, D. "End of Life. The Buddhist View." *Lancet*, No. 366, 2005, DOI: 10.1016/S0140-6736(05)67323-0, pp. 952–955.

Knack, A. V. "Compulsory vaccination with or without conscientious objection clause." *Hippokrates*, Vol. 24, No. 18, 1953, pp. 565–567.

Krukowski, J. "Godność człowieka podstawą konstytucyjnego katalogu praw i wolności jednostki." In: *Podstawowe prawa jednostki i ich sądowa ochrona*, ed. L. Wiśniewski. Warszawa, 1997, pp. 38–50.

Krüper, J. "Religionstradition und Rechtskonvention: Die Unzulässigkeit religiöser Knabenbeschneidung," *ZJS*, No. 4, 2012, pp. 547–552. http://www.zjs-online.com/dat/artikel/2012_4_602.pdf.

Landau, S. et al. "Pharmacist interest in and attitudes toward direct pharmacy access to hormonal contraception in the United States." *Journal of the American Pharmacists Association*, Vol. 49, 2009, pp. 43–50.

Lawrence, R. E., Rasinki, K. A., Yoon, J. D. and Curlin, F. A. "Obstetrician-gynecologists' beliefs about assisted reproductive technologies." *Obstetrics and Gynecology*, Vol. 116, 2010, pp. 127–135.

Lawrence, R. E. and Curlin, F. A. "Physicians' beliefs about conscience in medicine: A national survey." *Academic Medicine*, Vol. 84, No. 9, 2009, pp. 1276–1282.

Lincoln, A. "Second Inaugural Address", http://avalon.law.yale.edu/19th_century/lincoln2.asp

Locke, J. An Essay *Concerning Human Understanding*, 13th ed. London, 1849.

Locke, J. *Two Treatises of Government*, a New Edition. London, 1824.

Madison, J. "Memorial and Remonstrance against Religious Assessments." 1785, http://press-pubs.uchicago.edu/founders/documents/amendI_religions43.html

King Jr., M. L. "Letter from Birmingham Jail." In: *Why We Can't Wait*. Signet Classics, 2000.

Mazurek, F. J. *Godność osoby ludzkiej podstawą praw człowieka*. Lublin, 2001.

Miller, F. G. and Brody, H. "The internal morality of medicine: An evolutionary perspective." *Journal of Medicine and Philosophy*, Vol. 26, No. 6, 2001, pp. 581–599.

More, T. *The Last Letters of Thomas More*. Ed. Alvaro de Silva. Grand Rapids, Michigan and Cambridge, England: William B. Eerdmans Publishing Company, 2000.

Mrozek, M. "Tomasz z Akwinu «Komentarz do sentencji Piotra Lombarda» II, D. 24, Q.2, A. 3–4." *Forum Teologiczne*, Vol. 15, 2014, pp. 175–191.

Muñoz, P. V. "The original meaning of the establishment clause and the impossibility of its incorporation." *University of Pennsylvania Journal of Constitutional Law*, Vol. 8, 2006.

Nawrot, O. "Klauzula sumienia w zawodach medycznych w świetle standardów Rady Europy." *Zeszyty Prawnicze BAS*, Vol. 9, No. 3, 2012, pp. 12–16.

Nawrot, O. "Prawa człowieka, sprzeciw sumienia i państwo prawa." In: *Sprzeciw sumienia w praktyce medycznej – aspekty etyczne i prawne*, eds. P. Stanisz, J. Pawlikowski, and M. Ordon. Lublin: Wydawnictwo KUL, 2014, pp. 105–116.

Orr, R. D. "Autonomy, Conscience and Professional Obligation." *Virtual Mentor. American Medical Association Journal of Ethics*, Vol. 15, No. 3, 2013, pp. 244–248. (https://journalofethics.ama-assn.org/sites/journalofethics.ama-assn.org/files/2018-05/msoc1-1303.pdf).

Orzeszyna, K. "Godność ludzka podstawą praw człowieka." In: *Człowiek - jego prawa i odpowiedzialność*, ed. R. Tabaszewski. Lublin: Wydawnictwo KUL, 2013, pp. 11–14.

Otis, J. "The Rights of the Colonies asserted and proved." In: *Colonies to Nation, 1763–1789*, ed. Jack P. Greene. New York: Norton & Co., 1975.

Pawlikowski, J. "Prawo do sprzeciwu sumienia w ramach legalnej opieki medycznej. Rezolucja nr 1763 zgromadzenia Parlamentarnego Rady Europy z dnia 7 października 2010 roku [The right to the conscientious objection in lawful medical care. Resolution 1763 of the Parliamentary Assembly of the Council of Europe of 7 October 2010]." *Studia z Prawa Wyznaniowego*, Vol. 14, 2011, pp. 313–338.

Pawlikowski, J., Jarosław Sak, and Krzysztof Marczewski. "Religijność lekarzy a kontrowersyjne moralnie procedury medyczne." *Wiadomości Lekarskie*, Vol. 5, 2010, pp. 5–16.

Pawlikowski, J. "Spór o klauzulę sumienia z perspektywy celów medycyny i etyki lekarskiej." In: *Sprzeciw sumienia w praktyce medycznej – aspekty etyczne i prawne*, eds. Piotr Stanisz, Jakub Pawlikowski, and Marta Ordon. Lublin: Wydawnictwo Naukowe KUL, 2014, pp. 145–170.

Pellegrino, E. D. *For the Patient's Good: The Restoration of Beneficence in Health Care*. New York: Oxford University Press, 1988.

Pellegrino, E. D. "Toward a reconstruction of medical morality." *American Journal of Bioethics*, Vol. 6, 2006, pp. 65–71.

Pellegrino, E. D. and D. C. Thomas. *The Virtues in Medical Practice*. New York: Oxford University Press, 1993.

Petrie, K. A., Torgal, A. H. and Westhoff, C. L. "Matched-pairs analysis of ovarian suppression during oral vs. vaginal hormonal contraceptive use." *Contraception*, Vol. 84, No. 5, 2011, pp. 1–4.

Piechowiak, M. *Filozofia praw człowieka. Prawa człowieka w świetle ich międzynarodowej ochrony*. Lublin: Towarzystwo Naukowe KUL, 1999.

Pierson, R. A., Archer, D. F., Moreau, M. et al. "Ortho Evra/Evra versus oral contraceptives: follicular development and ovulation in normal cycles and after an intentional dosing error." *Fertility and Sterility*, Vol. 80, No. 1, 2003, pp. 34–42.

Prusak, M. "*Opinie studentów farmacji na temat wątpliwości moralnych wobec sprzedaży środków antykoncepcyjnych oraz możliwości wprowadzenia klauzuli sumienia*", (summary of the presentation delivered to XXII Naukowy Zjazd Polskiego Towarzystwa Farmaceutycznego in 2013). *Biuletyn Stowarzyszenia Farmaceutów Katolickich Polski* im. bł. Marii Sagrario, Vol. 45, No. 1, 2014, pp. 61–62.

Prusak, M. *Sprzeciw sumienia farmaceutów. Aspekty etyczne, teologiczne i prawne*. Kraków: Wydawnictwo św. Stanisława BM, 2015.

Prusak, M. "Sprzeciw sumienia w praktyce aptecznej." In: *Sprzeciw sumienia w praktyce medycznej – aspekty etyczne i prawne*, eds. Piotr Stanisz, Jakub Pawlikowski, and Marta Ordon. Lublin: Wydawnictwo Naukowe KUL, 2014, pp. 211–226.

Radziwiłł, K. "Odmowa leczenia z perspektywy art. 7 Kodeksu Etyki Lekarskiej." In: *Sprzeciw sumienia w praktyce medycznej – aspekty etyczne i prawne*, eds. Piotr Stanisz, Jakub Pawlikowski, and Marta Ordon. Lublin: Wydawnictwo Naukowe KUL, 2014, pp. 191–195.

Rousseau, J. J. *Du contract social ou principes du droit politique*. Lyon, 1792.

Sachedina, A. "End-of-life. The Islamic View." *Lancet*, Vol. 366, No. 9487, 2005. pp. 774–779.

Sarnecki, P. "Komentarz do art. 53 Konstytucji RP." In: *Konstytucja Rzeczypospolitej Polskiej. Komentarz, Rozdział I. Rzeczpospolita*, ed. L. Garlicki. Warsaw, 2003.

Schenker, J. G. "Assisted reproductive practice: religious perspectives." *Reproductive Biomedicine Online*, Vol. 10, No. 3, 2005, pp. 310–319.

Shapiro, I and Adams, R. *Integrity and Conscience*. New York: New York University Press, 1998.

Skwarzyński, M. "Orzecznictwo Europejskiego Trybunału Praw Człowieka w zakresie klauzuli sumienia." In: *Aktualne problemy wolności myśli, sumienia i religii*, eds. P. Stanisz, A. M. Abramowicz, M. Czelny, M. Ordon, and M. Zawiślak. Lublin, 2015, pp. 286–291.

Skwarzyński, M. "Sprzeciw sumienia w adwokaturze." In: *Standardy bezstronności światopoglądowej władz publicznych*, eds. A. Mezglewski and A. Tunia. Lublin, 2013, pp. 201–220.

Skwarzyński, M. "Sprzeciw sumienia w europejskim i krajowym systemie ochrony praw człowieka." *Przegląd Sejmowy*, Vol. 21, No. 6, 2013, pp. 9–26.

Sobczak, J. and Sobczak, W. "Komentarz do art. 10 KPP (Comments to Article 10 of the Charter of Fundamental Rights)." In: *Karta Praw Podstawowych Unii Europejskiej. Komentarz*, ed. A. Wróbel. Warsaw: C.H. Beck, 2012.

Spreng, J. E. "Pharmacists and the 'duty' to dispense emergency contraceptives." *Issues In Law & Medicine* 2008, Vol. 23, 2008, pp. 215–277.

Stanisz, P. "Klauzula sumienia." In: *Prawo wyznaniowe*, A. Mezglewski, H. Misztal, and P. Stanisz. Warszawa: C.H. Beck, 2011, pp. 117–124.

Stanisz, P., Pawlikowski, J., and Ordon, M., eds. *Sprzeciw sumienia w praktyce medycznej – aspekty etyczne i prawne*. Lublin: Wydawnictwo KUL, 2014.

Stanisz, P., Pawlikowski, J. "Il diritto dei medici all'obiezione di coscienza in Polonia: recenti sviluppi." *Quaderni di diritto e politica ecclesiastica*, Vol. 2, 2017, pp. 459–473.

Stępkowski, A. ed. *Protection of Human Life in its Early Stage, Intellectual Foundations and Legal Means*. Frankfurt ma Main: Peter Lang, 2014.

Strauss, L. *Natural Right and History*, Chicago Illinois: Chicago University Press, 1965.

Strickland, S. L. M. "Conscientious Objection in Medical Students: a Questionnaire Survey." *Journal of Medical Ethics*, Vol. 38, 2012, pp. 22–25.

Sulmasy, D. P. "What is conscience and why is respect for it so important?" *Theoretical Medicine Bioethics*, Vol. 29, 2008, pp. 135–149.

Sulmasy, S. L. and Mueller, P. S. "Ethics and the legalization of physician-assisted suicide: An American college of physicians position paper." *Annals of Internal Medicine*, Vol. 167, No. 8, 2017, pp. 576–578.

Sutkin, G. et al. "Opinions of West Texas pharmacists about emergency contraception." *Pharmacy Practice*, Vol. 4, 2006, pp. 151–155.

Szostek, A. "Kategoria sumienia w etyce." In: *Sprzeciw sumienia w praktyce medycznej – aspekty etyczne i prawne*, eds. P. Stanisz, J. Pawlikowski, and M. Ordon. Lublin, 2014, pp. 15–25.

Tocqueville, A. de. *Democracy in America*. New York: Random House, 1945.

Tozzi, P. A. "Sovereignties: Evaluating Claims for 'Right to Abortion' under International Law." In: *Protection of Human Life in its Early Stage. Intellectual Foundations and Legal Means*, ed. Aleksander Stępkowski. Frankfurt ma Main: Peter Lang, 2014, pp. 49–67.

Tuleja, P. "Prawo naturalne i prawo pozytywne jako podstawa konstytucyjnych praw człowieka." *ETHOS*, Vol. 12, No(s). 1–2 (45–46) , 1999, pp. 200–212.

Veatch, R. "Internal and External Sources of Morality for Medicine." In: *The Health Care Professional as Friend and Healer*, eds. D. C. Thomasma and J. L. Kissel. Washington: Georgetown University Press, 2000.

Ventura-Juncá, P. "Objection of Conscience, Witness in Medical Health Practice: The Case of Emergency Contraception." In: *Christian Conscience in Support of the Right to Life*, eds. E. Sgreccia and J. Laffitte. Vatican, 2008, pp. 115–122. (http://www.academiavita.org/_pdf/assemblies/13/christian_conscience_in_support_of_the_right_to_life.pdf).

Vischer, R. K. *Conscience and the Common Good: Reclaiming the Space between Person and State*. Cambridge: Cambridge University Press, 2009.

Washington, G. "Thanksgiving Proclamation," http://lcweb2.loc.gov/ammem/GW/gw004.html.

Washington, G. "Farewell Address," http://avalon.law.yale.edu/18th_century/washing.asp.

Wenger, N. S. and Carmel, S. "Physicians' religiosity and end-of-life care attitudes and behaviors." *The Mount Sinai Journal of Medicine*, Vol. 71, No. 5, 2004, pp. 335–343.

Wicclair, M. "Is conscientious objection incompatible with a physician's professional obligations?" *Theoretical Medicine and Bioethics*, Vol. 29, 2008, pp. 171–185.

Wiśniewski, A. *Koncepcja marginesu oceny w orzecznictwie ETPCz*. Gdańsk, 2008.

Witherspoon, J. "The Dominion of Providence over the Passions of Men." In: *Political Sermons of the American Founding Era, 1730–1805*, ed. Ellis Sandoz. Indianapolis: Liberty Press, 1991, pp. 531–558.

Wolfe, Ch. *The Rise of Modern Judicial Review: from constitutional interpretation to judge-made law*, rev. ed. Lanham - London: Rowan & Littlefield, 1994.

Zajadło, J. "Godność jednostki w aktach międzynarodowej ochrony praw człowieka." *Ruch Prawniczy Ekonomiczny i Socjologiczny*, No. 2, 1989, pp. 103–117.

Zoll, A. "Klauzula sumienia." In: *Sprzeciw sumienia w praktyce medycznej – aspekty etyczne i prawne*, eds. P. Stanisz, J. Pawlikowski, and M. Ordon. Lublin, 2014, pp. 77–85.

Zoll, A. "Prawo lekarza do odmowy udzielenia świadczeń zdrowotnych i jego granice." *Prawo i Medycyna*, Vol. 5, No. 13, 2003, pp. 18–20.

Decisions and Judgments

Human Rights Committee:

Atasoy v. Turkey, communication nos. 1853/2008 and 1854/2008, UN Doc. CCPR/C/104/D/1853-1854/2008.

L.T.K. v. Finland, Communication no. 185/1984, UN doc. CCPR/C/25/D/185/1984.

Min-Kyu Jeong et al. v. Republic of Korea, communication nos. 1642-1741/2007, UN Doc. CCPR/C/101/D/1642-1741/2007.

Yoon v. Republic of Korea and *Choi v. Republic of Korea*, communication nos. 1321/2004 and 1322/2004, UN Doc. CCPR/C/88/D/1321-1322/2004.

Sweden:

Swedish Discrimination Ombudsman, cases 2014/12 2014/226 2014/227, 10 April 2014.

District Court of Jönköping (Jönköpings tingsrätt) case no T 1781-14, 12 Nov 2015.

District Court of Nyköping (Nyköpings tingsrätt) case no T 2153-15, 4 Nov 2016.

Swedish Labor Court (Arbetsdomstolen) case no B 10/16, 12 April 2017.

Decision of the Swedish Labor Court (Arbetsdomstolen), case no B 124/16, 9 May 2017.

The Court of Justice of the European Union:

Germany v. Y and Z (nos.C-71/11 and C-99/11).

Oliver Brüstle v. Greenpeace e.V (C-34/10, 18 October 2011).

The European Committee of Social Rights:

Federation of Catholic Family Associations in Europe (FAFCE) v. Sweden, (Complaint No. 99/2013, 17 March 2015).

International Planned Parenthood Federation – European Network (IPPF EN) v. Italy (Complaint No. 87/2012, 10 September 2013).

The European Court of Human Rights:

A. B. & C. v. Ireland (no. 25579/05).

Baykara v. Turkey (no. 34503/97).

Bayatyan v. Armenia (no. 23459/03).

Bukharatyan v. Armenia (no. 37819/03).

Chassagnou and others v. France (no. 25088/94, 2833/95, 2844/95).

Evans v. United Kingdom (no. 6339/05).

Eweida and Others v. United Kingdom (nos. 48420/10, 59842/10, 51671/10, 36516/10).

Hasan and Chaush v. Bulgaria (no. 30985/96).

Hirst v. United Kingdom (no 2), Application no. 74025/01, [GC].

McFarlane v. United Kingdom (no. 36516/10).

Metropolitan Church of Bessarabia and others v. Moldova (no. 45701/99).

P. and S. v. Poland (no. 57375/08).

Parrillo v. Italy (no. 46470/11).

R. R. v. Poland (nos. 27617/08, 27617/04).

Thlimmenos v. Greece (no. 34369/97).

Tysiac v. Poland (no. 5410/03).

Vartic v. Romania (No. 2) (no. 14150/08).

Von Hannover v. Germany (no. 2), (nos. 40660/08 and 60641/08).

Vo v. France (no. 53924/00).

X, Y, and Z v. United Kingdom (no. 21830/9).

Yumak and Sadak v. Turkey (no. 10226/03).

Polish Constitutional Tribunal:

Ruling of the Constitutional Tribunal of 15 January 1991, File No. U 8/90, OTK ZU 1991, No. 1, item 8.

Ruling of the Constitutional Tribunal of 7 October 1992, File No U 1/92, OTK ZU 1986–1995, Vol. 3/1992.

Ruling of the Constitutional Tribunal, 7 October 2015, No. K12/14 2015, OTK 9A, n. 143.

US Supreme Court:

Burwell v. Hobby Lobby Stores, Inc., 573 U.S. (2014).

Doe v. Bolton, 410 U.S. 179 (1973).

Employment Div. v. Smith, 494 U.S. 872 (1990).

Masterpiece Cakeshop v. Colorado Civil Rights Commission, 584 U.S. (2018).

Obergefell v. Hodges, 576 U.S. (2015).

Roe v. Wade, 410 U.S. 113 (1973).

Storman, Inc. v. Wiesman, 579 U.S. (2016).

Washington v. Glucksberg, 521 U.S. 702 (1997).

Wisconsin v. Yoder, 406 U.S. 205 (1972).

Other US Courts:

Little Sisters of the Poor v. Burwell, No. 13–1540 (10th Cir. 2015).

Elane Photography v. Willock, N.M. 309 P.3d 53 (2013).

Ingersoll v. Arlene's Flowers and *State of Washington v. Arlene's Flowers* (Wash SC, En Banc, No 91615-2; 16 Feb. 2017).

Miller v. Davis, (D.C. for Kentucky (Ashland), No. 15–44-DLB; 12 August 2015.

Other resources:

"2015 Final State Legislative Session Report." Americans United for Life. July 14, 2015. http://www.aul.org/wp-content/uploads/2015/10/Final-Session-Report-2015.pdf

Abortion views cost job." BBC. 7 October 2000. http://news.bbc.co.uk/2/hi/health/961169.stm

"Aborträtten hotas av samvetsfrihet" (English: "The Right to Abortion is threatened by freedom of conscience"), *Aftonbladet*, 12 November 2015.

"Background about Euthanasia in the Netherlands." Patients Rights Council. http://www.patientsrightscouncil.org/site/holland-background/

"Citizens' initiative calls for right to conscientious objection in health care." Helsinki Times. 28 August 2014. http://www.helsinkitimes.fi/finland/finland-news/domestic/11797-citizens-initiative-calls-for-right-to-conscientious-objection-in-health-care.html

Code de la santé publique (CSP). http://droit-finances.commentcamarche.net/download/telecharger-286-code-de-la-sante-publique-2017-pdf

"Dog efter förlossning – barnmorskebrist bakomliggande orsak" (*Eng.* Died in childbirth – lack of midwives the underlying reason, *Swedish National Television* (SVT), 2 October 2017.

Ethical Framework for Gynaecologic and Obstetric Care. https://www.figo.org/sites/default/files/uploads/wg-publications/ethics/English%20Ethical%20Issues%20in%20Obstetrics%20and%20Gynecology.pdf

FIGO Guidelines Regarding Informed Consent. https://www.figo.org/sites/default/files/uploads/wg-publications/ethics/English%20Ethical%20Issues%20in%20Obstetrics%20and%20Gynecology.pdf

"Holland's Euthanasia Law." Patient's Rights Council. http://www.patientsrightscouncil.org/site/hollands-euthanasia-law/

"Protocol No. 15 amending the Convention on the Protection of Human Rights and Fundamental Freedoms." http://www.echr.coe.int/Documents/Protocol_15_ENG.pdf

"Safe Abortion: technical and policy guidance for health systems." 2012. http://apps.who.int/iris/bitstream/10665/70914/1/9789241548434_eng.pdf?ua=1.

"Sahlin jämställde jihadister med abortmotståndare" (English. "Sahlin compared jihadists with those who refuse abortion"), Världen idag, 9 February 2015.

Swiss national advisory commission on biomedical ethics; Prise de position n° 9/2005 Avis unanime http://www.nek-cne.ch/fileadmin/nek-cne-dateien/Themen/Stellungnahmen/fr/suizidbeihilfe_fr.pdf

The WMA Medical Ethics Manual https://www.wma.net/what-we-do/education/medical-ethics-manual/

Ulrica Söder Bergstedt, "Politiker vakna – nu är läget i vården akut" ("Politicans wake up – the situation within the hospitals is acute"), *Aftonbladet*, 18 June 2015.

Contributors

Danuta Brańska
She gained her Master's degree from the Medical University of Warsaw. For more than 10 years, she was working in the pharmaceutical concern in the sales department, then in an open pharmacy and now at the hospital pharmacy. Since 2009 member of the Association of Catholic Pharmacists in Poland.

Dorinda C. Bordley
Vice President, Senior Counsel of Bioethics Defense Fund, a public-interest organization that creates winning arguments for life to benefit lawmakers, courts, students and citizens across the United States and abroad. Dorinda received her B.A. in Finance, summa cum laude (1987), and Juris Doctor (1990) from Loyola University, New Orleans, where she served as managing editor of the law review. She clerked for the Chief Justice of the Louisiana Supreme Court before joining a practice in law enforcement defense.

Robert Clarke
Barrister and Director of European Advocacy for ADF International. He specializes in religious freedom issues and cases before the European Court of Human Rights as well as leading efforts across Europe in defence of life, family, and religious freedom. Prior to joining ADF International, Clarke was counsel of the Nursing and Midwifery Council in London, prosecuting cases of medical misconduct.

Jakob Cornides

Doctor of Law (University of Vienna). He has served as an official for the European Commission since 1997, first in the Directorate General for Consumer Protection and Health, and since 2002 in the Directorate General for Trade.

David F. Forte
Professor of Law at Cleveland State University, where he was the inaugural holder of the Charles R. Emrick, Jr. Calfee Halter & Griswold Endowed Chair. He served as the Garwood Visiting Professor at Princeton University in the Department of Politics and Visiting Fellow at the James Madison Program in American Ideals and Institutions. He also held the position of Consultor to the Pontifical Council for the Family under Pope St. John Paul II and Pope Benedict XVI. In 2003, Dr. Forte was a Distinguished Fulbright Chair at the University of Trento and returned there in 2004 as a Visiting Professor. He was the Senior Visiting Scholar at the Center for the Study of Religion and the Constitution in at the Witherspoon Institute in Princeton, New Jersey. He holds degrees from Harvard College, Manchester University, England, the University of Toronto, and Columbia University.

Claire de La Hougue

She holds a Ph.D. in law. She worked at the International Institute of Human Rights René Cassin and has become a lawyer registered at the Bar of Strasbourg. She is a Research Fellow at the ECLJ since 2010.

Roger Kiska

Legal Counsel at Christian Legal Centre, President of the Mum, Dad & Kids Association. He earned his Juris Doctor degree at Ave Maria School of Law in Ann Arbor, Michigan. He is admitted to the State Bar of Michigan and successfully completed the United Kingdom's Solicitor's Transfer Exam – the British equivalent of the American Bar exam.

Nikolas T. Nikas

Co-founder, president and general counsel of Bioethics Defense Fund (BDF), a public-interest organization that creates winning arguments for life to benefit lawmakers, courts, students and citizens across the United States and abroad. Nikas received his B.A. (1979) and M.A. (1981) in government and international relations from the University of Notre Dame, with his masters focusing on political theory. He received his Juris Doctorate, magna cum laude, in 1986 from Arizona State University College of Law.

Jakub Pawlikowski

Graduated in medicine, philosophy and law. Head of the Department of Sociology of Medicine at the Medical University of Lublin (MUL). Visiting Associate Professor at Harvard T.H. Chan School of Public Health at Harvard University, Department of Epidemiology (2016–2017). Member of the experts advisory boards at the Polish Ministry of Science and Higher Education (panel for the protection of human rights in research) and Ministry of Health (Agency for Health Technology Assessment and Tariff System).

Grégor Puppinck

Holds his Ph.D. with a dissertation in legal theory. He graduated from Paris II Law School and from the "Institut des Hautes Etudes Internationales." From 2003 to 2008, he has taught human rights, European law, and constitutional law at the Law School of the University of Haute-Alsace, France. Currently serves as Director General of the European Centre for Law and Justice (ECLJ), the ACLJ's international affiliate in Strasbourg, France, with consultative status at the U.N. He is also a Member of the OSCE Panel of Experts on Freedom of Religion or Belief and an Expert to the Council of Europe. He takes part in the Committee of Experts on the Reform of the European Court of Human Rights.

Konstanty Radziwiłł

Doctor in medical sciences. He is a specialist in family medicine. He is a lecturer in the Department of Family Medicine of the Warsaw Medical University. In 2001–2010, he was the president of the Polish Chamber of Physicians and Dentists, in 2010–2014 its vice-chairman, and since 2014 is its secretary general. In 2010–2012, he was the president of the Standing Committee of European Doctors (CPME). In 2015–2018, he was a Ministry of Health of the Republic of Poland.

William L. Saunders

Graduate of the Harvard Law School, who has been involved in issues of public policy, law and ethics for thirty years. He is Of Counsel at Americans United for Life, chairman for the Federalist Society's Religious Liberty Group. He is a regular columnist for the National Catholic Bioethics Quarterly. Mr. Saunders has written widely on these topics, as well as on Catholic social teaching. He has given lectures in law schools and colleges throughout the United States and the world. He is the Director of the Program in Human Rights for the Institute for Human Ecology and Co-Director of the Center for Religious Liberty at The Catholic University of America in Washington, DC.

Michał Skwarzyński

Doctor of Law, with a specialization in Human Rights. Associate Professor in the Department of Human Rights, the John Paul II Catholic University of Lublin, Faculty of Law, Canon Law and Administration. He is practicing as an attorney specializing in human rights protection.

Aleksander Stępkowski

Professor of law at the Faculty of Law and Administration University of Warsaw. Director of the Sociology of Law Chair. Holds Ph.D. and post-doctoral degree (habilitation) in legal sciences. His research activity focus on private and public comparative law as well as political and legal thought (including Polish republican tradition). Fellow of the Foundation for Polish Science (2000 and 2001), scholar at the University of Manchester (1999), the University of Oxford (2002), and Katholieke Universiteit Leuven (2003). In 2015–2016, Undersecretary of state responsible for legal, treaty and human rights issues in the Polish Ministry of Foreign Affairs. Founder and first president of the Ordo Iuris Institute for Legal Culture. In February 2019 he has been appointed judge within the Polish Supreme Court.

David Thunder

He earned his BA and MA in philosophy at University College Dublin, and his Ph.D. in political science at the University of Notre Dame. David Thunder is a researcher and lecturer at the Institute for Culture and Society, University of Navarra in Pamplona, Spain, since September 2012. He is a recipient of the prestigious Ramón y Cajal grant (with a five-year duration, from 2017 to 2021), awarded by the Spanish government to support outstanding research activities. Prior to his appointment to the University of Navarra, he held several research and teaching positions in the United States, including visiting assistant professor at Bucknell and Villanova, and Postdoctoral Research Fellow in Princeton University's James Madison Program.

Ad Fontes

Schriften zur Philosophie

Herausgegeben von Tadeusz Guz

Band 1 Dominik Lusser: Individua Substantia. Interpretation und Umdeutung des Aristotelischen ουσια-Begriffs bei Thomas von Aquin und Johannes Duns Scotus. 2006.

Band 2 Magdalena Börsig-Hover: Zur Ontologie und Metaphysik der Wahrheit. Der Wahrheitsbegriff Edith Steins in Auseinandersetzung mit Aristoteles, Thomas von Aquin und Edmund Husserl. 2006.

Band 3 Tadeusz Guz (Hrsg.): Das Naturrecht und Europa. 2007.

Band 4 Erik M. Mørstad: Der Tod und die Erinnerung. Eine kulturphilosophische und theologische Auseinandersetzung mit der Erinnerung an Jesus von Nazaret und an den Menschen. 2007.

Band 5 Magdalena Börsig-Hover: Romano Guardini (1885-1968). Wegbereiter des 21. Jahrhunderts. 2009.

Band 6 Tadeusz Guz / Elżbieta Szczurko / Leszek Bruśniak (Hrsg./eds.): Metaphysik heute / Metaphysics today. 2009.

Band 7 Anton Hilckman: Gesammelte Werke. Schriften zur Kulturwissenschaft. Teil 1: Die Wissenschaft von den Kulturen. Bearbeitet, kommentiert und herausgegeben von Tomasz Stępień. 2011.

Band 8 Anton Hilckman: Gesammelte Werke. Schriften zur Kulturwissenschaft. Teil 2: Grundlagen des Abendlandes. Bearbeitet, kommentiert und herausgegeben von Tomasz Stępień. 2011.

Band 9 Manfred Balkenohl: Plädoyer für das Leben. Philosophisch und theologisch. 2011.

Band 10 Aleksander Stępkowski (ed.): Protection of Human Life in Its Early Stage. Intellectual Foundations and Legal Means. 2014.

Band 11 Igor Nowikow: Der Freiheitsbegriff bei Kant. Eine philosophische Untersuchung im Rückblick auf das christliche Freiheitsverständnis. 2014.

Band 12 Heinz-Georg Kuttner: Paradoxien der soziologischen Vernunft und ihre Überwindung. 2015.

Band 13 Kateryna Vaskivska / Oksana Khymych / Paweł Marzec: Planning and Regulation of Investment Operations at Meso Level. Management, Intensification, Mechanisms. 2016.

Band 14 Aleksander Stępkowski (ed.): Contemporary Challenges to Conscience. Legal and Ethical Frameworks for Professional Conduct. 2019.

www.peterlang.com

www.ingramcontent.com/pod-product-compliance
Ingram Content Group UK Ltd.
Pitfield, Milton Keynes, MK11 3LW, UK
UKHW041826100926
8556IPUK00002B/42

9 783631 775554